PHOTOSHOP ELEMENTS 2024 USER GUIDE

A Complete Practical Guide to Learn and Master Adobe Photoshop Elements 2024 with all the Features and Updated Tips

CHARLES SHERER

TABLE OF CONTENT

INTRODUCTION

Adobe Photoshop Element is a software for editing and handling digital images, web developers, graphic designers, and photographers always make use of it, and all those who work with images use Adobe Photoshop, users of Photoshop can create high-quality images and artwork using diverse features and tools embedded in it. A general tool for editing images and graphics is Adobe Photoshop, users of Adobe Photoshop can create wonderful images, and for numerous professional photographers and graphic designers, it has advanced into the industry standard. All thanks to the program's user-friendly interface and widespread feature set. Adobe's Photoshop Elements is filled with all the photo editing tools you need to apply to transform your images amazingly and astonishingly. And with the assistance of this Photoshop Elements 2024 mini-book, you will discover everything about editing your image from ordinary to extraordinary with all the tricks for simple, one-click fixes, before jumping into more advanced editing features. Enhance colors, add filters, and make your images amazing. In this mini-book, you will learn how to, build eye-catching images and improve your design, Boost contrast enhance color, and sharpen your images, and you will also understand the fundamentals of Photoshop Elements and speedily improve your photos and you will also get to discover more advanced Photoshop tools like layers, and so on.

CHAPTER ONE

SLIGHT IDEA ABOUT PHOTOSHOP ELEMENTS 2024

Adobe Photoshop Elements 2024 is a photo editing application generated for enhancing, improving, editing, and sharing forms of photos. Photoshop Element 2024 comes with an entirely refreshed UI with a dedicated dark mode and simple-to-access features. Photoshop Elements is a helpful software that can assist you in collecting, organizing, and editing diverse categories of media such as photos and videos, and distributing them by using diverse platforms like Instagram, Twitter, and Facebook to friends and families. Adobe Photoshop Elements is for all categories of users, it is used for making photos look better and more-finer than they used to be, it is also a one-time purchase that is to say you will continue enjoying this application for an unlimited period as you desire without any interval payment, if you are a beginner or you have gathered some knowledge in photo editing and desire to create amazing images or have a mission for creating excellent photos with little energy. However, Photoshop 2024 is released with powerful features that can assist you in creating outstanding effects over an image.

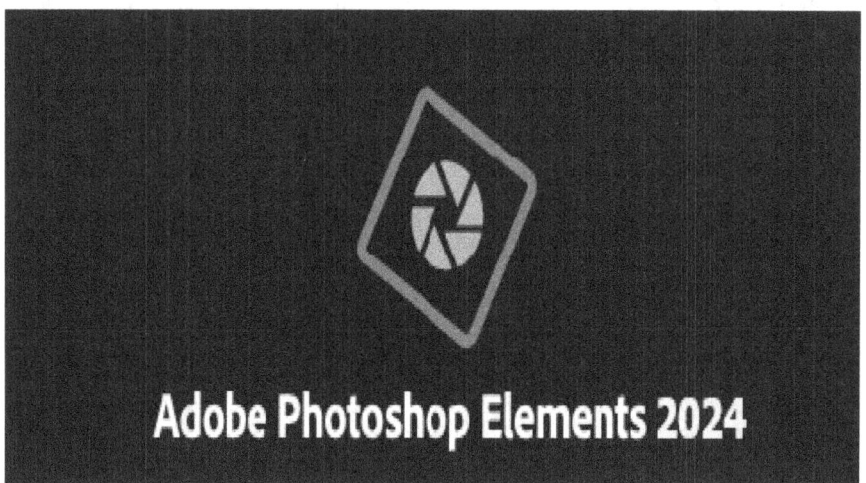

INTRODUCTION TO IMAGE EDITING

Image editing can be humbly put as mixtures, adjustments, and changes that you make to the content of your image. Majorly all images require one or two touches to make your pictures attractive, irrespective of the current appearance of your image you can do something to refine its appearance.

Photoshop Elements is all that you need to create important edits to your image, this chapter will enlighten you on the fundamental steps you have to take to improve the content of your image.

DISCOVERING YOUR WAY AROUND THE ELEMENT HOME SCREEN

You have to find your way to the **Home Screen** if you want to get started with image editing. To gain access to the Home Screen, you need to install the element into your PC, you can now launch the Photoshop Element application from the list of applications you have on your PC to have the right to use the Home Screen. The Home Screen is where the editing work started, See the image below.

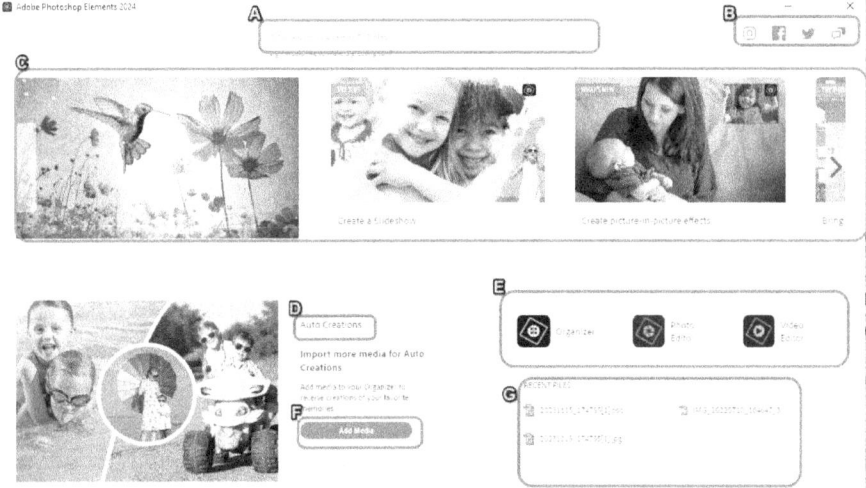

Element 2024 Home screen allows you to carry out these numerous tasks:

A. **Search Box:** The search box permits you to search for a certain task you want to study, you just need to type the task you want to learn then click enter, and the search box will show the corresponding results.

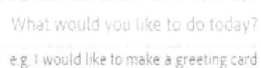

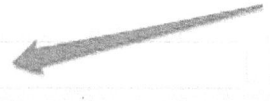

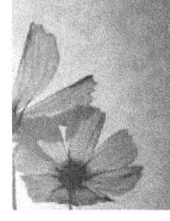 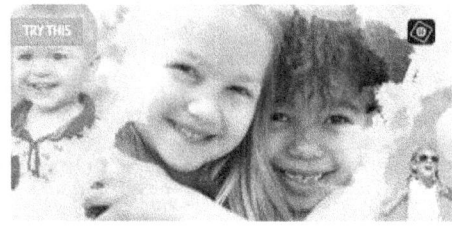 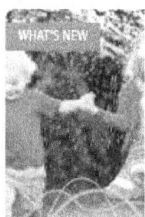

B. **Instagram, Facebook, Twitter, and Help button:** you can access and share images or files on the first three social media applications, the fourth button is to find help from Element possibly on what you did not understand.

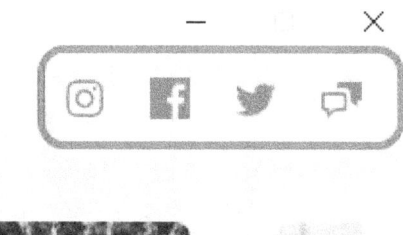 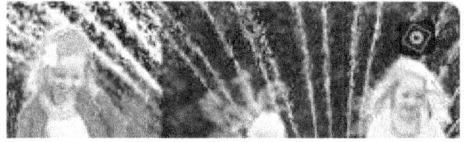 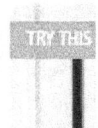

C. **The Container of cards and more button:** The container cards comprise Try This, what's New, and Guided Edits, they are the features that can assist you in performing exceptionally on the Elements, the cards comprise different themes, while **more button** is used to move to the right or left of the container to view more container cards, beneath are the explanation of the three cards:

- **What's new:** it is the card with the blue color with children playing, it gives you access to the new features that are available in Photoshop elements 2024, you can access the what's new features by mousing over what's new and clicking the open link that displays forth.

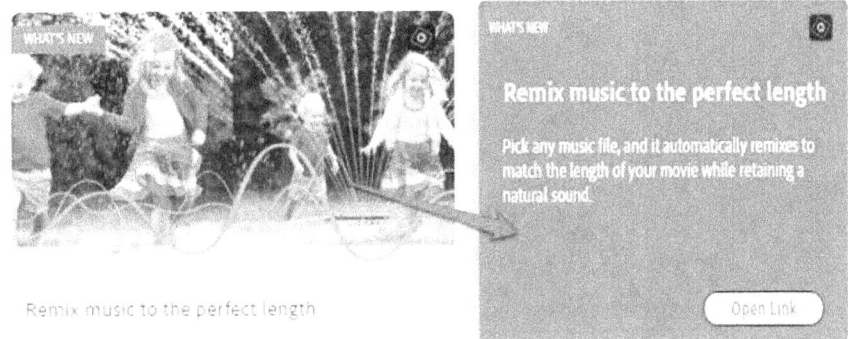

Remix music to the perfect length

- **Try this:** it is a card with a green color, and it permits you to try new inspiring features. This card brings numerous new features you can try based on the current activities you are trying to do on the Photoshop Element. Access the **Try This** feature by mousing over it and then clicking on the Try This button that comes into sight.

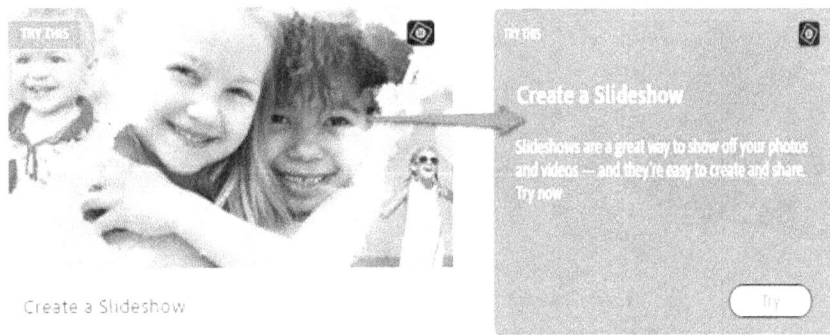

Create a Slideshow

- **Inspiration:** the card's orange color; provides instances of the features that are performed by another user to stimulate inspiration. Access inspiration features by mousing over its card and clicking on the view button that comes into sight.

D. **Auto creation:** Auto creation is the sequences of personalized creation such as slides, photo collages, and video collages. You can see Auto creation by clicking on View All. Auto creation is created from media that you added to the Photoshop Elements through Add media.

E. **Add Media:** this is used to add numerous media into the auto-creation, such as photos, images, etc., when you add media, the media button will evaporate from the Home screen but you can add more media from the Organizer.

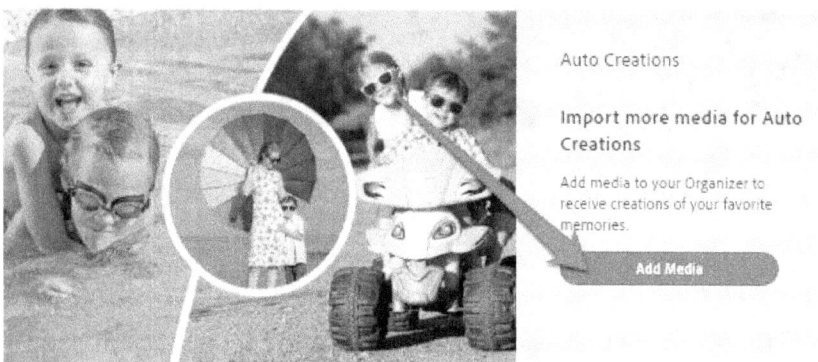

F. **Program launcher:** this can be found at the bottom right of the Home screen and it comprises three icons to launch various Photo applications. Click on the respective button to launch each application such as Photo Organizer, Photo Editor, and Video Editor.

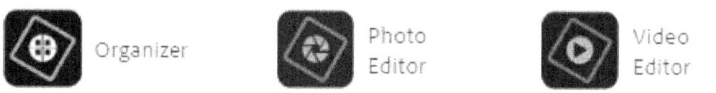

G. **Recent Files:** this is the file of the images you have recently worked on. It is shown on the Home screen for quick access perchance the user desires to continue editing on them. Clicking any resent file will make them open in the Photo Editor application.

BEGINNING WITH THE PHOTO EDITOR

Photo Editor is the main Photoshop elements tool designed for different photo amendments and corrections, such as color, effects, brightness, repairing and fixing of the image, and so on. For you to start on the Photo Editor, you need to:

Visit the **program launcher** beneath the Home screen and click on the **Photo editor** icon to access Photo Editor.

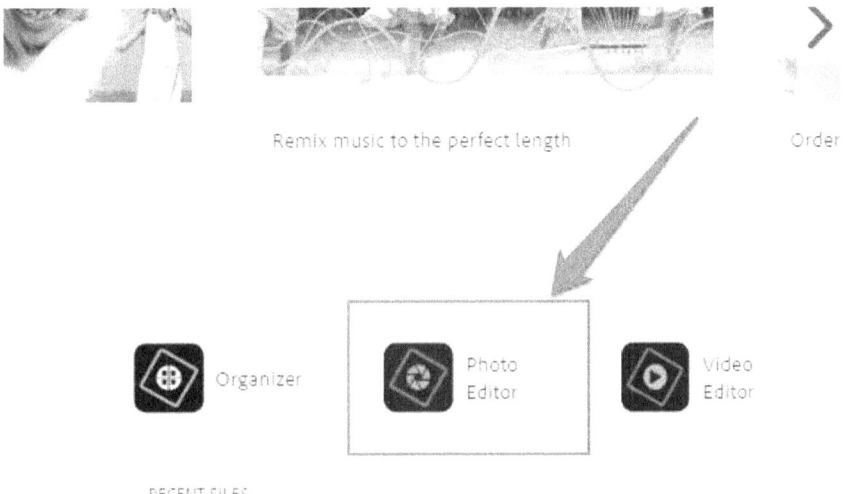

Photo Editor will be opened on the next screen with the Quick tab which is the default mode whenever you launch into the Photo Editor, Quick mode tools have fewer tools compared to other modes but it is a faster mode for passing out editing to your picture such brightness, sharpness, contrast, and color as well.

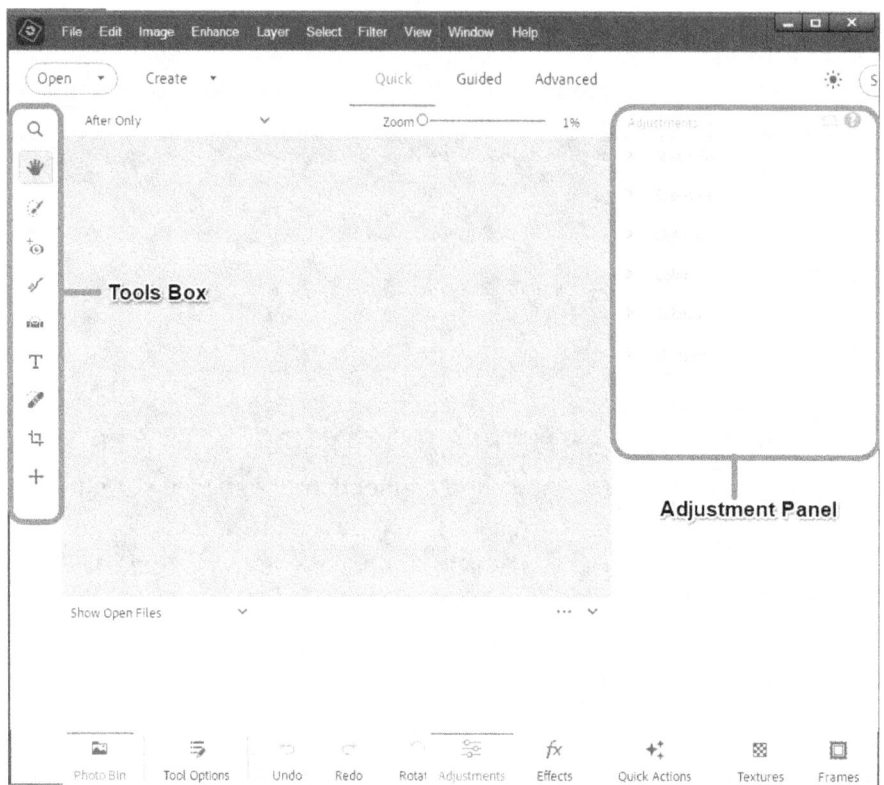

After the Quick mode, the remaining two modes are **Guided and advanced** the three modes have diverse tools at various locations, nevertheless, particular tools can be found in the three modes. For instance, in Quick mode, at the right-hand side of the workspace, there is an adjustment panel for editing, and at the left-hand side there is a tools box, the tools box works together with the panel bin. With the combination of those tools such as image editing, refining, and correction, basic editing is performed over the image. I will be explaining each of the modes in particular as we proceed.

BUILDING SIMPLE EDITS WITH THE QUICK MODE

Quick mode assists the user in building amazing editing on the image in a very simple way. Quick mode was referred to as the Beginner's mode by many people because it is easy to handle for image editing thought with limited tools. Quick mode as different tools such as the Hand tool, Zoom tool, and so on, you can position the mouse across those tools to discover their names, the tools work exactly in advanced modes. However, the **advanced mode** has many tools. **The Menu bar** is also present in Quick modes, such as Edit, File, Image, and so on. However, all the features are not available here because it is a beginner's mode, for example, in the layer tab if you click on any feature on the layer tab, it won't respond which means those features are not available.

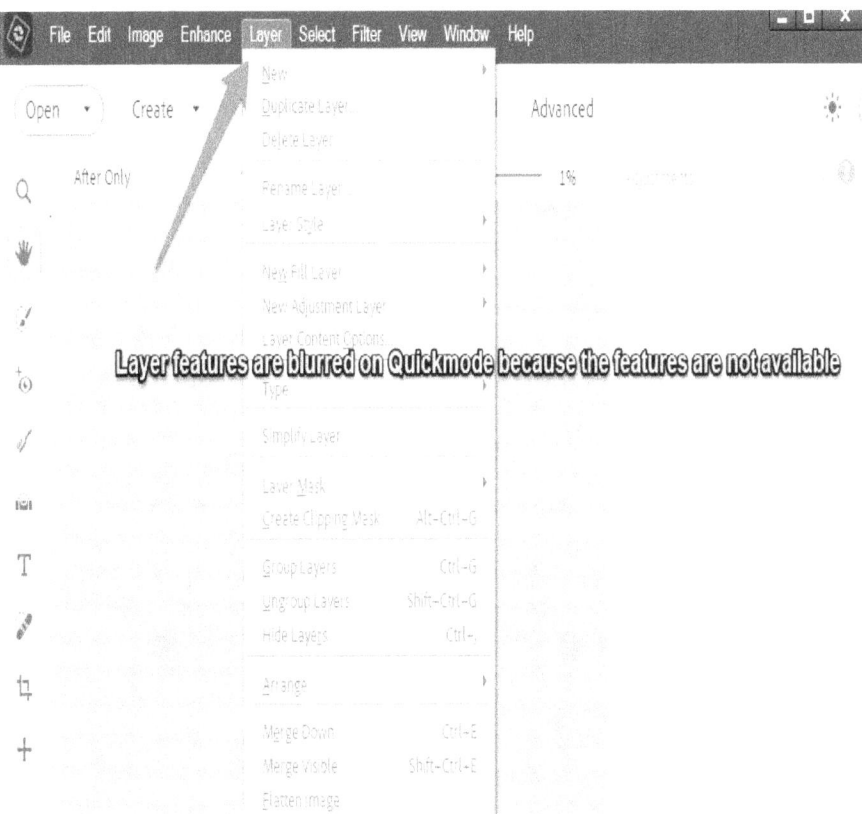

Layer features are blurred on Quickmode because the features are not available

At the left-hand side of the Quick mode is the **Panel bin** that comprises numerous photo fixes such as **adjustment panel, Effect panel** and so on that can easily be used to improve, adjust, and correct the content of your image. For example, let us make us of the Adjustment layer to quickly adjust the color of an image, you will have to click on the down arrow beside the fixed name you want to use, then drag the slider or other control to adjust and improve your image, or ask Photoshop elements to do the fixing for you by clicking the **Auto button.**

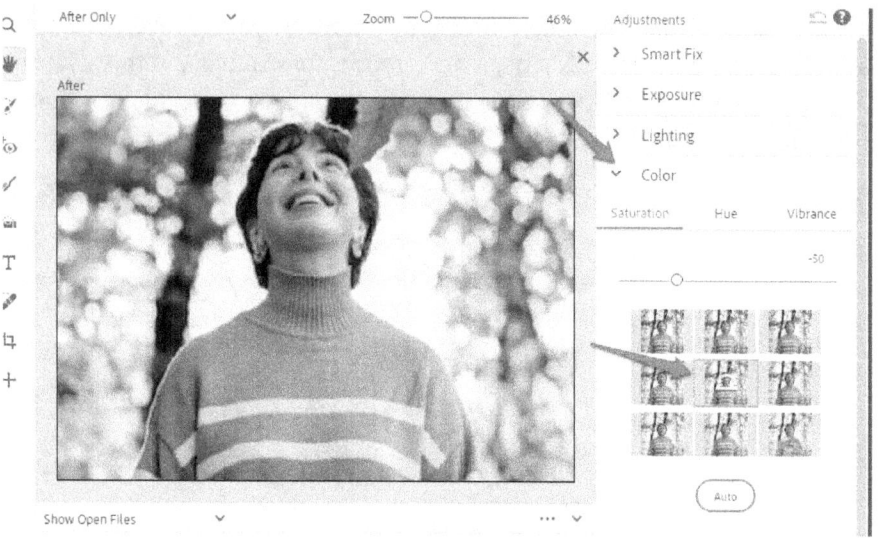

You can start to edit an image in Quick mode by following these steps:

➢ Click **Photo Editor** from the Home screen by default it will unlock in **Quick mode** at the middle top if you have already unlocked Photo Editor in a different Mode

➢ Click on the **File tab** and pick **Open** to access the Open dialog box.

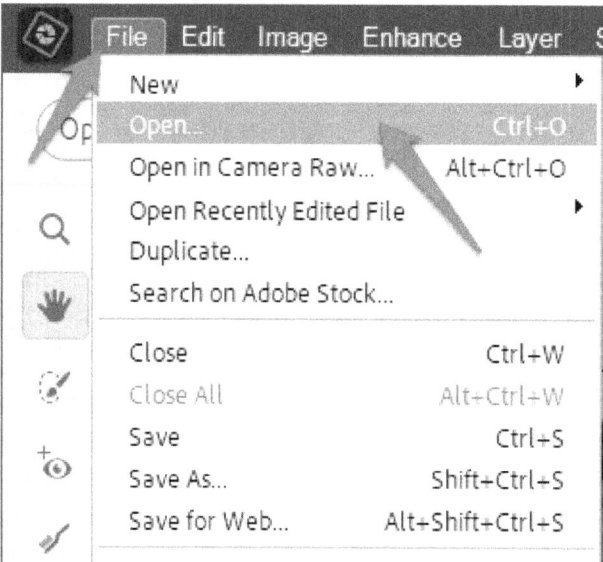

➢ Search and choose **the file** that needs improvement and click on the **Open** button.

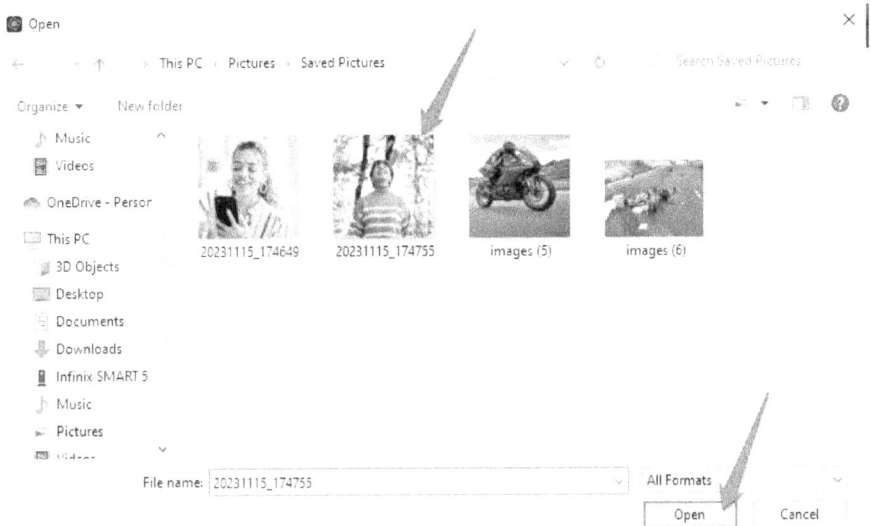

> ➢ The photo will be unlocked on the Quick mode workspace, click on the **view down arrow** and pick **Before & After Horizontal** to inspect the adjustments you are making on the original image compared to the initial image as an outcome of the editing you are passing over it.

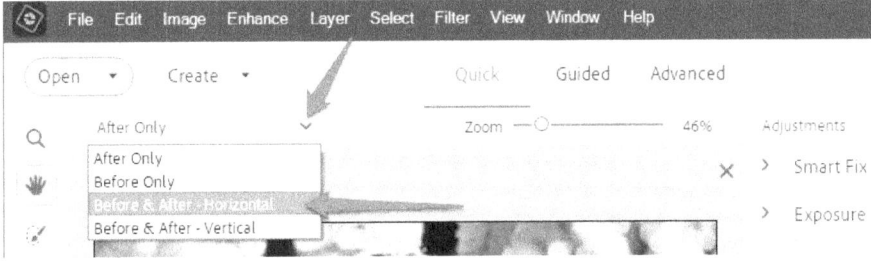

> ➢ You may quickly apply the **Smart Fix** in the panel bin by clicking on its arrow and dragging the slider button. You can also use the **Crop and Hand Tools** in the tools box, The **crop tool** assist you in cutting the unnecessary part out while the **hand tool** assists you in seeing any aspect of the image just for a simple remodeling.

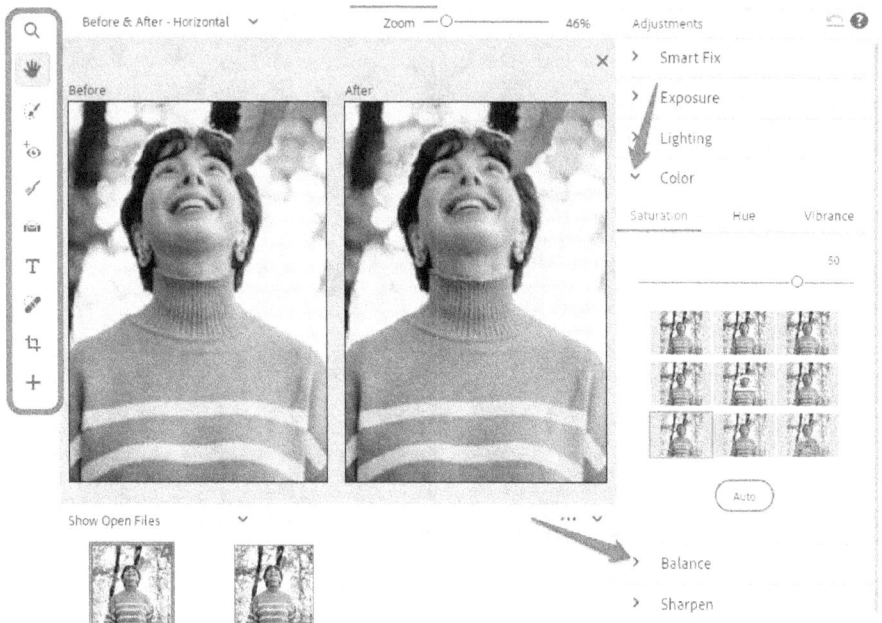

> After the simple correction, you can save your photo, by going back to the **File tab** and **Save As** to access the Save As dialog box, input a different name from the original name into the **file name,** and click on **Save** Button.

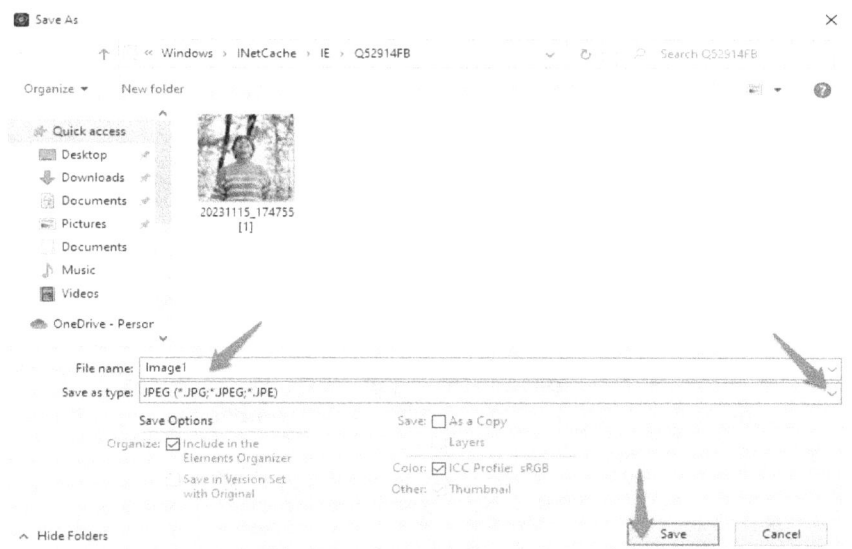

Note: saving your photo with a different name and Save AS commands keep your original image content untouched and save the edited photo as a separate photo.

CHAPTER TWO

UPLOADING PHOTOS WITH PHOTOSHOP ELEMENTS

Photoshop Elements allows you to share the photo you edited with Photoshop application to social media platforms such as Facebook, Twitter, Instagram, and so on. You can also share the following media on the internet:

- **Video and Audio:** both video and audio tracks can be uploaded to families and friends on the internet.
- **Album:** you can add numerous pictures together and send them to the internet.
- **Slide Show:** you can also make a slide show presentation and send it to the internet.

Photoshop Elements pictures can be shared on the internet through the Organizer and Photo Editor, to share pictures to the internet through Organizer, kindly:

1. Click the **Organizer** from the Photoshop Elements Home screen.
2. Click on **Media** from the Organizer screen, then select the **pictures** you want to upload (Ctrl+click for numerous pictures selection).
3. Click on the **Share** menu and choose the **Social media** button where you are sending the pictures.

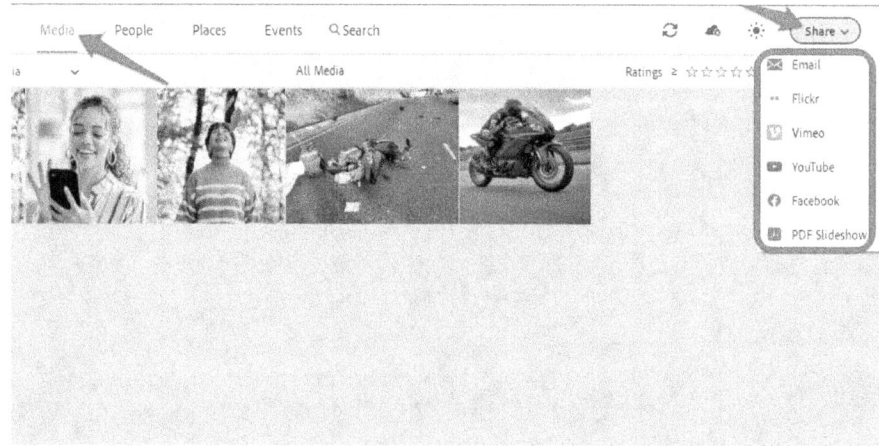

To make use of **Photo Editor** in uploading photos, kindly:

1. Launch into **Photo Editor** from the Photoshop Elements Home screen.
2. Choose the **Photos** you are sending to the internet from the Photo Bin (Ctrl+Click for numerous image selections).
3. Click on the **Share** menu and choose the social media where the Photos are going.

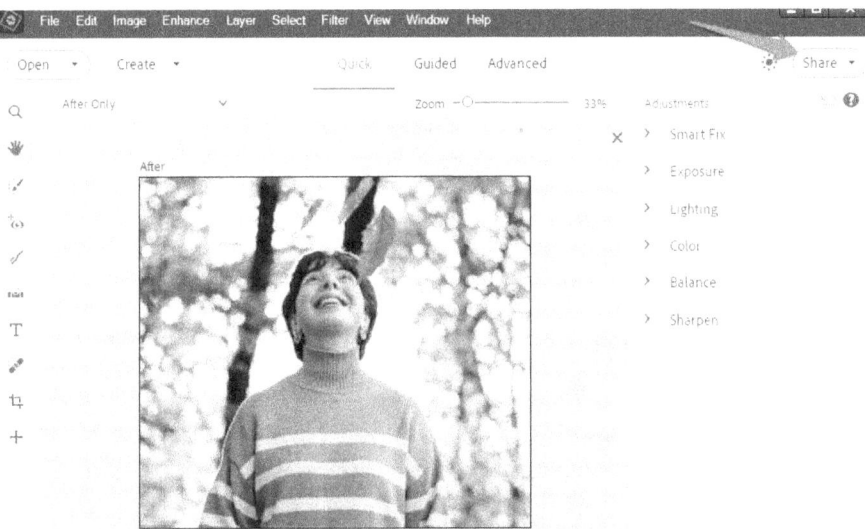

APPLYING UNDO AND REDO BY TRACKING EDITING STEPS

Undo and redo are influential tools for tracking your previous image editing work. Whenever you discover unwanted editing on the photo you are editing, Undo is needed, you can easily trace the editing with Undo or (Ctrl+Z), and you continue pressing Undo or Ctrl+Z until you backstage to the editing steps you need. Nevertheless, you can apply Redo to forward editing steps peradventure you have used the Undo command too much, Redo will assist you in tracking it forward again. Redo is inactive till you Undo an action because it only works when an action is undone. To track or trace editing steps forward or backward to correct a certain error, kindly follow these instructions:

➤ Click on the **Edit tab** and choose Undo or press **Ctrl+Z** to remove the previous editing step you do not need.

➤ Click on **Redo** or press **Ctrl+Y** in case you have undone too many steps.

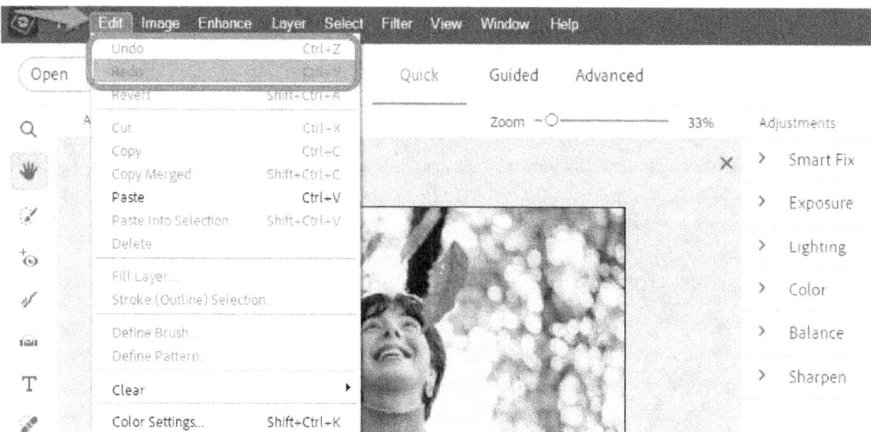

REMOVING EDITING STEPS WITH HISTORY BOX

Immediately you start editing an image, each step you took on the image is passed on into the History box. History Box can only be accessed under Advanced mode; it will not work out if you try it on Quick mode. Follow these instructions to undo some unwanted steps in your image with the History box.

➤ Move to the **Advanced mode** by clicking the **Advanced** at the top of the Photo Editor.

➤ Click on the **Window tab** and choose the **History** button from the drop-down list.

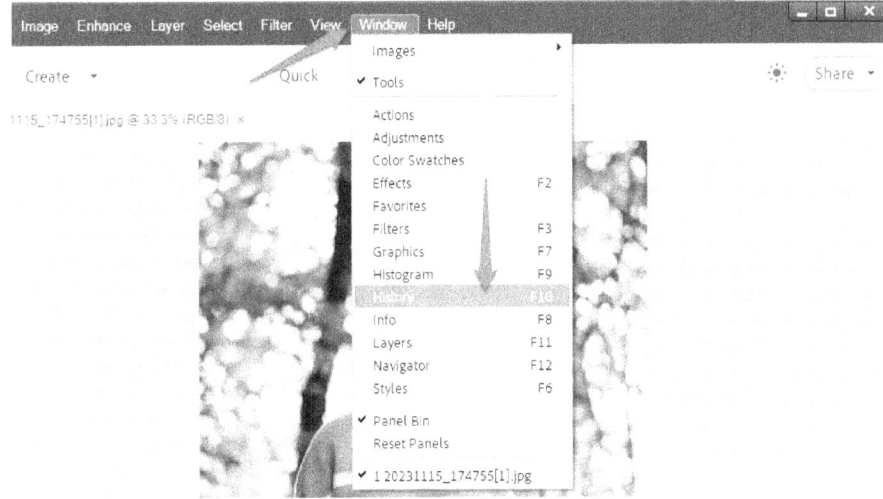

> The History box begins the listing of the state from the later editing to the earlier editing, which means the oldest states inhabit the top while the recent ones inhabit the bottom of the list. Click on each step to undo them. In case you click earlier editing (that is from the top) you automatically inform Photoshop Element to undo the later editing steps (the steps that follow it).

> Each step you undo will become **dull,** you may redo it with a single click one more time in the history box.

MANAGING THE HISTORY BOX

For instance, if you have about 700 states editing on the history box, these 700 states inhabit the system memory which may negatively affect the system operation especially if the PC does not have enough storage space. To manage the History box, apply these two techniques:

1. **Clear the content on the History/clipboard:** the operation system will be affected by slowing down the rate of operation when the history box/clipboard is crowded with too much content, so it is essential to always clear the content on the History box/clipboard, to do that, kindly follow the step below:

> Click the **Edit tab** and click the **Clear** menu from the drop-down list, then choose **Clear History, Clipboard content, or Both to clear** some space for the memory.

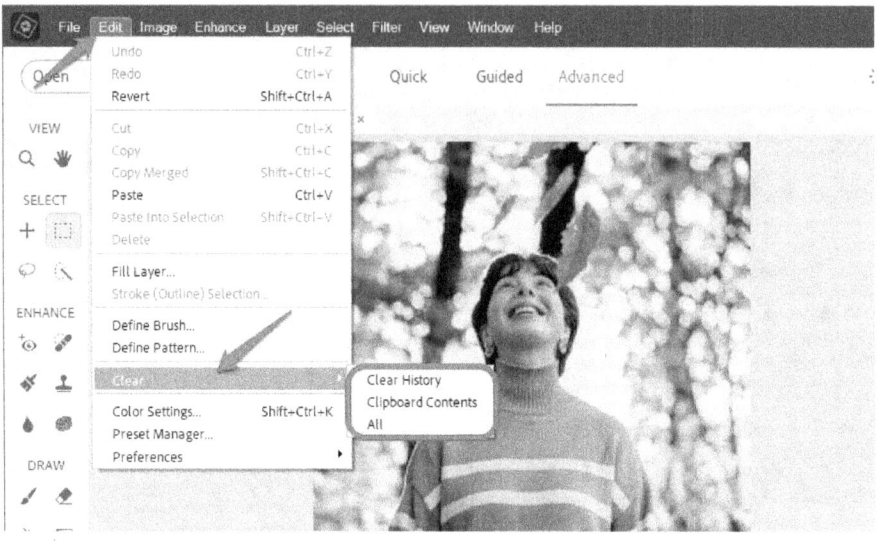

2. **Maintaining the default History state:** though Element permits you to have a maximum of 1000 history states, it is advisable to maintain 70 history states to create enough space memory for the operating system, raising history capacity above 100 states may affect the PC operating system negatively. Follow these steps to set the maximum history state for your history box:

➤ Click on the **Edit** menu and click on the **Preferences menu,** then lastly choose performance to open the Preferences dialog box by activating the performance tab.

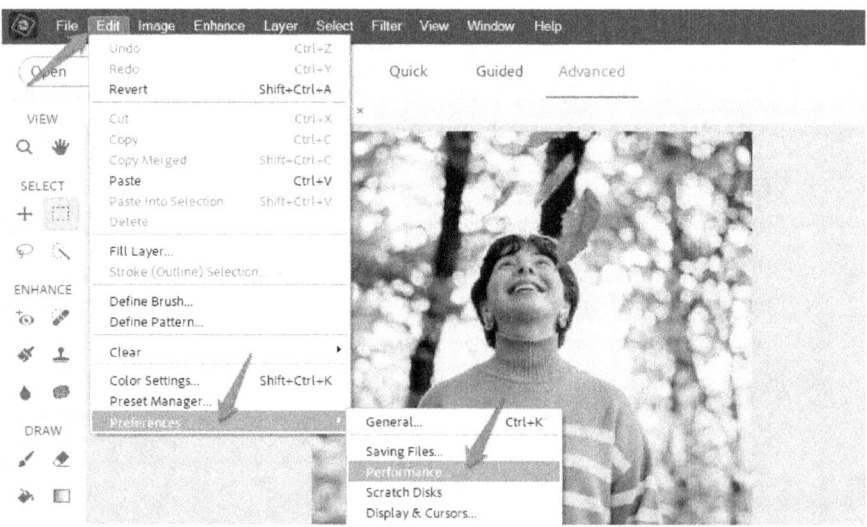

➢ Shift to History & cache beneath the Performance tab, then clear the **history state and input the maximum history states** which must not be more than 100 states for the sake of the PC operating system, then click OK.

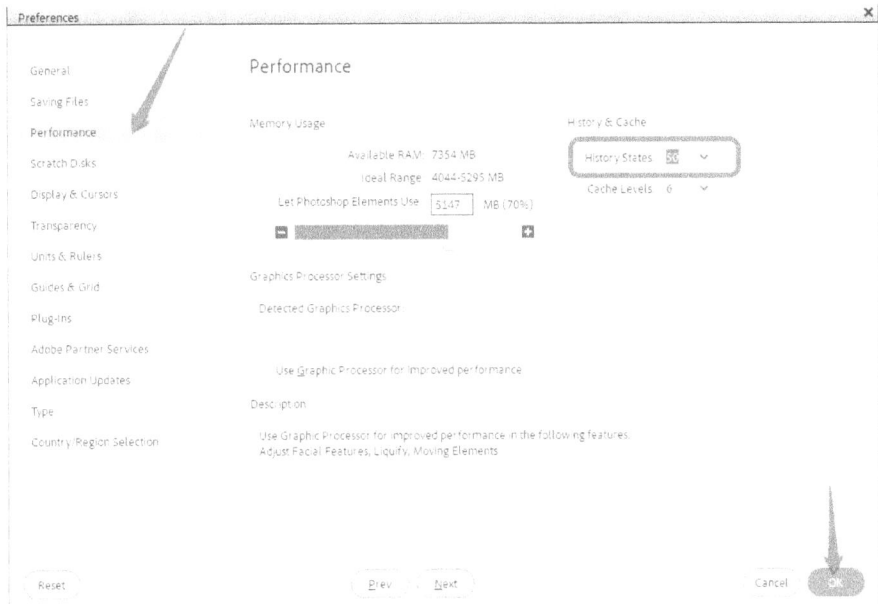

REMOVING EDITS TO THE LAST SAVE WITH REVERT COMMAND

Perhaps you want to remove particular editing you made after the last save, Element will assist you in doing that if you carry out your editing saving one after the other. To erase the editing action till the last saved action, follow the steps below:

1. Bang on the **Edit tab** and click **Revert** to remove the edit task till the last saved.

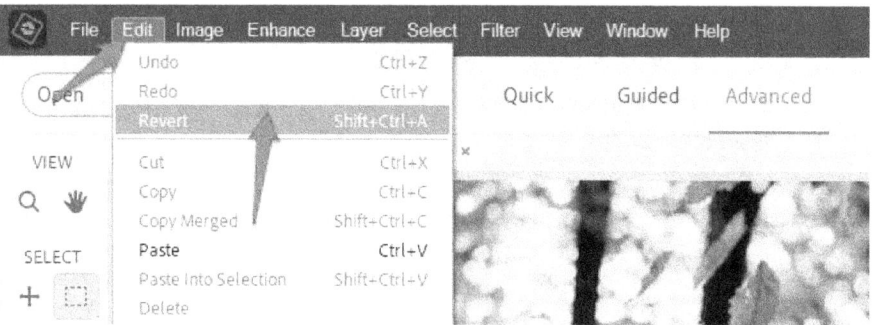

GAIN ACCESS TO MORE INSTRUCTION WITH THE HELP COMMAND

Help command provides you with instructions when you need certain assistance which you may not find inside the manual guide. To ask Elements for a precise direction on any aspect that relates to the Element assignment, see the following guides as listed beneath the Help menu:

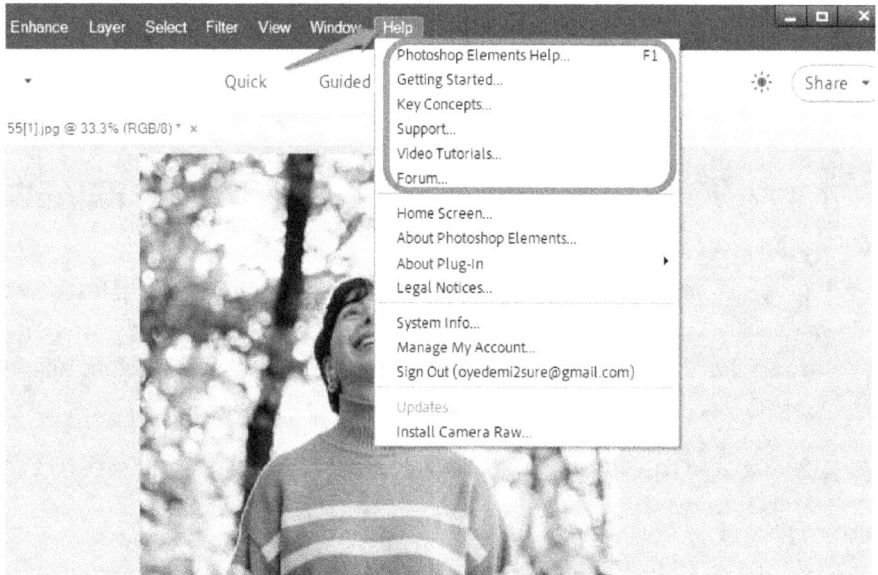

1. **Photoshop Elements Help:** this is the first option instantaneously you click on the Help tab, and you can also press F1 to access Photoshop Elements Help. Input any information you want from the Elements Help and press the Enter key to process the outcome for you.

2. **Getting Started:** this option provides you with the fundamental knowledge and information you need to start any task on Element.
3. **Key Concept:** the key concept provides you with significant terminology and concepts that are necessary for you to know when dealing with Element assignments.
4. **Support:** this option provides you with any support you may need on Element by importing you to the Official website of Adobe www.adobe.com, to obtain the support of any kind.
5. **Video tutorial:** it helps you to obtain any video that relates to obtaining some task done on Photoshop Elements from the Adobe Website.
6. **Forum:** the last option is the community of Adobe where you can meet others and discuss with other Adobe users who may have more knowledge than you.

DIVERSE REASONS FOR SAVING FILES DIFFERENTLY

The last thing to do when you are done doing justice to the image by purifying the image and its environment is to save such image in different names, formats, and folders which I will be discussing vividly one after the other below.

SAVING THE IMAGE AS THE ORIGINAL

Saving an image as the original means you are saving the image without duplicating any copy, that is to say, you have only the copy of the image saved. Follow the steps below to do that:

➢ Click the **File** tab and choose the **Save** command to access the Save/Save As dialog box.

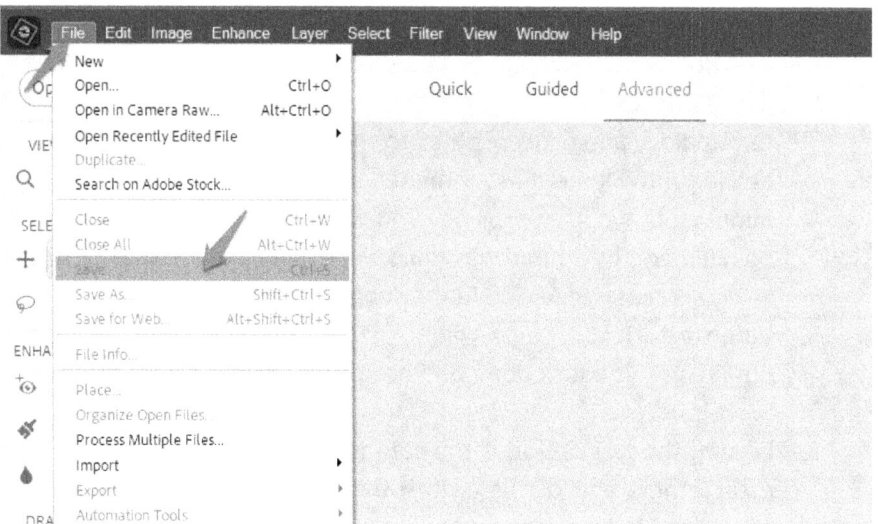

> ➤ Input the **name** you want for the file name into the file name box and choose the Format you want for your file from the **Save as type** drop-down list. Click on the **Save** button for verification.

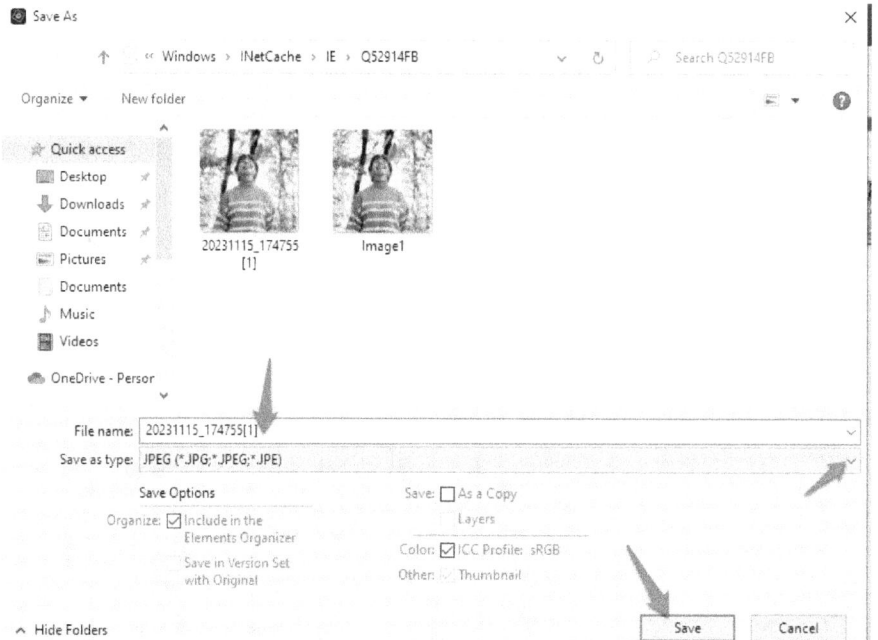

SAVING IMAGE TO DUPLICATE THE IMAGE FILE

Saving in this manner is very helpful, it will not let you lose the original image and you simply go back to the original image and start editing again whenever you lose the duplicated one. To save files and keep the original, follow the steps below:

➢ Click the File tab and choose the **Save As** command to access the Save/Save As dialog box.

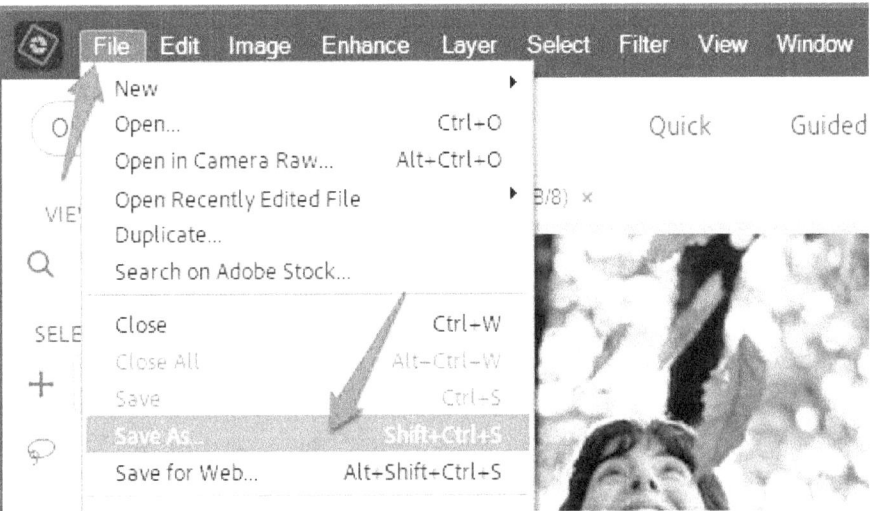

➢ Input the **name** you want for the file name into the file name box and choose the Format you want for your file from the **Save As Type** drop-down list.
➢ Click on the **Save** button for verification.

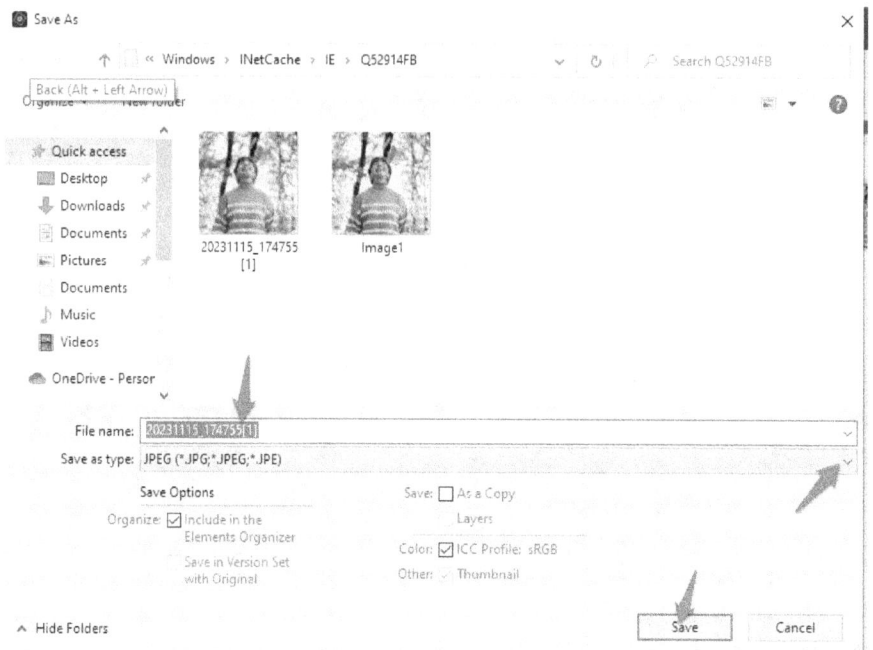

Element Save/Save As dialog box has exceptional saving options which set it apart from other Save/Save As dialog boxes, those options are discussed below:

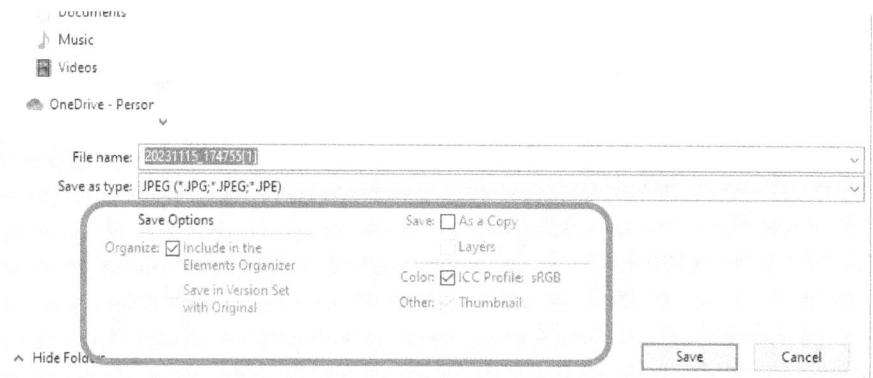

- **Include in the Element organizer:** put a mark beside this check box to add the image you are about to save to the organizer list.

- **Save in Version Set with Original:** putting a mark in this check box will assist you in saving the version of the original image file though this option is only available in Quick mode.

- **As a Copy:** putting a mark in this check box assists you in saving a copy of the original image without terminating the original image's contents.

- **Layers:** it works for the image with layers, to protect the image layers, put a mark on this check box.

- **ICC Profile:** putting a mark on this check box assists you in preserving the color profile of the image.

- **Thumbnail:** positioning a mark on this check box allows you to view the small copy of the image anytime you are viewing it on the document or desktop, you have to select **ask** in the Saving file preference. The check box will be available for you to activate or deactivate. But if you select **always**, it will pick activate itself automatically, if you choose **never**, it will deactivate itself automatically.

SAVING FILES INTO DIFFERENT FILE FORMATS

There are numerous formats for saving the file in Elements, and you have to select one of them to save your file, which ever file you pick will affect the structure of your file, you can have a glimpse of how they are listed in the **Save As dialog box** under Save As type menu.

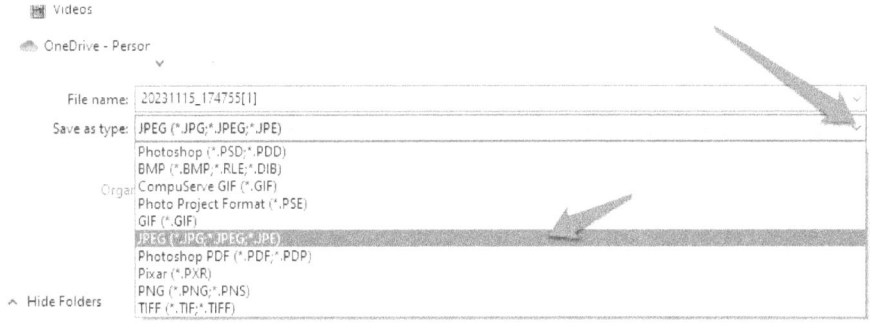

I will be using JPEG as a template for how to save files.

JPEG (JOINT PHOTOGRAPHER EXPERTS GROUP)

This is generally used by all users for saving because it is characterized by a small file size. Follow these steps below to save your file in JPEG format:

> Click the **File tab** and choose **Save As.**

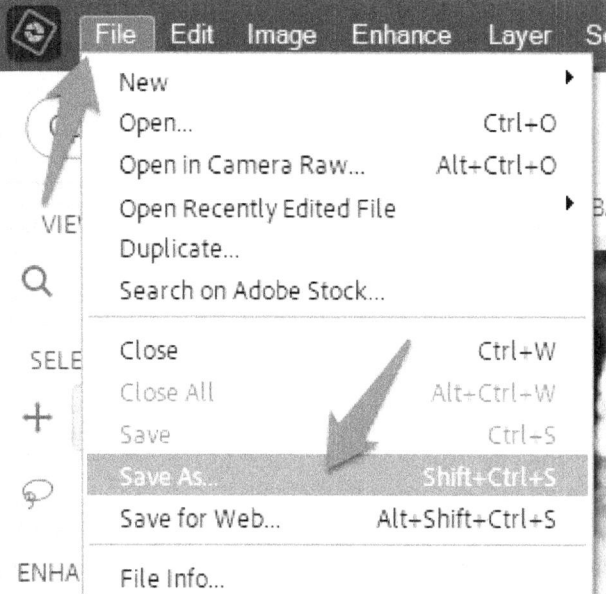

> Choose the location where to save the file and enter the name you want for the file into the file name.

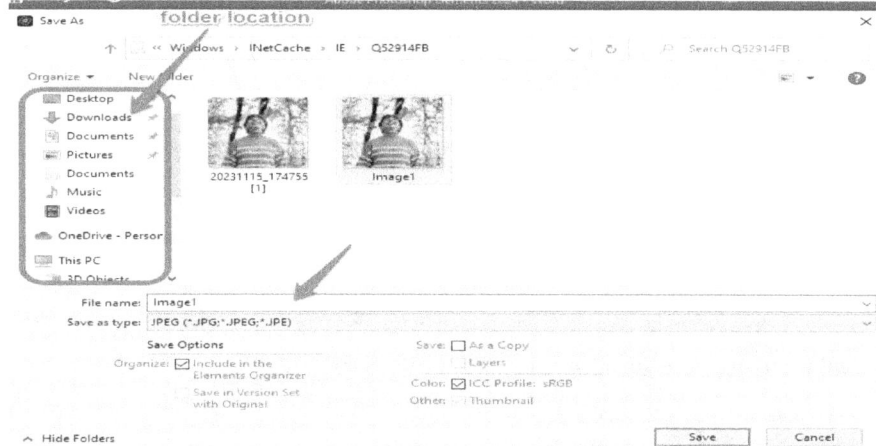

➢ Click on the **Save as type** menu, then choose the format you want in this case I will be choosing **JPEG** format.

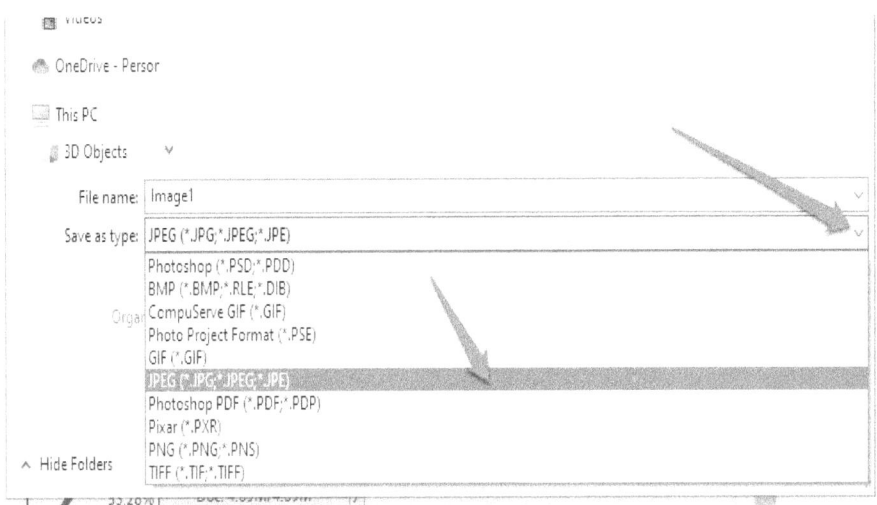

➢ Click on the **Save** button to access the JPEG dialog box.

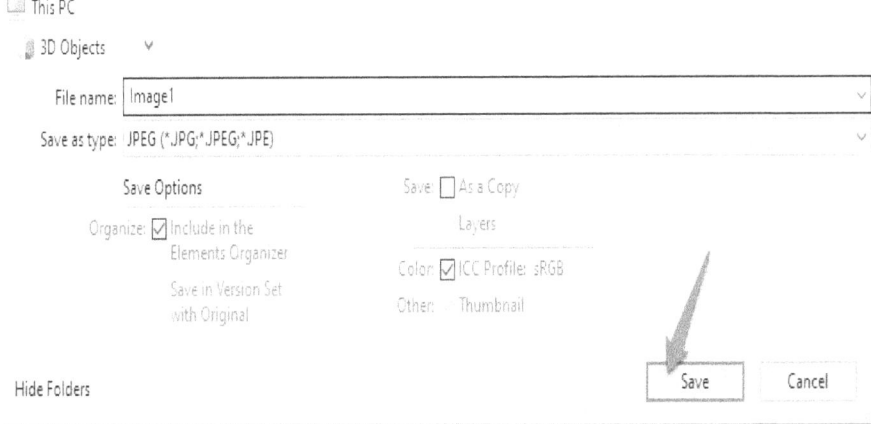

➢ Choose a color to simulate the background of your file if it has a transparency background, adjust the quality of your image by clicking on the **Quality** menu and choosing from low to large or dragging the quality slide to set your file quality.
➢ Choose the file option you want by clicking any of the three **Format Options** and clicking OK.

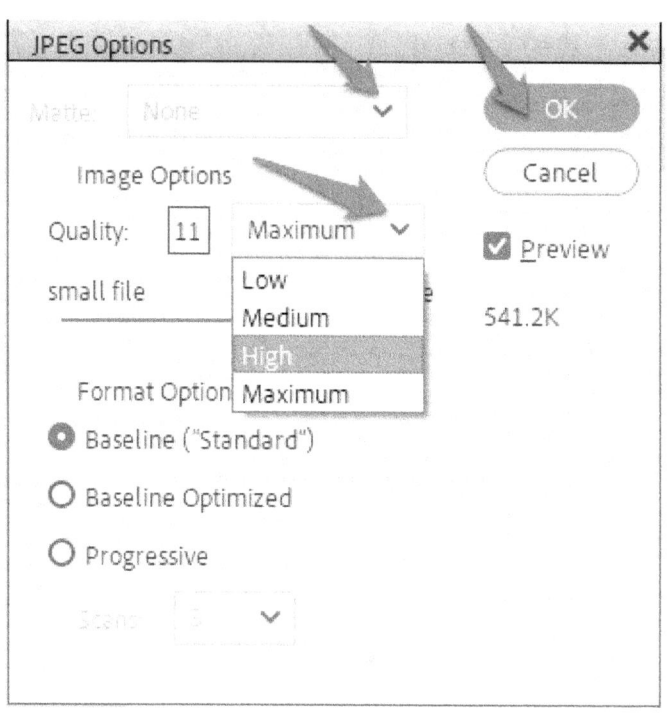

CHAPTER THREE

IMPORTANT REQUIREMENT FOR IMAGE EDITING

It is very important to familiarize yourself with the fundamental requirements before moving to the image editing scene to get the finest and greatest editing outcome, such as Resolution, Dimension, Pixel, and Color mode (profile).

THE WORD PIXEL

Pixels are the short form for Picture Elements, Pixels are the little lines organized in a two-dimensional grid known as a square, for illustration, an image that contains 204 pixels in width and 146 in height has a combination of 29784 pixels.

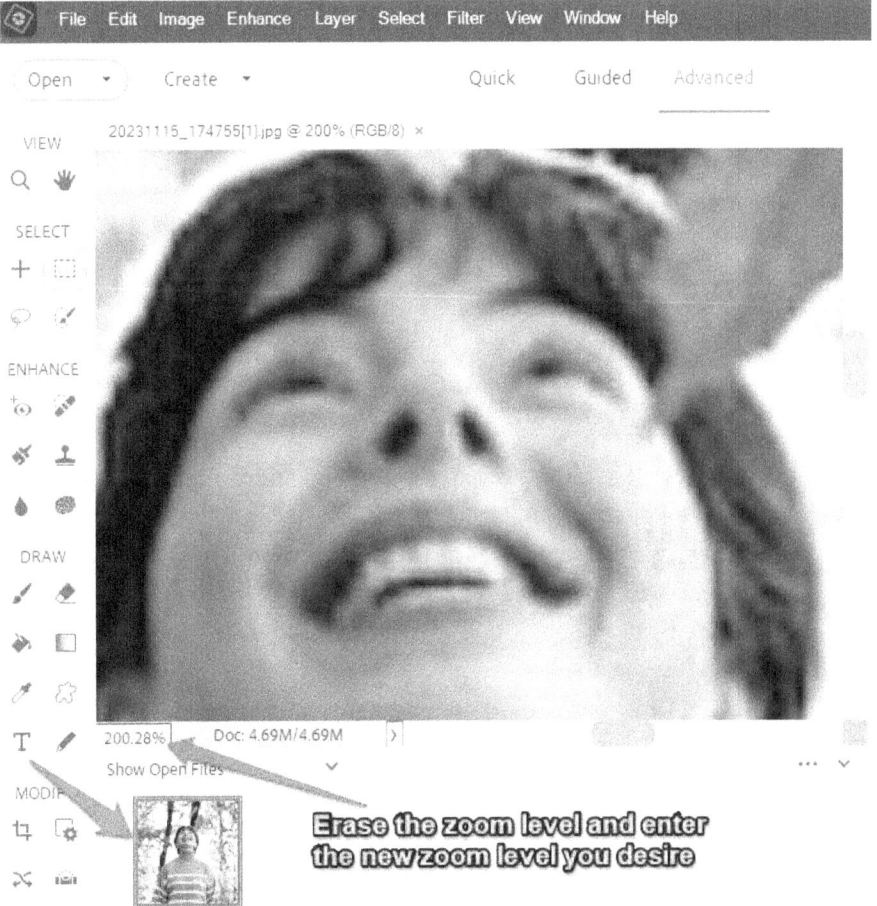

DEALING WITH IMAGE RESOLUTION

Resolution refers to the number of pixels that an image has that is to say pixels are the major determinant of Resolution. Resolution is measured by pixels per inch (PPI).

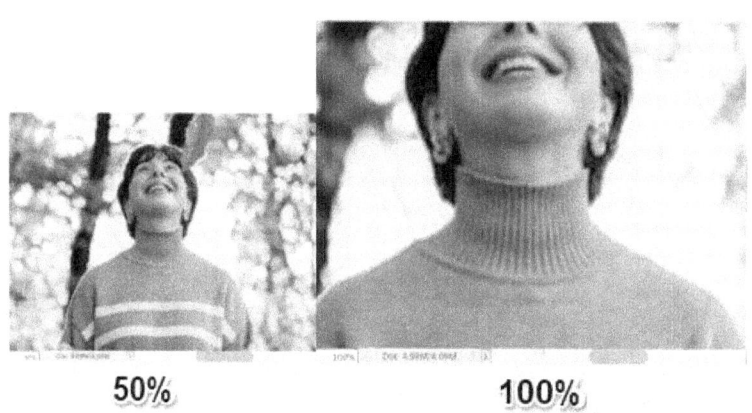

Image resolution is very important when editing an image especially if it is for these two motives:

1. **Image Printing:** based on experiment and knowledge, the resolution measurement that will give the greatest and finest outcome or result image for printing is 300 ppi on all the printers, setting a resolution too high will give an unnecessarily large file size while setting a resolution too low will gives low image quality when printing, so balancing is required.
2. **Viewing Onscreen:** based on experience and experiment, 100 ppi or thereabout always works well on all monitors while 75 ppi or thereabout will work better on a Macs monitor.

IMAGE DIMENSION

Image dimension can refer to the length and width of an image, it is always measured in pixels, nevertheless, some graphics measure their image dimension in points, inches, centimeters, and so on.

DIFFERENCE BETWEEN RESAMPLING AND RESIZING AN IMAGE

Resampling is an act of modifying the image resolution, which is an act of removing or adding numerous pixels in the image. Sampling up means you are increasing the number of pixels meanwhile sampling down means you are reducing the number of pixels.

Resizing on the other hand simply means decreasing or increasing the size of the pixels of an image.

TECHNIQUE OF RESAMPLING AN IMAGE

To get started in resampling an image, you will need to make use of the image size dialog box, then follow the instructions below:

1. Click the image tab, then click on the **Resize** menu from the image drop-down list, select **Image Size** from the Resize drop-down menu to access the image dialog box, or press **Ctrl+Alt+I**

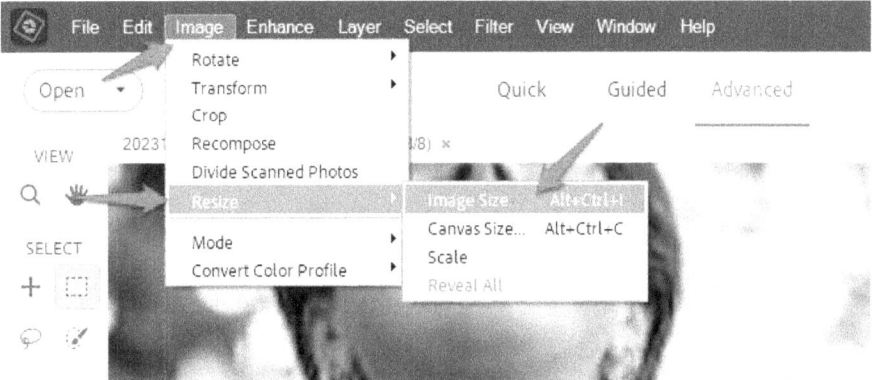

2. **Scale styles:** put a checkmark on the scale styles to allow you to add many style effects to your image such as border, and framework, it will appear the same as the size of the image you choose it for.
3. **Constraint Proportion:** make sure you tick this check box always, it assists in conveying your picture so that it will not be inaccurate.

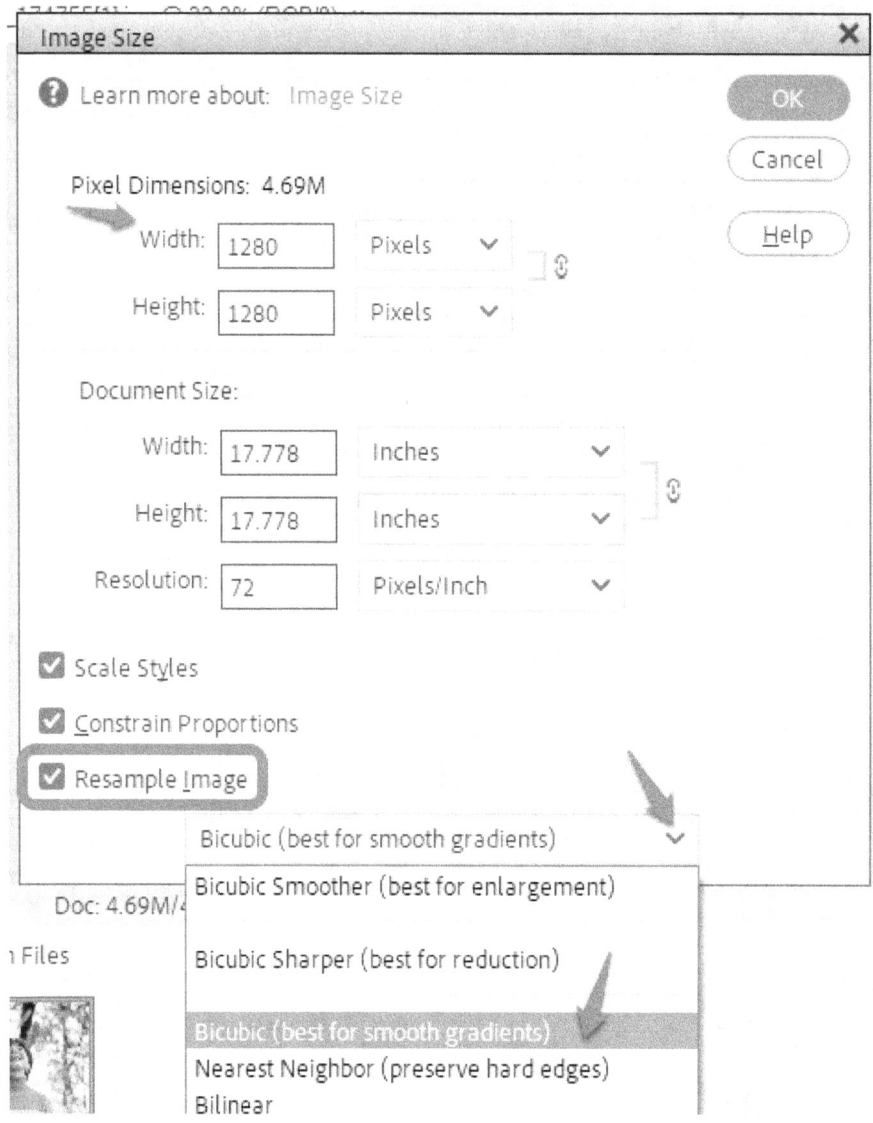

4. **Resample Image:** position a mark on the Resample Image check box, for you to modify the height and width dimension, or else you will not be permitted to edit the height and width dimension of the image and again to make the scale styles and constraint options active.

5. you may then modify the width of the image now, immediately you modify the width and height will be adjusted spontaneously.

6. You can now select any technique of **Resampling** you want among the following
- **Bicubic smoother**
- **Bilinear**
- **Bicubic**
- **Bicubic sharpener.**
7. You can also modify the **Resolution** but it will affect the image dimension, nevertheless, if you desire to modify the resolution alone without affecting the image dimension, cancel the mark on the Resampling image text box. Then press OK.

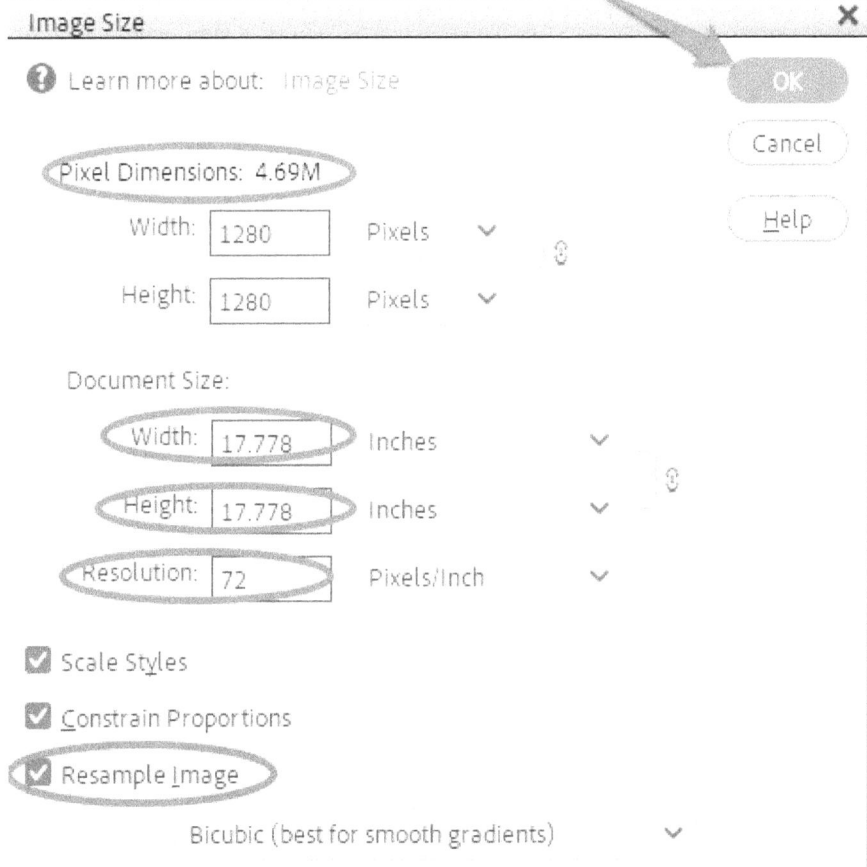

ACQUAINTANCE WITH THE USAGE OF COLOR

Color option is very dominant in Photoshop Element, you cannot ignore it, the fundamental thing you need to know is the type of color that you will be dealing with while working on Photoshop Element, RGB is known as Primary color and is grouped into three components, they are Red, Blue, and Green. Let us take a glance at the level of color to check each component:

1. Click on the **Enhance** menu and choose the **Adjusted Lighting menu.**
2. Choose **Levels** from Adjust lighting fly-out to access Level's dialog box.

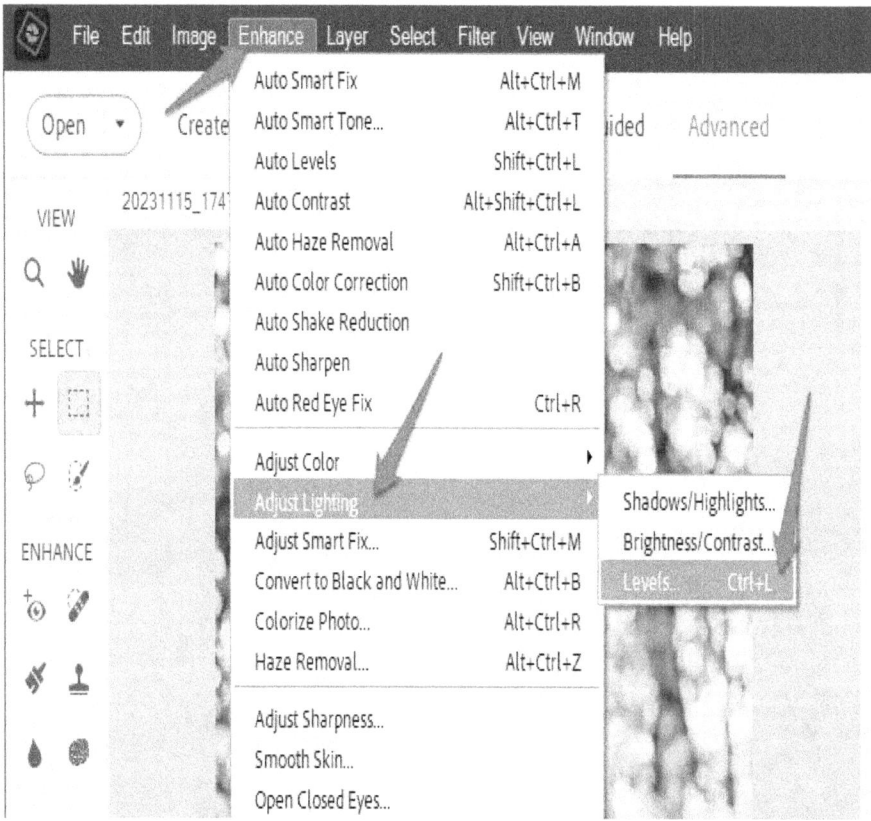

3. The dialog box reveals to you the **RGB** as a complete and distinct component that makes up **RGB** immediately after you click on the **RGB** menu, each component can permit you to modify the balance of your image lightness.

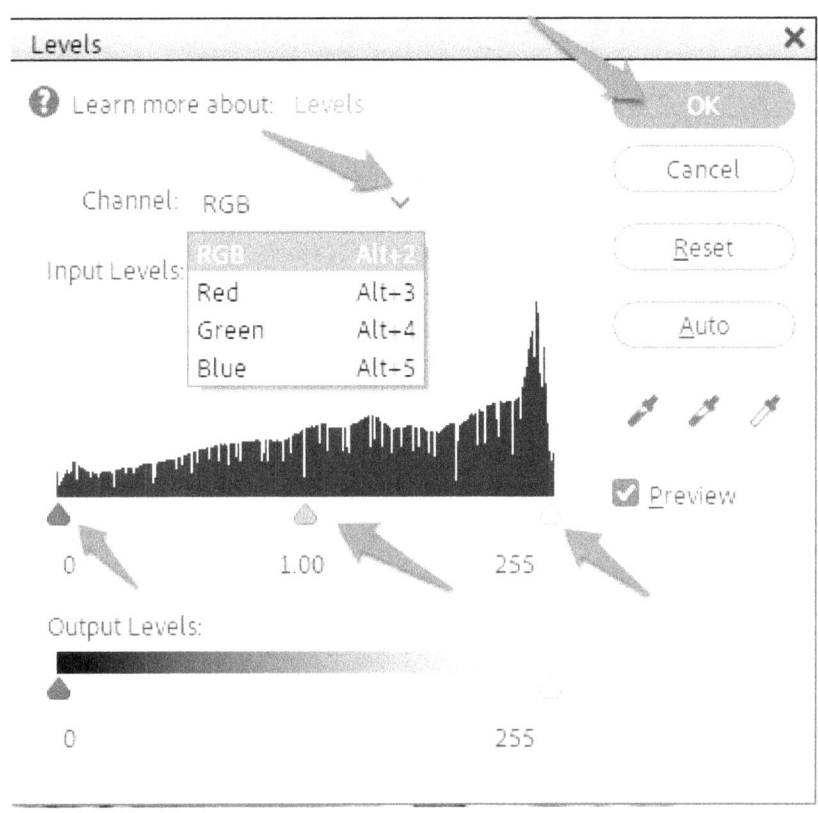

The quantity of darker color is positioned at the left and the quantity of lighter color is positioned at the right.

CHAPTER FOUR

UNDERSTANDING PHOTO EDITOR WORKSPACE

There is one Editor workspace in Photoshop Elements which is called Photo Editor, and there are three modes in Photo Editor which are Quick mode, Guided mode, and Advanced mode. The Quick mode has been explained earlier in this mini-book, therefore I will be jumping to Advanced mode which is one of the new features in Photoshop Element 2024, so let us quickly take a glance at each tool in the Advanced mode workspace to fast-track your process when editing an image on Elements. The image below displays the Photo Editor Workspace in Advance mode.

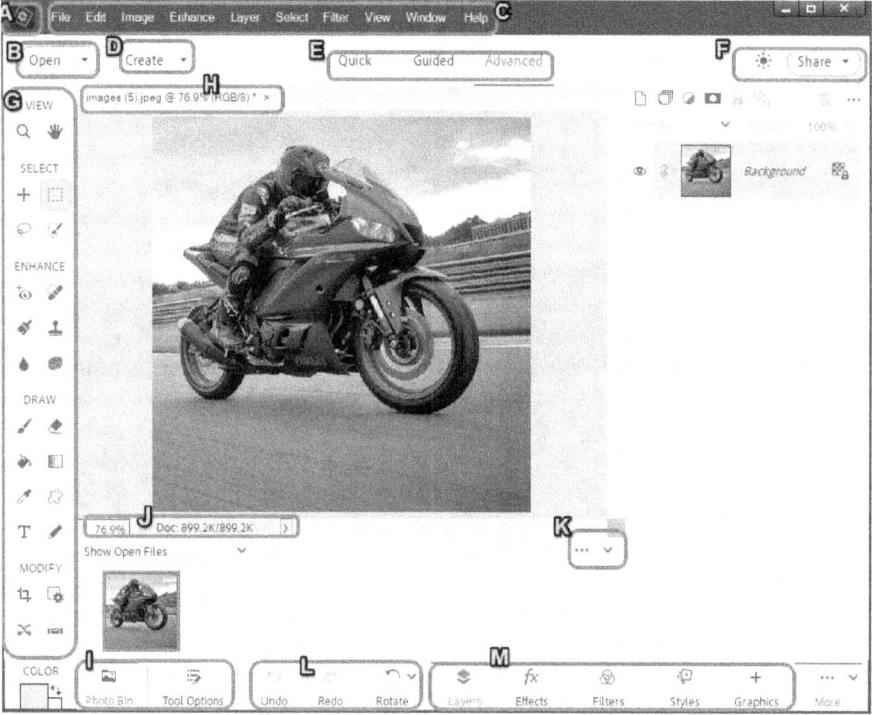

A. **System menu button:** this comprises a simple drop-down menu such as Move, Restore, Size, and so on.

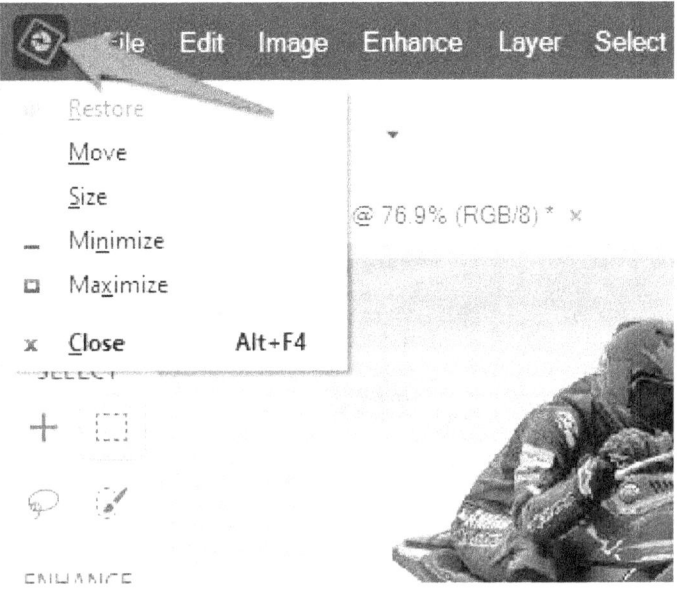

B. **Open button:** this can be found at the top of the tools box, it comprises a drop-down menu of the image you have recently unlocked and the creation of the new blank file.

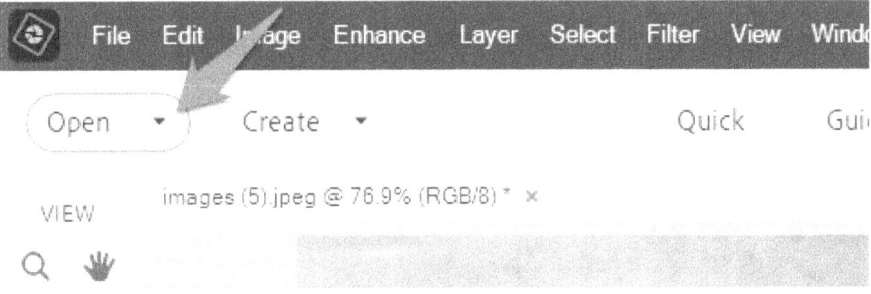

C. **Menu bar:** this can be located at the top of the Photo Editor, it comprises tasks, such as Edit, Image, File, and so on. Each of the categories contains numerous subcommands beneath them for executing many tasks that cannot be found in the toolbox.

D. **Create:** this includes numerous options for creating and image.

E. **Photo editor mode:** this permits you to shift between the three Photo Editors (Quick, Guided, and Advance).

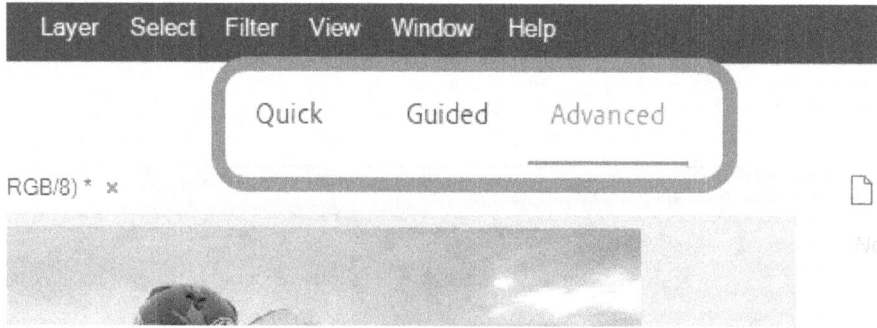

F. **Share button:** this button contains numerous options for sharing an image.

G. **The tools box:** this houses the tools you can use for image editing and improvement such as the Hand tool, Move tool, Crop tool, and so on.

H. **Image tabs:** this is the tab for all the images that you unlocked in the Photo Editor.

I. **Photo Bin & Tool option:** these two features can be located beneath the status bar. The photo bin permits you to view and choose photos meanwhile Tool option provides you information about the chosen tool.

J. **Status bar:** it shows the information about the image that you are presently working on.

K. **Photo bin option:** this gives you more options on the unlocked image such as Show Grid, Save Bin as an Album, and so on.

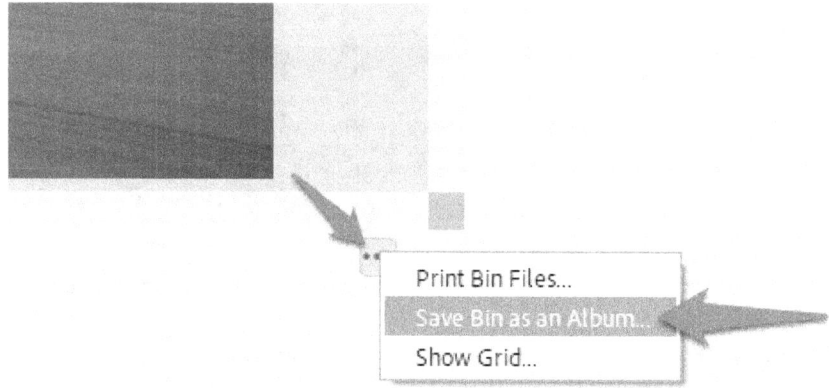

L. **Undo, Redo, and Rotate:** these three buttons are positioned beside the photo bin and tool option beneath the screen. Undo is used to reverse a mistake you made while Redo is used to reverse undo an action. Then Rotate has a drop-down you can apply to rotate an image from one side to another.

THE IMAGE WINDOW

The image window is the workspace where different image editing is being carried out, to unlock the image window, kindly follow the steps below:

➢ Click the **File tab** and select **Open** from the drop-down menu to view the Open dialog box.

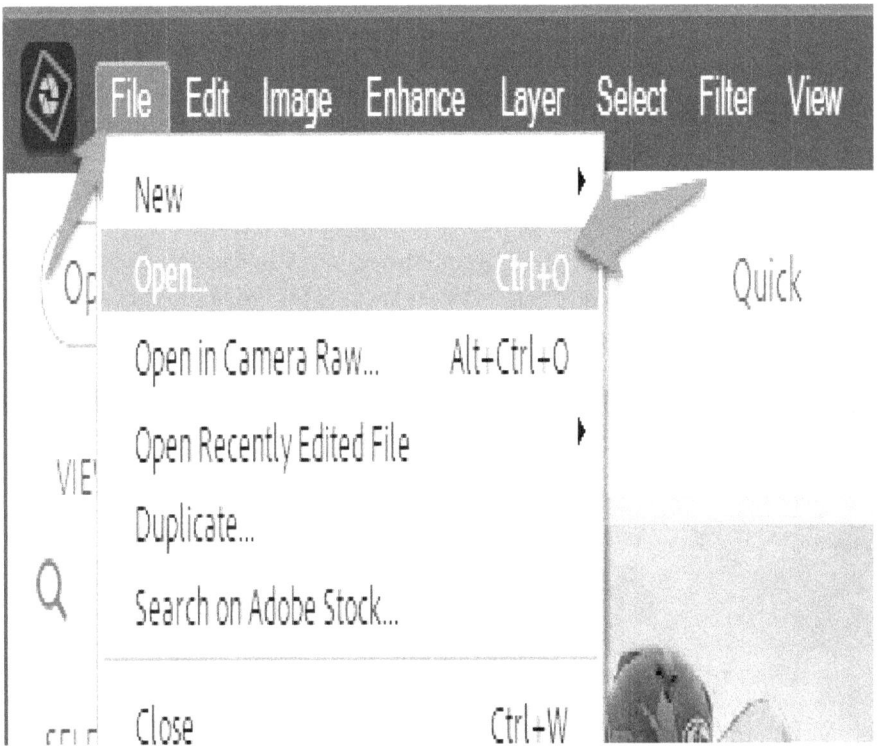

➢ Unlock the folder where the picture you want to edit can be found, then look for the Photo you want to use, click on it, and also click on the **Open** button.

45

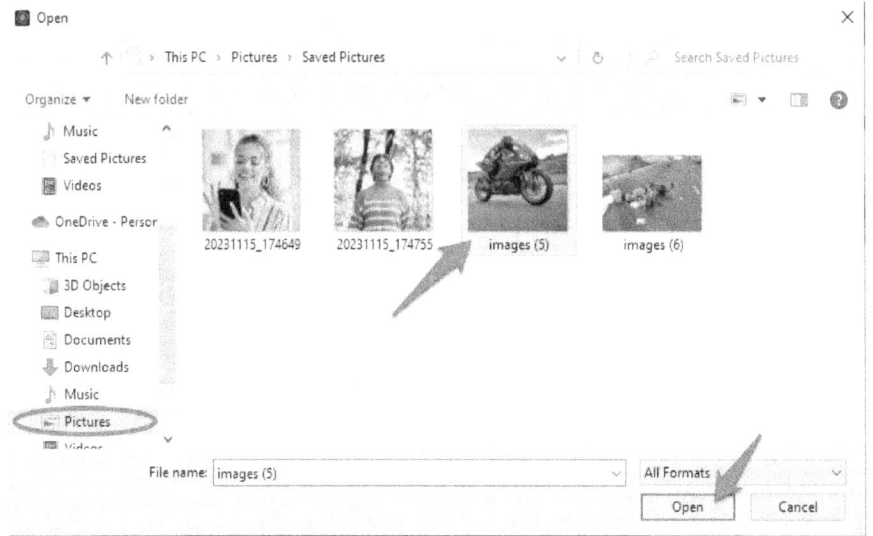

> ➢ Instantly you open the image, such an image will be opened up in the image window.

You can select many images, the more you include images the more the thumbnails you will have in the Photo Bin. You can also use Ctrl-click to select numerous images. Let us speedily move around the image window to have clarity of each piece of data there:

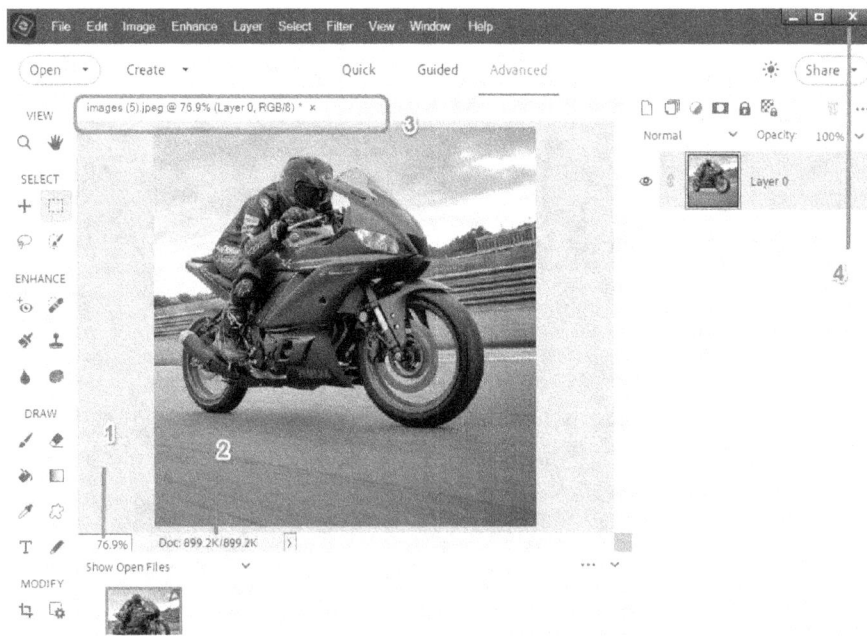

1. **Magnificent box:** this box helps you to know how the image is being zoomed in.
2. **Information bar:** it shows information about the image you are working on in the image window by applying the drop-down menu to choose any information you need.

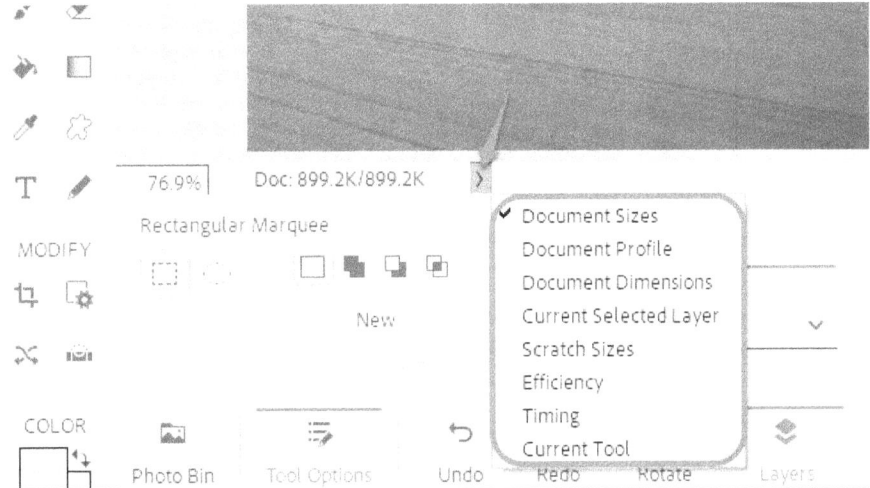

3. **Filename:** this is the name of the image unlock in the Photo Editor.
4. **Close button:** if you want to close the image click on the icon(X).

CONTEXT MENU

This is a commands menu that shows on the active tool when you right-click a chosen area with the mouse. Do these if you want to discover the context menu:

➢ Position your mouse on an image and right-click the image with the tool you are making use of.
➢ Then apply any commands you want from the context menu that comes into sight.

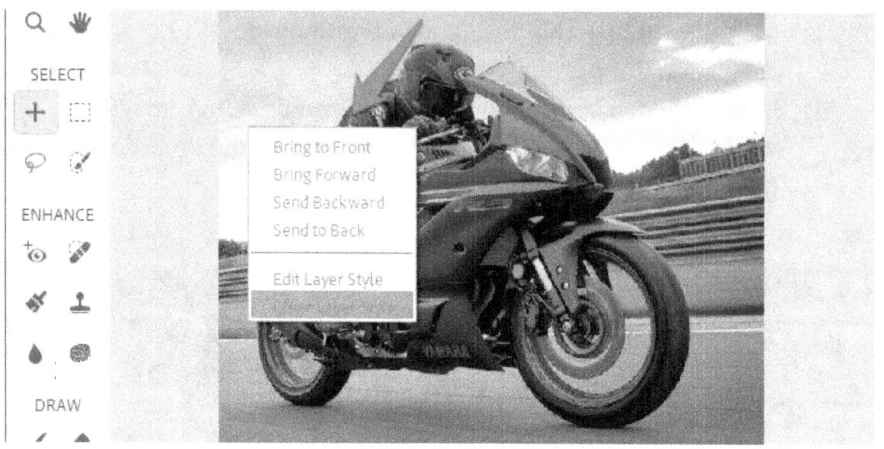

FAMILIARIZING WITH THE FUNCTIONS OF EACH ELEMENT TOOL

Elements give you numerous tools for image manipulation, let's observe them on each side of the Quick mode and Advanced mode.

QUICK MODE TOOLS BOX

The following tools are the tools that can be located in the Quick mode: Hand tool, Crop tool, Selection tool, and so on. I will be discussing them in the Advanced mode because they serve the same motive in both modes.

EXPERT MODE TOOL BOX

Advanced mode contains more practical tools than the Quick mode tool because it is created for professionals who can manipulate the image for any purpose. Therefore, we shall be looking at the function of each tool based on the Advanced tools categories with their keyboard shortcuts.

View group tools

Tool Icon and Shortcuts	Functions
Zoom Tool (Z)	It is created for zooming in and out an image
Hand Tool (H)	To move within the image to show aspects of the image that need unusual attention.

Select Group Tools

Tool Icon and Shortcut	Functions
Lasso tool (L)	It is used to draw free-form selections to make a curved selection on the image.
Elliptical Marquee tool (M)	It is used to define an aspect of an image by drawing an elliptical all over the aspect you want to edit.
Move tool (V)	It is used to move the selected aspect of the image and layer.
Rectangular Marquee tool (M)	This is used to define an aspect of the image by drawing a rectangular box all over the area you want to edit.
Auto Selection tool (A)	This automatically chooses the area you draw around within an image area.
Refine Selection tool (Y)	This is used to add or remove an aspect to the selection aspect for spotting the image edge automatically.
Magic wand tool (A)	This is used to choose pixels within a similar color or tone range with a single click.
Selection Brush tool (A)	This is used for choosing an aspect to be painted with a brush.
Magnetic Lasso tool (L)	This is used for drawing a selection border which will select the pixel of the selected aspect automatically.
Polygonal Lasso tool (L)	This is used for drawing a straight-edge or straight-line selections.
Quick Selection tool (A)	This is used for choosing colors, edges, and features in the image area.

Enhance Group Tool

Tools Icon and Shortcuts	Functions
Smart Brush Tool	It changes the color and adds a tonal adjustment to the exact aspect of an image.
Spot Healing Brush Tool (J)	it is created to remove any spots from the chosen area of the image.
Eye Tool	this is used to correct closed eyes and remove the red-eye effect and pet-eye effect from the image.
Detail Smart Brush tool	it paints an area of the image to change the chosen area.
Clone Stamp Tool (S)	This is an image sample that can be used to paint an object in your image, remove image imperfections, or duplicate an object.
Pattern Stamp Tool (S)	This is used to paint a pattern on the chosen area of an image.
Sharpen Tool (R)	It aims at the soft edges of the image and sharpen such area to make is perfect
Blur Tool (R)	It is created to soften the hard edges or blur the chosen areas of an image by removing some elements.
Smudge Tool (R)	This is used to kindle a brush smearing wet paint.
Burn Tool (O)	This is used for the darkening aspect of an image.
Dodge Tool (O)	This is used for lightening an aspect of an image.
Sponge Tool	This is created to modify the saturation of an aspect in a photo.

Modify Group Tool

Tools Icon and Shortcuts	Functions

Perspective Crop Tool (C)	This is used for converting the cropped image from its perspective
Cookie Cutter Tool (C)	This is used for cropping an image to any shape you want
Crop Tool (C)	This is created to crop the aspect of an image for you to have the area you needed
Recompose Tool (W)	It is used to resize a picture without modifying the features and contents of the image
Straighten Tool (P)	This is used to organize the image vertically or horizontally
Content-Aware Tool (Q)	This is used for shifting objects and transferring them to different positions within the image.

Draw Group Tool

Tools Icon and Shortcuts	Functions
Brush Tool (B)	To improve airbrush methods and also to create hard or soft strokes of color
Impressionist Brush Tool (B)	To improve or modify the color and details of the image.
Color Replacement Tool (B)	This is used for editing particular colors in your image
Eraser Tool (E)	This is used to create the pixels in the image.
Pattern Tool (K)	It is used for applying a pattern to your image
Paint Bucket Tool (E)	For painting an aspect that is similar to the color value of the pixel you choose
Magic Erase Tool (E)	For changing every similar pixel
Background Eraser Tool (E)	For changing the color of pixels to transparent pixels for the simple removal of an object from its background

Types Tool (T)	It is an unusual tool used for creating and editing text on the image
Pencil Tool (N)	It was created to build hard-edged freehand lines.
Custom Shape Tool (U)	This permits you to draw numerous shape options such as ellipse, line, rectangle, and so no
Color Picker Tool (I)	This is used to copy the color of your image and generate a new background with the color
Gradient Tool (G)	This is used for applying a gradient to an aspect of an image

The explanation of each tool has been given, now it is essential to show you how to select them, follow these steps below to select any of the above tools:

1. Click the individual tool in the tools box.
2. Press the shortcut key of the tool you wish to choose, for instance, press **V** for the **Move tool.**

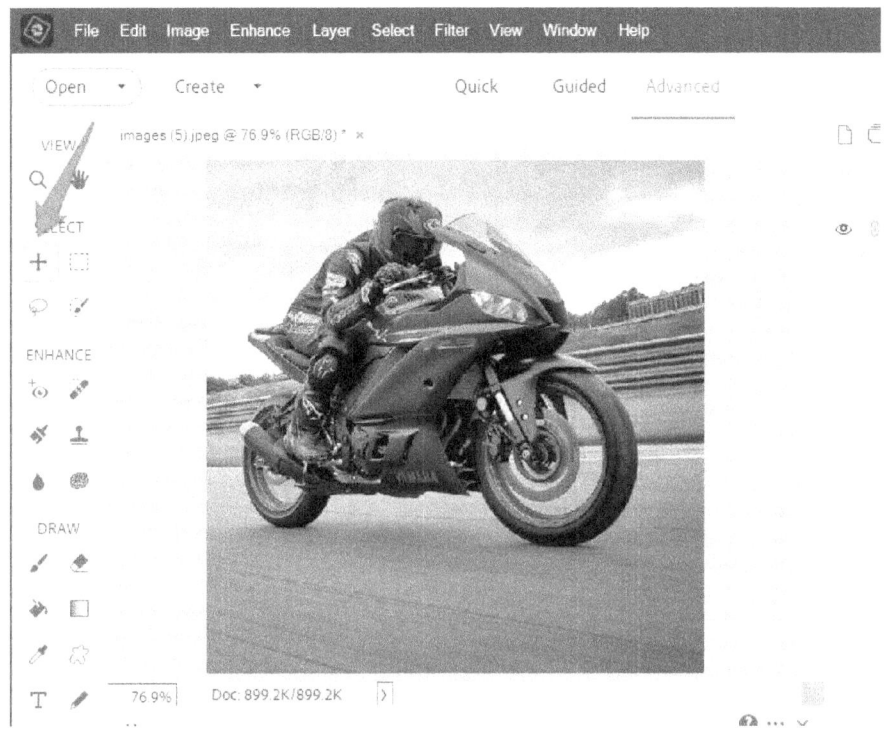

GAIN ACCESS TO MORE TOOLS WITH THE TOOLS OPTIONS

The tool option can be found beneath the Photo Editor Screen, though all the tools cannot be found in the group, immediately after you pick the connected tool, he remaining tool will come into sight in the tool option, for instance, if you click on the Quick Selection tool all other tools that are created for selection in that group will also come into sight in the Tool option such Selection Auto selection, Brush tool, Refine Selection, and others. Tool option also gives you numerous options for regulating the tool you chose in the tools box.

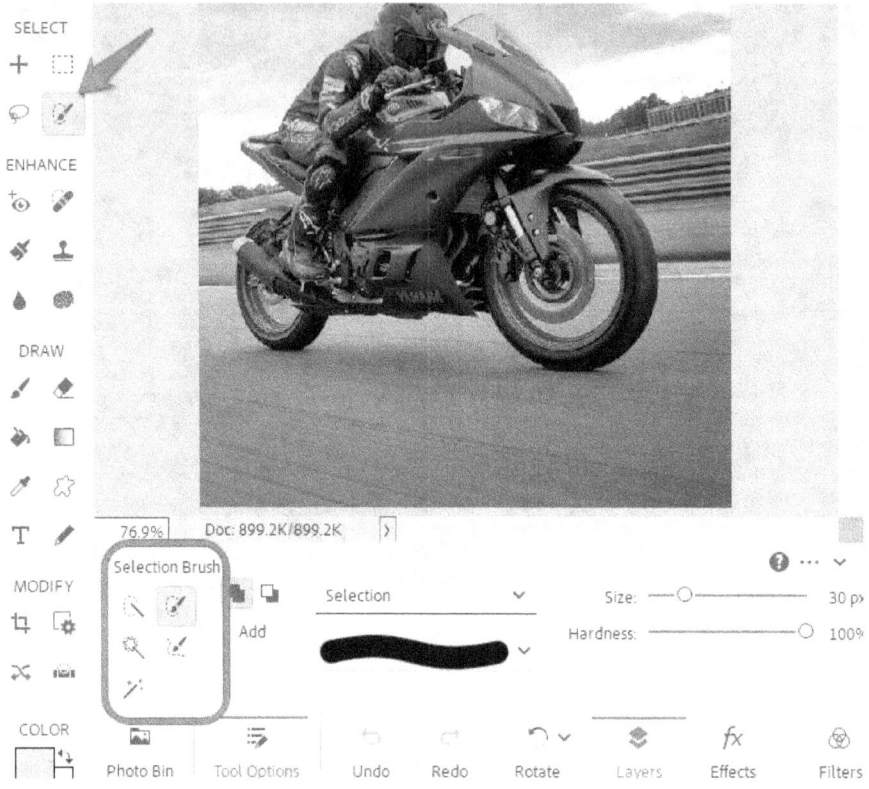

THE PANEL

The Panel can be found in both Quick mode and Advanced mode but they are different, the panel permits you to carry out certain amendment features on the image. Check the image below for you to locate the Panel Bin.

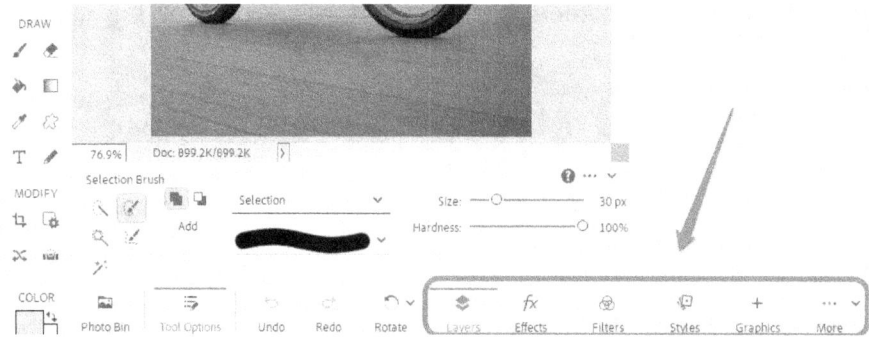

The Panel Bin items are as follows:

> **Layers:** it deals with the layer that you included in your image. It has numerous tools at the top which you can apply to edit the layer image.

> **Effects:** the effect panel contains tabs and a menu that you can apply to make different effects to your image such as special effects and automated color. The effect has two types Artistic and Classic. Click on the tab you desire and choose the type of effect you need in any category you pick.

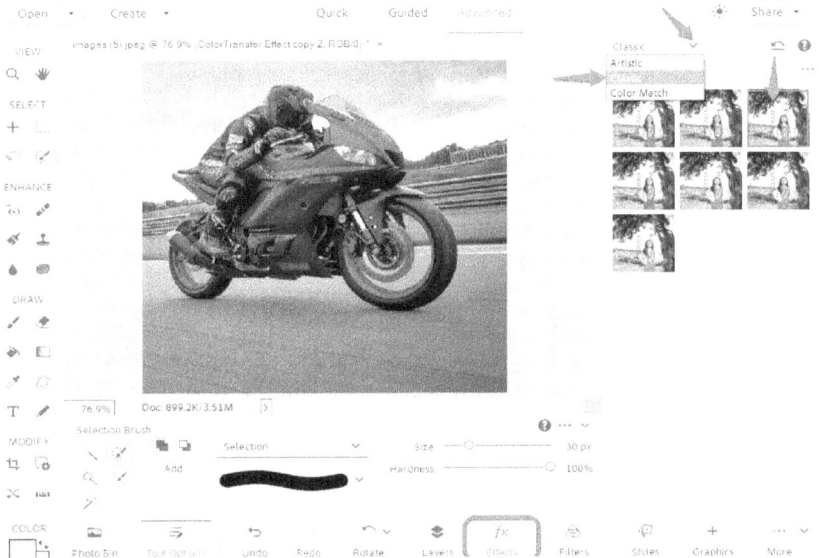

> **Filters:** These show the effect of the filter on the image. There are more than 80 filters that you can use on your image.

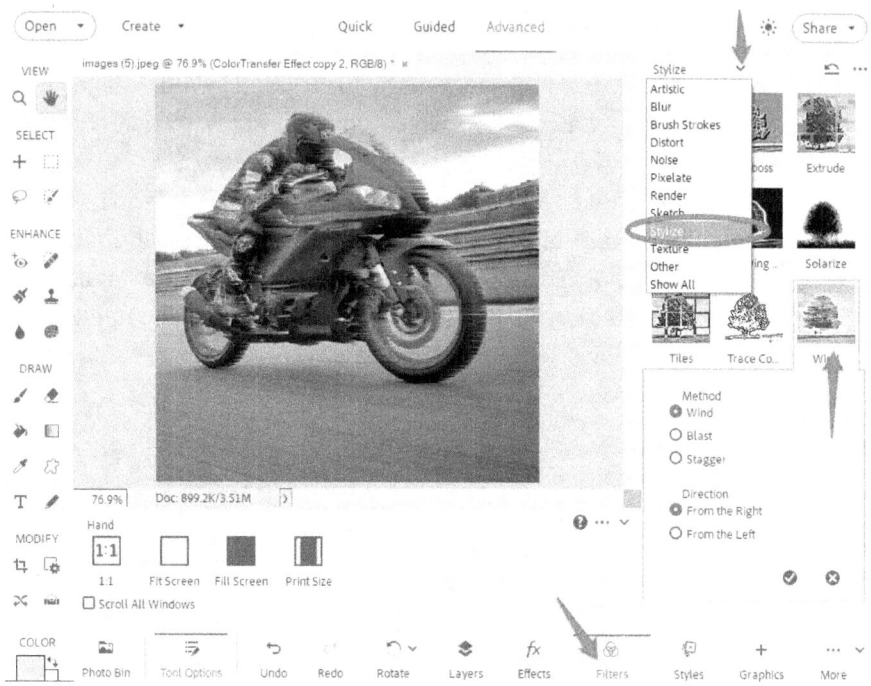

> **Styles:** This is used to apply an effect to the layer such as levels, glows, patterns, and so on to an image.

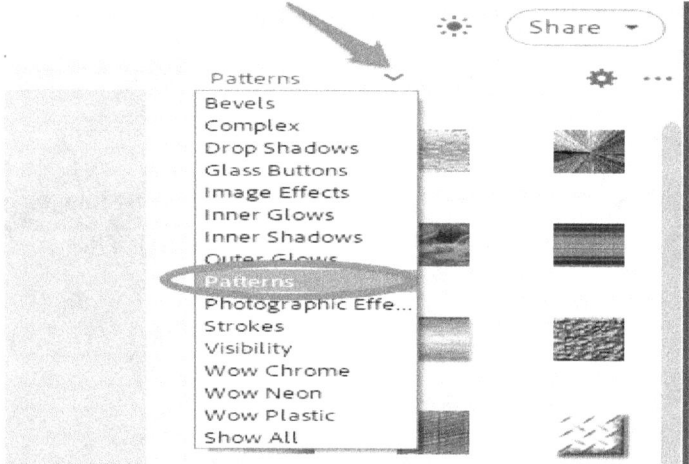

> **Graphics:** this contains numerous menus that can be added to your images, such as Picture frames, Clip art, and so on.

➤ **More:** this comprises additional panels, when you click on the more button, it will show all the panels beneath the more heading in the Panel bin.

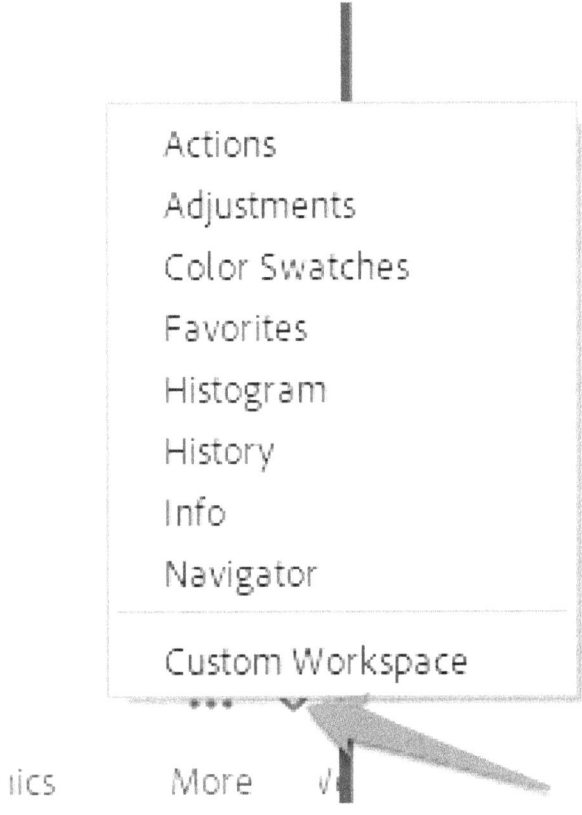

USING THE PHOTO BIN

The Photo Bin positions all the pictures you have unlocked in the image and displays their thumbnails consequently. With the Photo Bin, you can unlock, hide, view, and rotate an image.

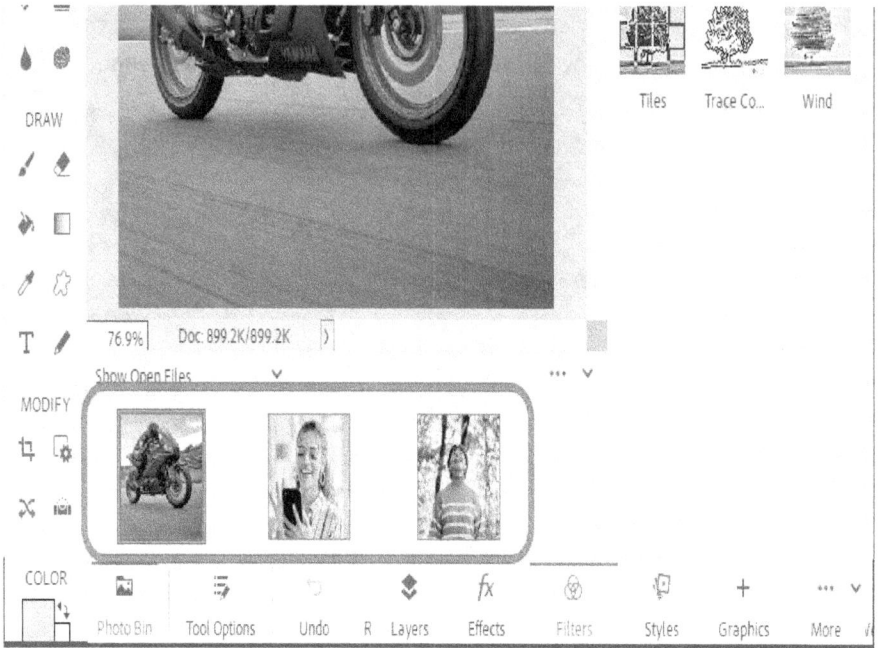

GETTING TO KNOW THE PHOTO BIN ACTIONS

The Photo Bin actions are the additional action you can execute on the image that is unlocked in the Photo Bin with the Bin menus. Below are the guides for making use of the Photo Bin menus:

> Click on the Bin menu to gain access to the Photo Bin actions which are itemized beneath

> • **Print Bin Files:** this is used to print an image by choosing the thumbnail of the image you want to print, click on the Print Bin Files to enter the Print dialog box, then click Print to send the image to the printer.

> • **Save Bin as an Album:** it is used to include images in the album through Photo Bin.

> • **Show Grid:** this automatically inserts a grid to all the images in the Photo Bin.

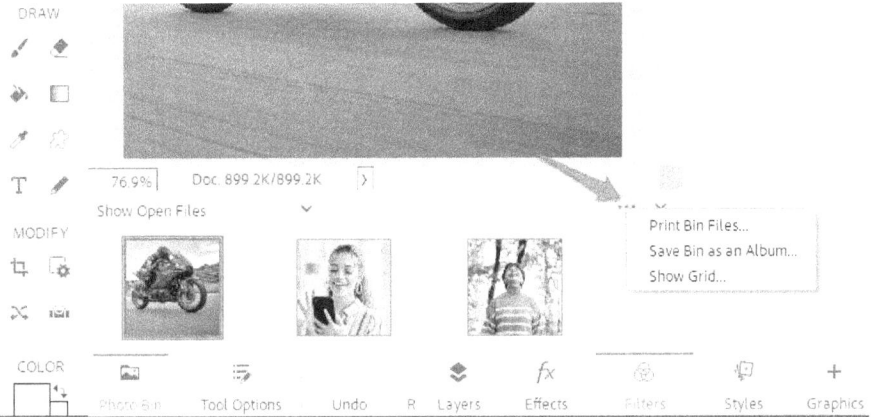

FORMULATING DIVERSE VIEWS FOR AN IMAGE

Diverse view simply means you are showing an image in two different places, most especially at the point when you need to zoom an image to edit a certain spot. To formulate a second view for an image, follow the steps below:

1. Unlock the image you want to show in diverse views, then click on its Thumbnail in the Photo Bin.
2. Click the **View tab** and choose the **New Window** for the file name of the image you want in a diverse view.

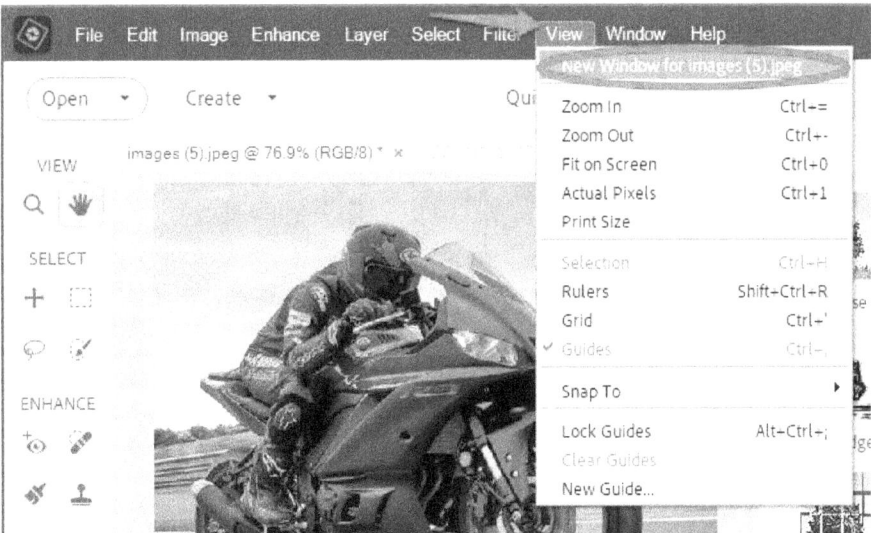

3. A new file name will appear in the image window, then you will be able to see the first and the second file in a different way.

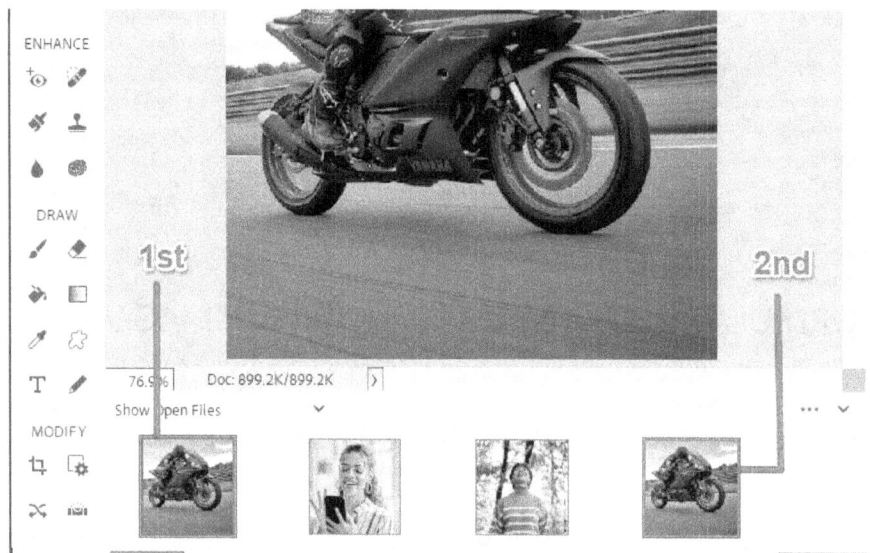

4. Select the **equivalent file name** to move to a different view. When you pick the initial file name you will see the original view and when you pick the other thumbnail you will be provided with the zoom view of the photo.

DIRECTING YOURSELF WITH GUIDED-MODE

The Guided mode is an amazing mode that assists you in going deeper into Photo Editor with step-by-step guiding backing for editing an image. To walk around Photo Editor with the Guided mode, Click Guided mode at the top of the Photo Editor with the Basics mode at default.

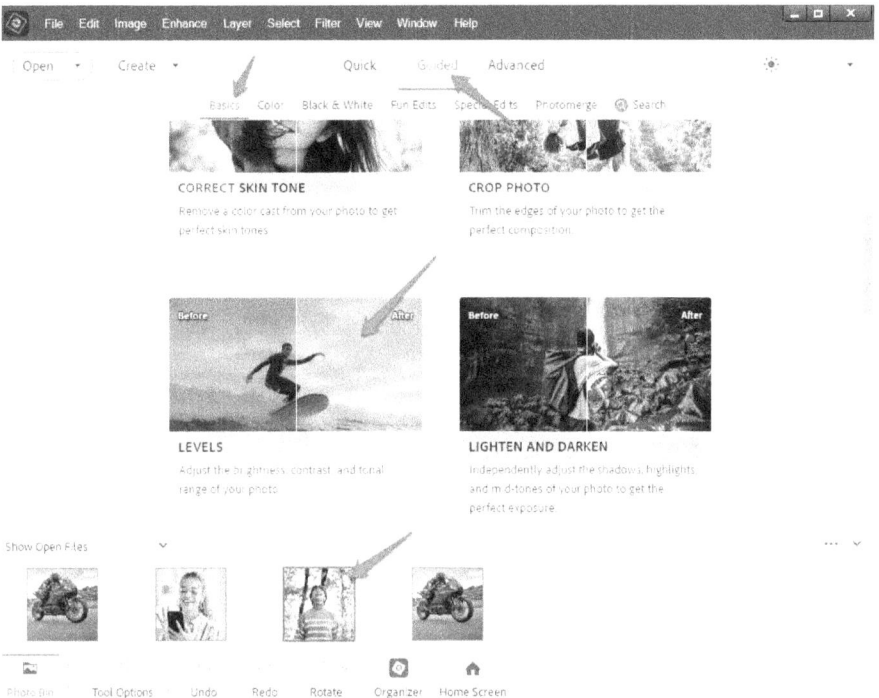

The tabs at the top of the Guide mode indicate numerous groupings of the Guide mode, which are itemized beneath:

- ➢ Basic group
- ➢ Color group
- ➢ Black and White group
- ➢ Fun Edits group
- ➢ Special Edits group
- ➢ Photomerge group

To view the list of photo editing options that are available in each group click on each tab or group, for example, if you click on Basics group you will gain access to Contrast and Brightness editing, and so on. To edit with Guided mode, select the Editing Option you want on the image you chose in the Photo Bin and a panel will be unlocked which comprises options or steps to correct your image. When you choose an editing option, your image will appear and the panel will be unlocked to help you with the chosen editing option. For example, **Level** assists in changing the contrast, brightness, and tonal range of your photo.

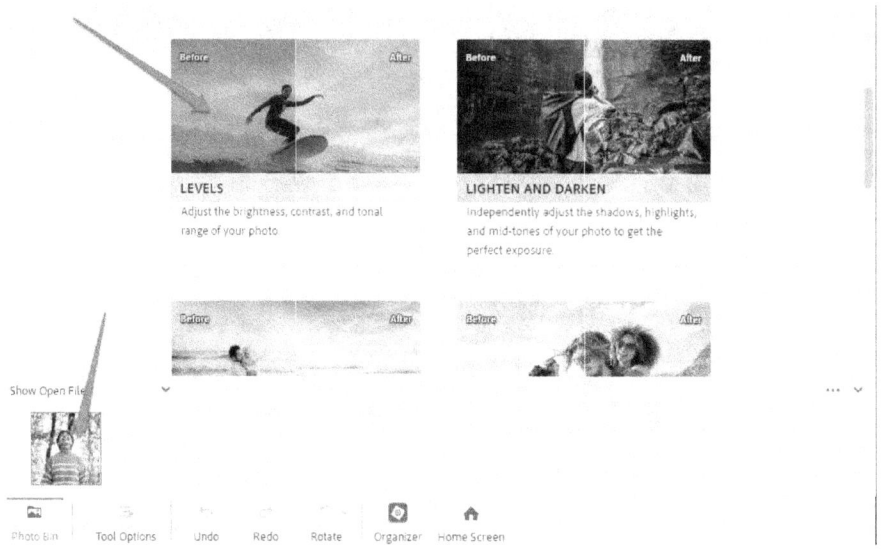

To do this, pick the **Level editing option,** instantly you will see numerous adjustment options, click **Create Level Adjustment** to enter create a level adjustment dialog box, then click on the OK button first in the New Layer dialog box to build a layer for the image so that you can make use of the adjustment on the layer.

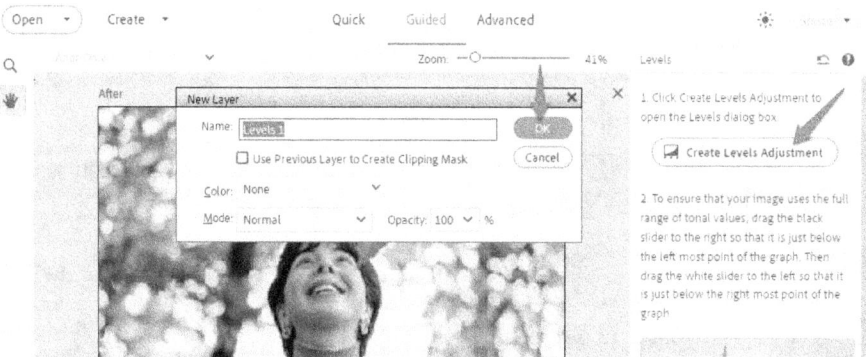

You can decide to click on Auto to change the contrast and sharpness automatically or apply the slider to change manually and click OK.

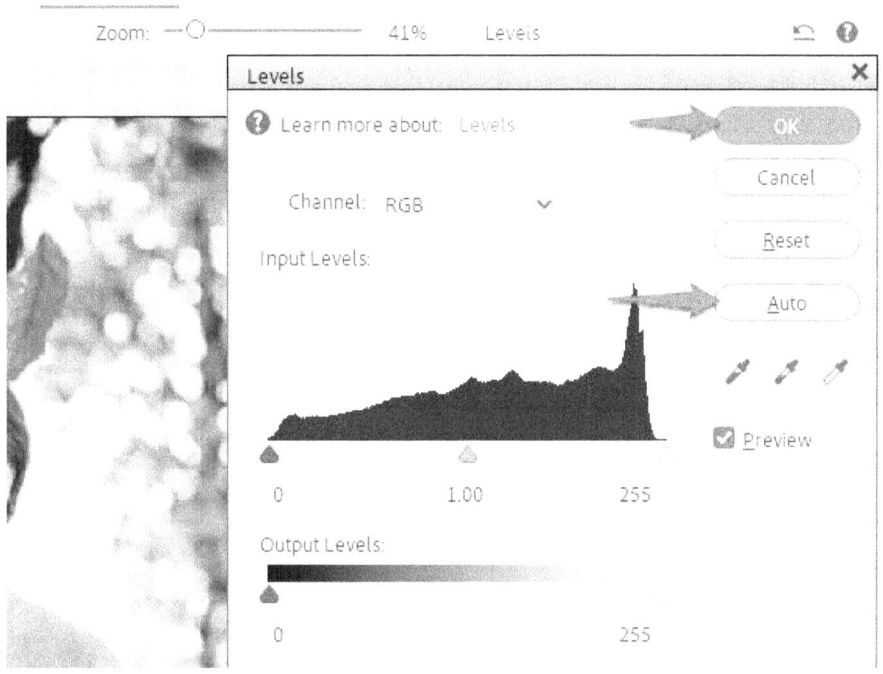

Then you may follow the remaining steps to perfect it if you want a better outcome.

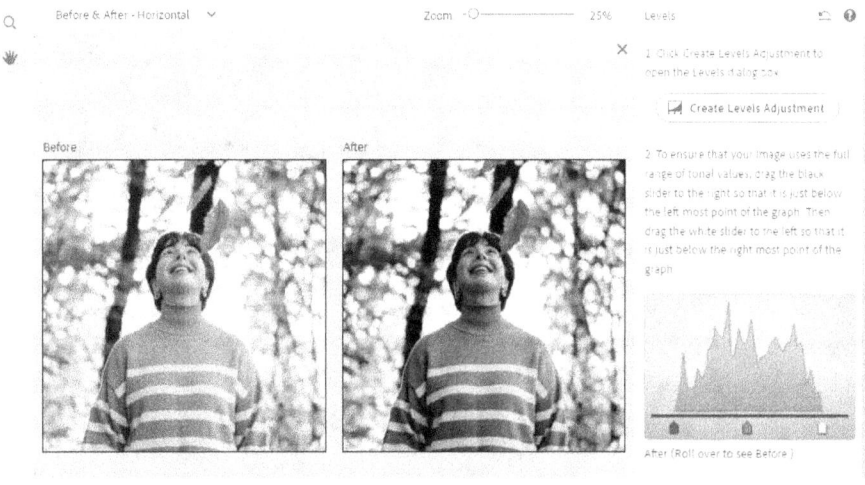

UNDERSTANDING THE PHOTO EDITOR ENVIRONMENT(PREFERENCE)

Element offers a way of changing and regulating the Photo Editor Environment for its users, the only way to do this is to unlock the Photo Editor dialog box and change its option to your tradition, follow the steps bellow to unlock the Photo Editor dialog box:

➤ Select the **Edit** tab and click on the **Preference** menu, then pick **General** from the drop-down list.

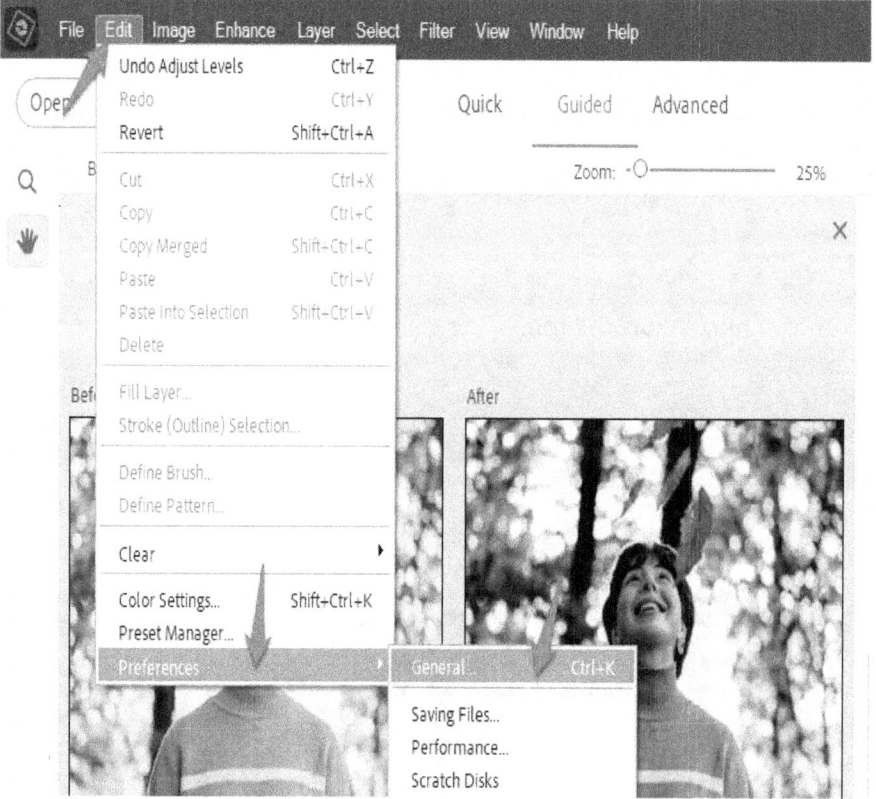

➤ The preference dialog box will appear, see the image below.

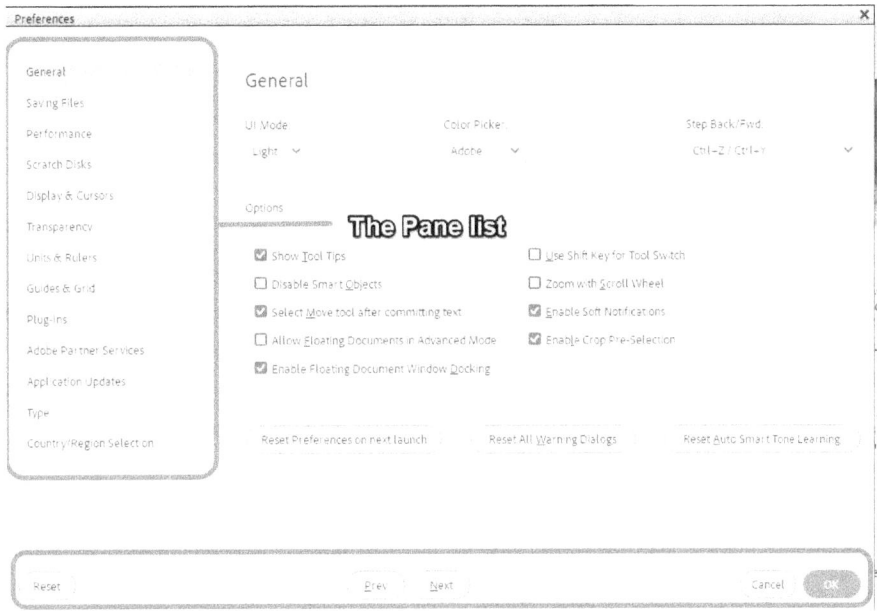

- **The Pane list:** this includes all the panes inside the Preferences dialog box, you can click on any pane, and change its option to your taste.
- **Reset:** this option is understandable. it is used to return to the preferences setting to default the way it was when you unlock the Preferences dialog box.
- **Cancel:** this is used to reserve the change you have made.
- **Ok:** it is used to confirm the changes you have made.

CHAPTER FIVE

FUNCTIONING WITH THE ORGANIZER

Organizer is an aspect of Elements that you can use to import, choose, view, and systematically arrange your images for effective image collection and image library. This chapter discusses all the essential instructions you need to know about Elements Organizer. Photo and media are the main elements that inhabit about 70% of your hard disk because of their uses and importance, therefore much effort must be placed on their proper arrangement, to make photo editing easier with Elements, you must include or import certain images that you need to the Organizer from the photo gallery.

IMPORTING IMAGES FROM THE REMOVABLE DISKS AND SYSTEM HARD DRIVE

> ➢ Unlock the **Organizer** application, then click the **File tab** and choose the **Get photos and Videos** menu, you may continue further to choose **From Files and Folders** from the drop-down list.

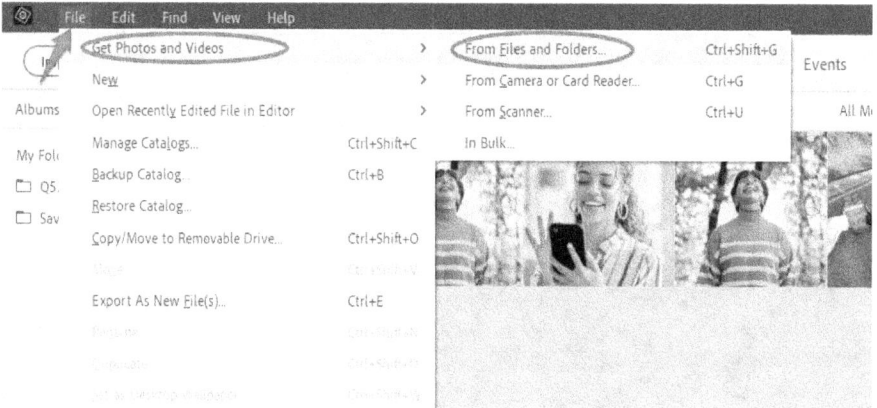

> ➢ The Get photos and videos from Files and Folders will be unlocked, you can now check your folders such as Picture, Hard Disk, Memory Card, USB, and other Devices that grasp the files you want to import.
> ➢ Choose the needed files and folders and select the Get Media button to include the carefully chosen files and folders in the Organizer.

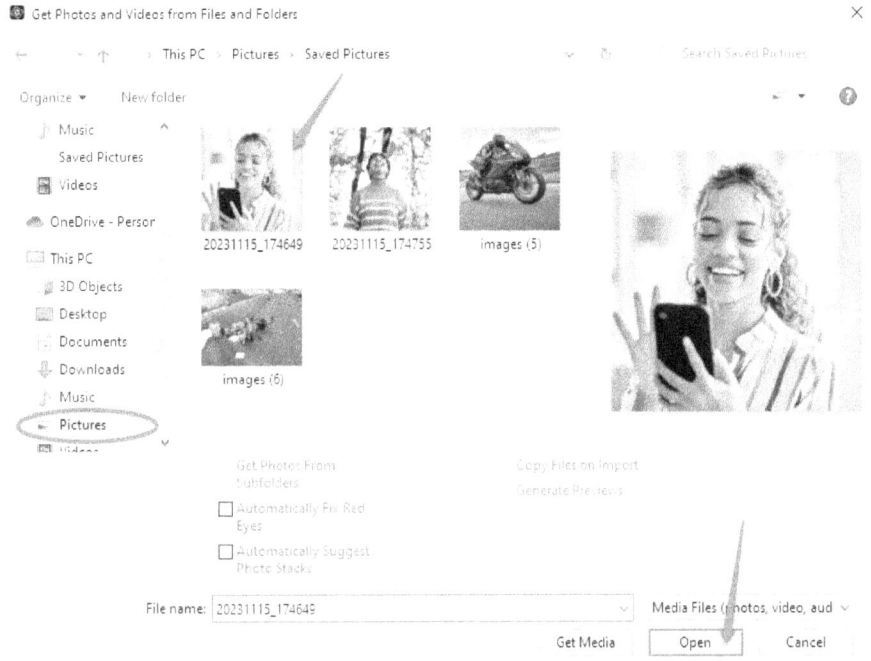

GETTING IMAGES FROM CAMERA AND CARD READER

You can import images into the Organizer by inserting the media card into the card reader and connecting it to your PC or when you take an image with your camera then connect the camera to your PC with a USB cable. Kindly follow these steps below to import images you took with your camera into the Organizer:

> Connect the **Camera** to your PC with the **USB cable** or insert the **Camera media card** into the card reader and connect it to your PC.
> Unlock the **Organizer** application and select the **File** tab, then pick **Get Photos and Videos** and choose **From Camera** or **Card Reader**.

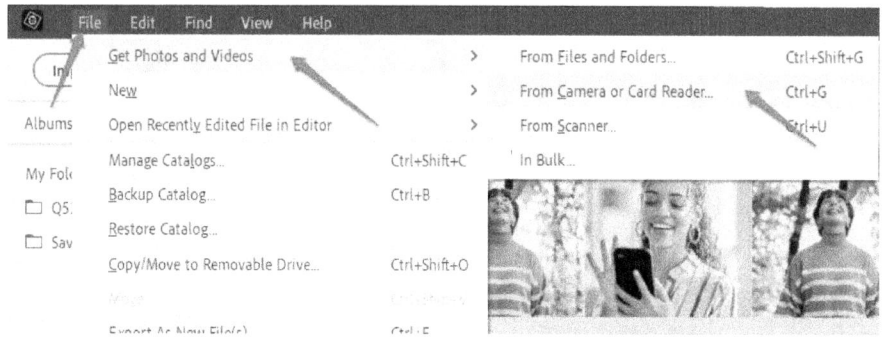

➢ The Adobe Photo Downloader dialog box will appear, then click on the **Get Photo From** menu and choose the name of your media card.

➢ Click on the Browse button and look for the folder then pick the photo you want to copy.

➢ Click on the **Get Media** button to add those photos to the Organizer.

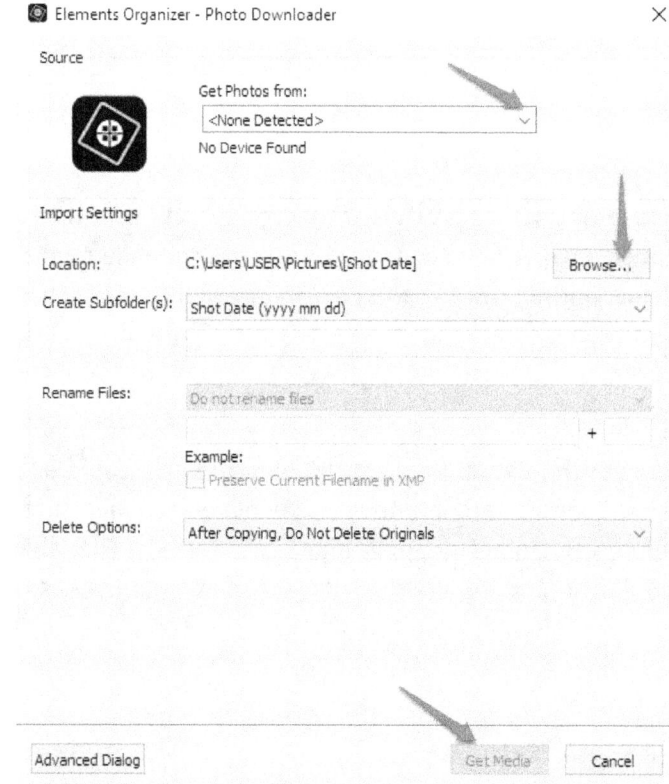

When the importing processing is finished you will have the picture in your organizer immediately and will be shown as the thumbnail in the Media tab of the Organizer.

IMPORTING PHONE PHOTOS TO THE ORGANIZER

Element permits you to import photos you have on your phone to the Organizer. Kindly follow the steps below to import your phone photos to the Organizer:

➢ Select the **File tab** and click on **Get Photos and Videos** menu, then select **From Files and Folders.**

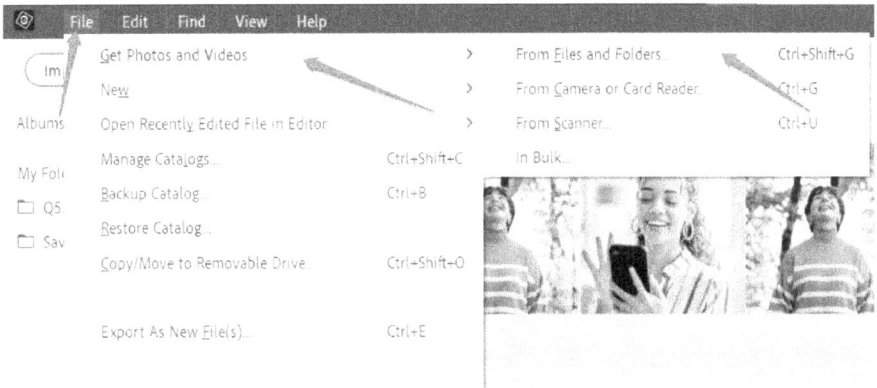

➢ Attach your Phone to the Computer with the USB cable and search through your phone folder to see where the photos to be imported are saved.

➢ **Get Photos and Videos from Files and Folders** will appear, then click on the **Browse** button to unlock the folder location and select the folder that holds the image you are sending to the Organizer.

➢ Click on the **Get Media** button to import the pictures to your Organizer.

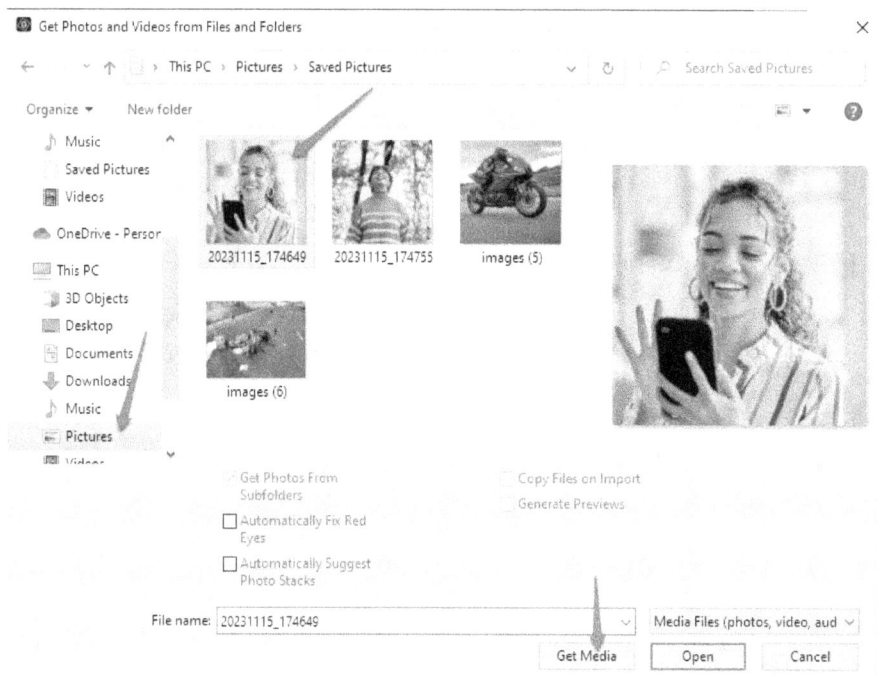

THE SCANNER

You can also obtain or import photos into the Organizer through the **Scanner,** therefore Organizer photos are not limited to the photos you obtain from a removable disk, camera, or hard drive. One thing you have to do is to attach the cable to your PC with the USB cable just like you did when you attach the camera or card reader. Follow the step below to import photos from the scanner:

1. Move to the scanner and attach it to the PC appropriately, click on the **File tab,** pick the **Get Photos and Videos** menu, then choose **From scanner** on the drop-down list.

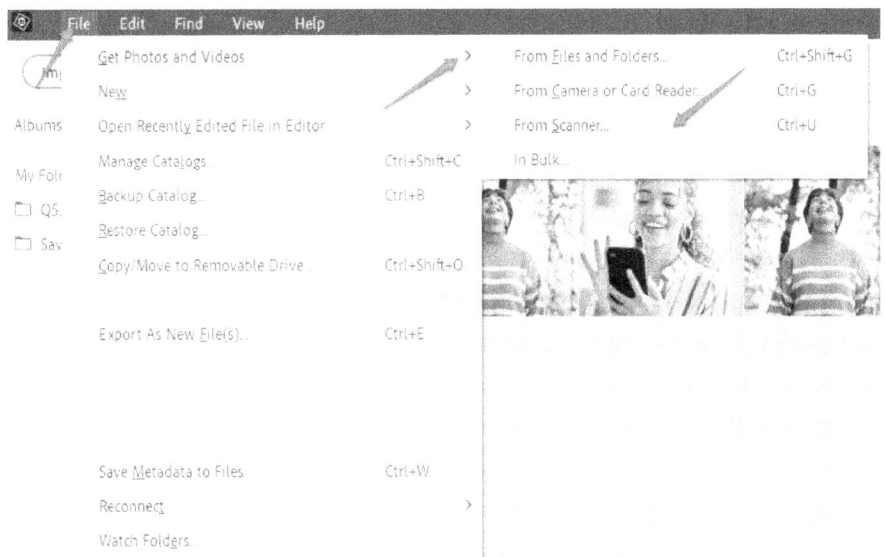

2. **Get Photos From Scanner** will appear, then choose Scanner name from the drop-down menu.

3. Click the **Browse** button and choose the photos of your choice then click OK.

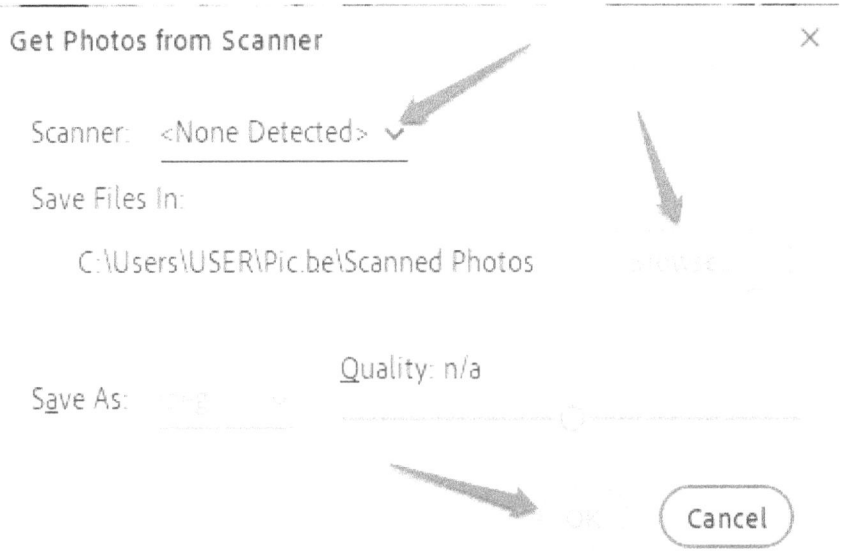

4. Check the **preview** of the scanning and if the preview satisfied you, then click on the scan button to forward it into the image window.

MODIFYING THE ORGANIZER ENVIRONMENT

You can customize your organizer environment to your taste, the same way you did to the Photo Editor environment. To do that, kindly follow the steps below:

➢ Click the **Edit tab** and choose the **Preference menu** and click **General** on the drop-down list.

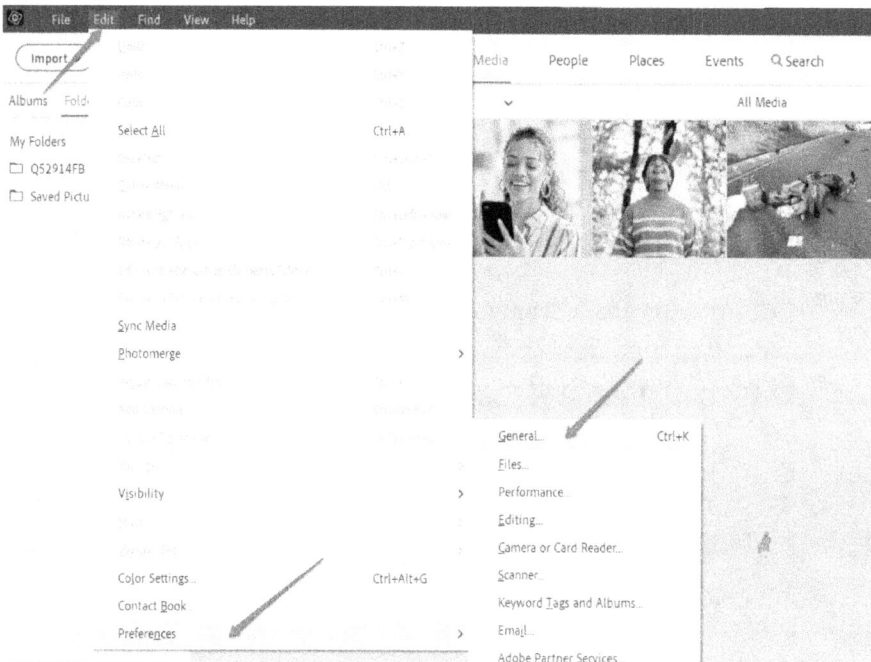

➢ The Preference dialog box appears; you can now make the necessary amendments to your Organizer environment.
➢ Click OK to confirm the amendment.

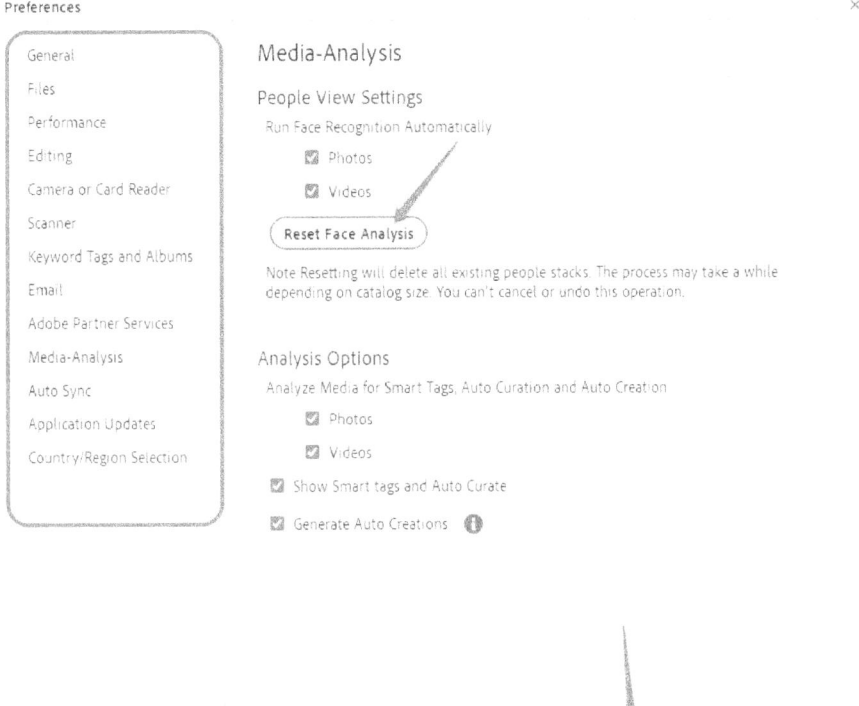

Preferences   ×

Media-Analysis

People View Settings

Run Face Recognition Automatically

☑ Photos

☑ Videos

(Reset Face Analysis)

Note Resetting will delete all existing people stacks. The process may take a while
depending on catalog size. You can't cancel or undo this operation.

Analysis Options

Analyze Media for Smart Tags, Auto Curation and Auto Creation

☑ Photos

☑ Videos

☑ Show Smart tags and Auto Curate

☑ Generate Auto Creations ⓘ

General
Files
Performance
Editing
Camera or Card Reader
Scanner
Keyword Tags and Albums
Email
Adobe Partner Services
Media-Analysis
Auto Sync
Application Updates
Country/Region Selection

(Restore Default Settings)   (OK) (Cancel) (Help)

CHAPTER SIX

MOVING AROUND THE ORGANIZER WORKSPACE

It is expedient to be familiar with each part of the organizer's workspace for appropriate exploration and making the best outcome out of the Organizer.

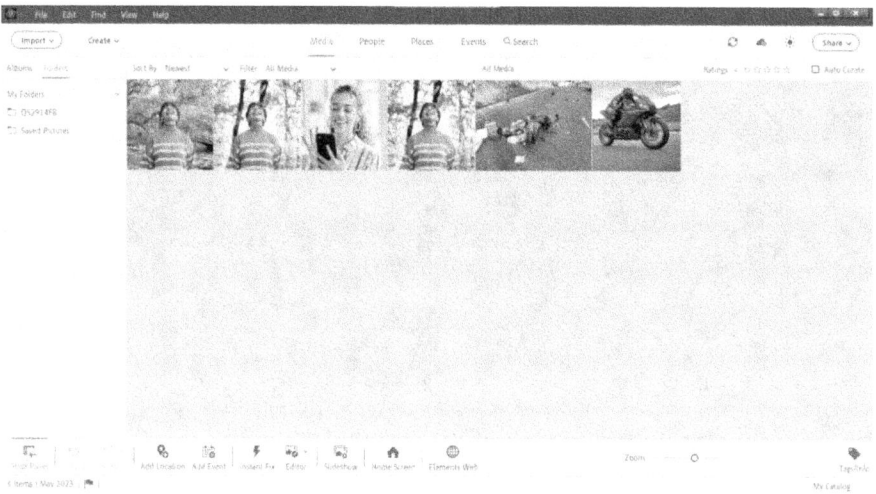

The following is the breakdown of Organizer components:

- **Menu bar:** this contains commands for executing numerous actions such as File, Edit, View, and Help, it can be located at the top of the screen.

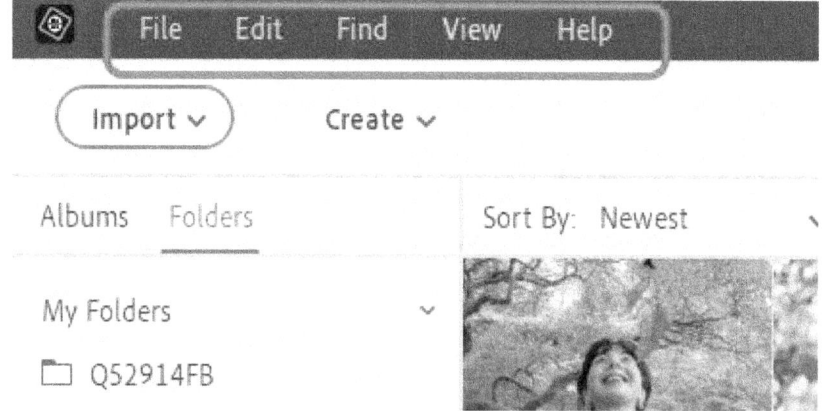

- **Import:** this button permits you to send or transfer photos to the Organizer through Files and folders, Card reader, Scanner, and Camera.

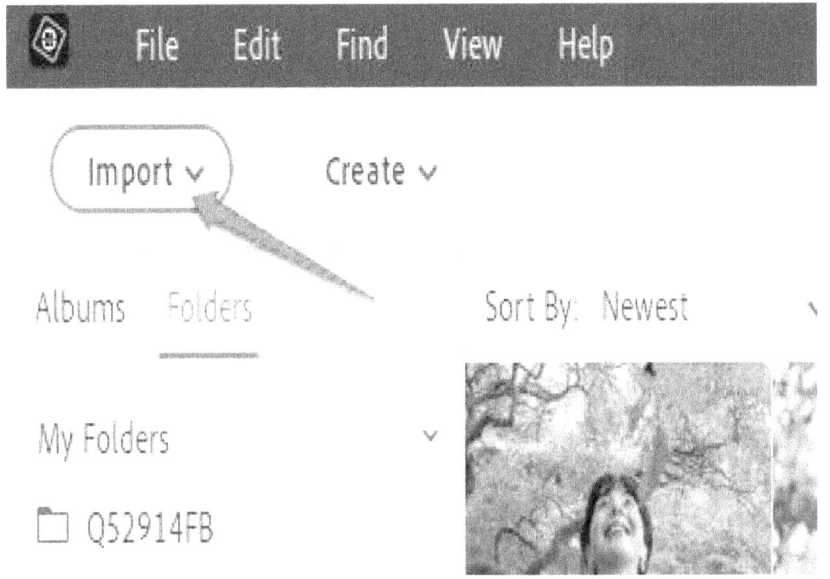

- **View button:** this permits you to navigate among Places, Media, People, and Locations.

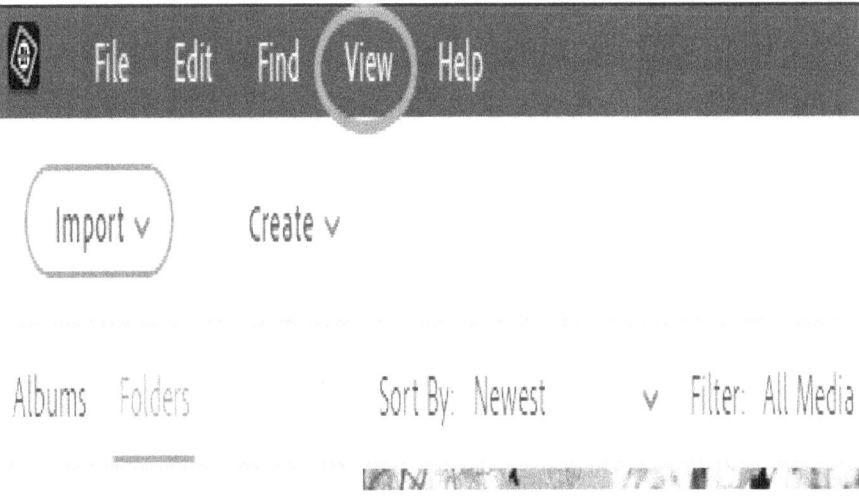

- **Search:** to access a new search page where you will be able to search for numerous tasks using diverse options, click on the Search icon.

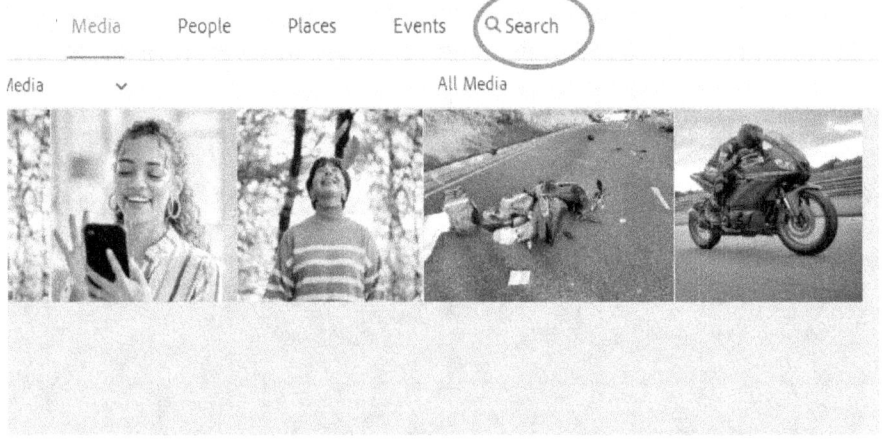

- **Special feature:** This involves three important buttons for an unusual task such as Close, Maximize, and Minimize buttons.

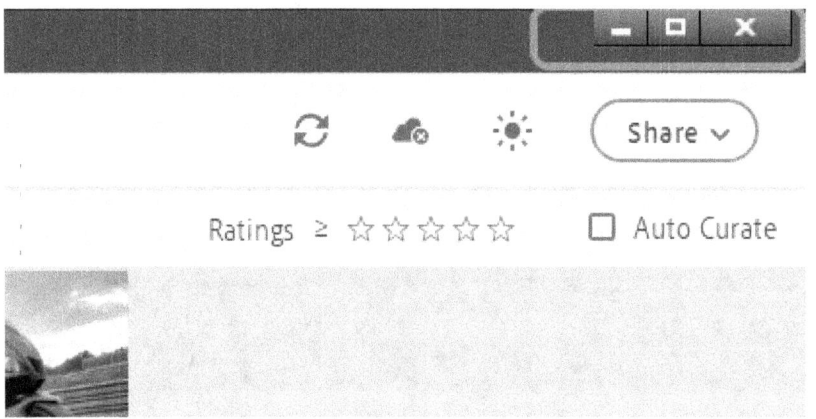

- **Create and share:** these two buttons can be located at the top of the screen, The create button is for creating a new task with the media while the share button is for sharing photos or media.

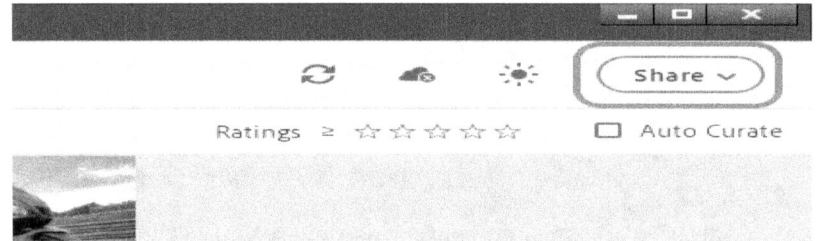

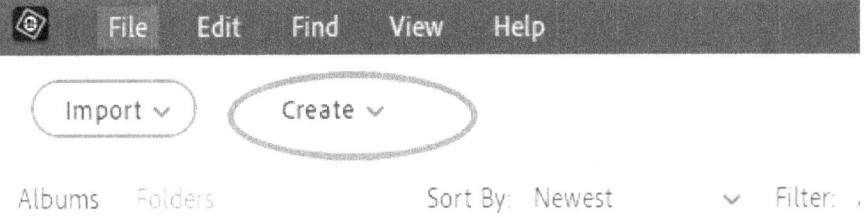

- **Album and folders:** the album is used for viewing any of the photos included in the album while the folder is created to view photos folder by folder.

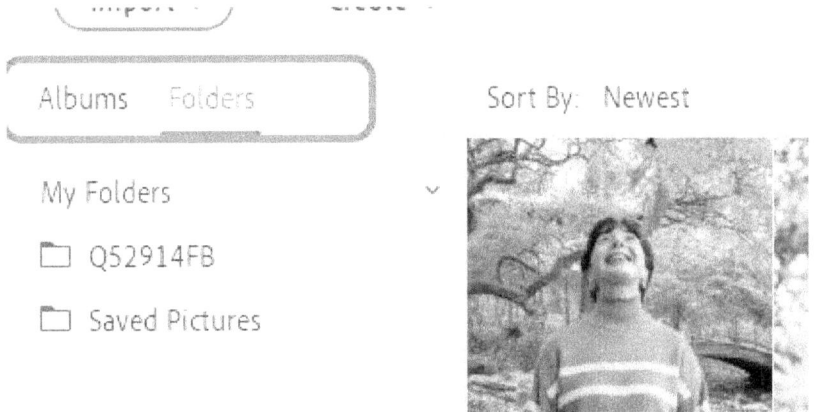

- **Folder button:** This is used for opening and showing the photos that are in each category of the folder.

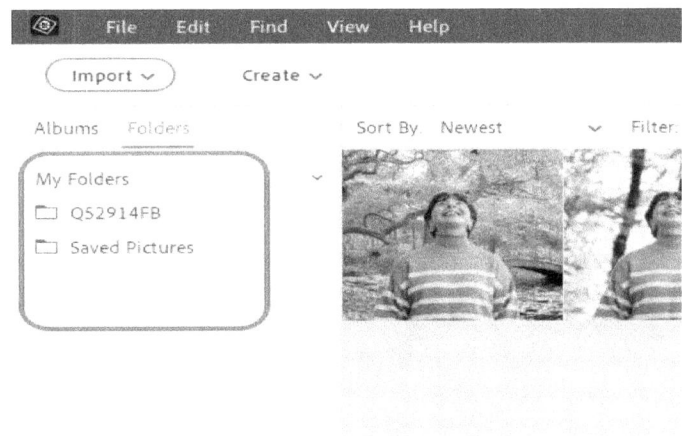

- **Rating and Auto curator:** this is used to display those images that have been rated while the Auto curator focuses on analyzing and managing photos for appropriate picturing.

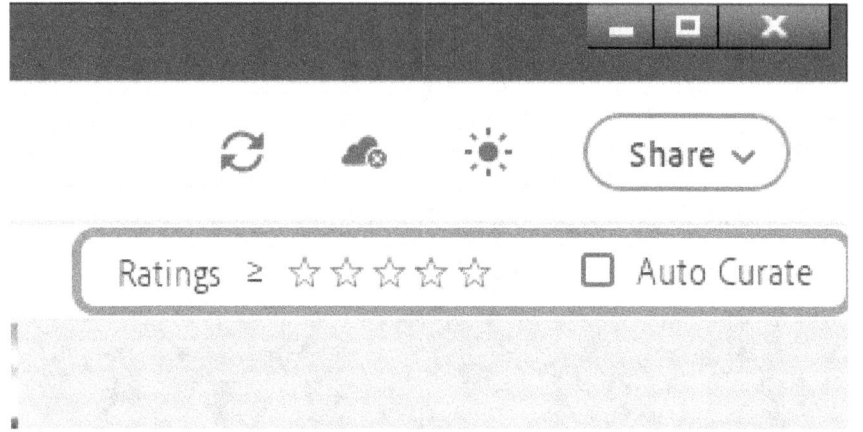

- **Sort By:** this is the aspect of the Organizer that allows you to arrange the media photo according to the newest, oldest, names, and batches.

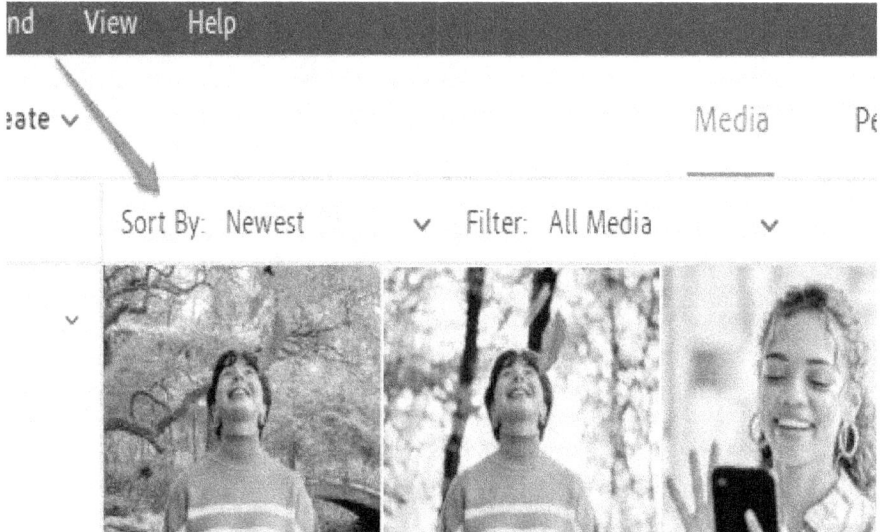

Now I will be breaking down the other components in numbers, kindly read further

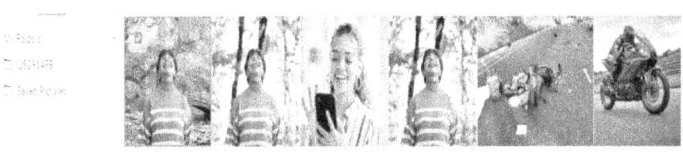

1

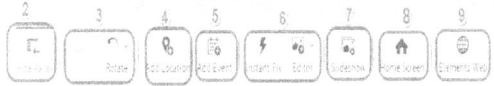 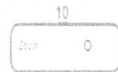

1. **Media Browser:** this is the window that shows all the photos you have transferred to the Organizer.
2. **Hide button:** this is used for hiding the left panel and thereby builds enough space for showing more photos.
3. **Rotate and undo:** the rotate button is used to swap an image anticlockwise and clockwise meanwhile the undo button provides two options to redo and undo an action performed on an image by clicking on the undo and picking undo or redo from the drop-down menu.
4. **Add location:** this button will assist you in including a location in your photo, when you choose a photo and click on the Add location button a dialog box will appear where you can type your location name and the picture will be added to the places panel automatically.
5. **Add Event:** the Add Event works the same way as Add Location but they differ in such a way that you have to type the event you are doing than typing location.
6. **Instant Fix and Editor:** the instant fix assists you in fixing and adjusting any irregularities in your photo in the Organization such as

cropping, red-eye fixing, and so on while the Editor is for navigating to Photo Editor from the Organizer.

7. **Slideshow:** to view the chosen photos as a slideshow, click on this button.
8. **Home Screen:** to move to the opening screen of Photoshop Elements, click on this button.
9. **Elements Web:** to go online, select this button.
10. **Zoom:** this is the button that permits you to see the aspect of a Photo in a larger way.
11. **Tag/info:** this button provides you access to the panel bin where you can choose your keyword tag.

THE ORGANIZER VIEW

The Organizer comprises four views that permit you to view your images. They include the following Media, People, Places, and Events.

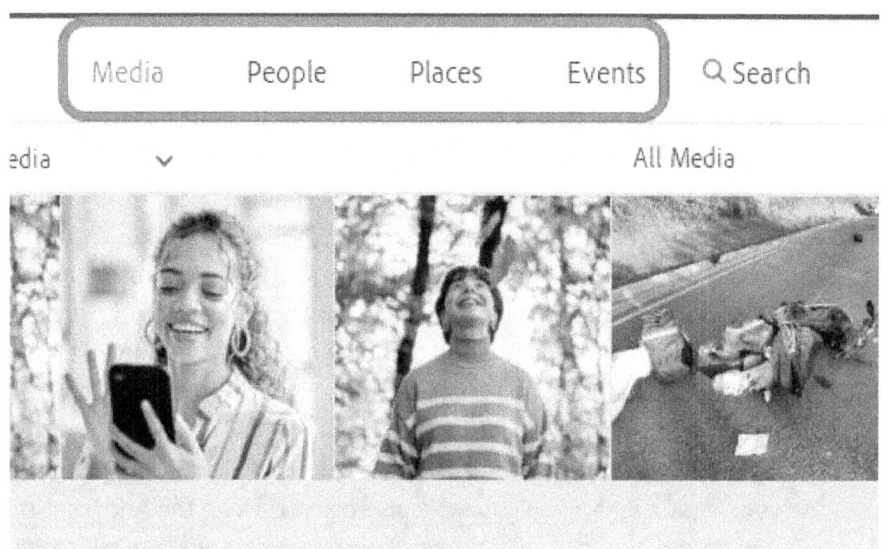

Here is the various Organizer breakdown:

➤ **Media:** this button shows all the buttons you have in the Organizer. It helps you to edit some irregularities in your photo immediately rather than moving to Photo Editor.

➤ **People:** this view displays only the photos you have with some people after you have tagged the chosen images with those people

- ➤ **Places:** this displays the images of the particular locations before you can have images in the Place tab.
- ➤ **Events:** this assists you to see those photos that you have created for certain events such as birthday parties, marriage, and so on.

GROUPING ORGANIZER PHOTOS WITH TAGS

The only means for the user is to tag your photos as necessary for appropriate sorting and finding. You can tag your images under four groups for easy access which are Keywords, People, Places, and Events, to tag photos into any of the four groupings, follow the steps below:

1. Choose the **Photos** you need to tag from the **Media Browser** and click the **Tag/info** beneath the screen on the right-hand side.

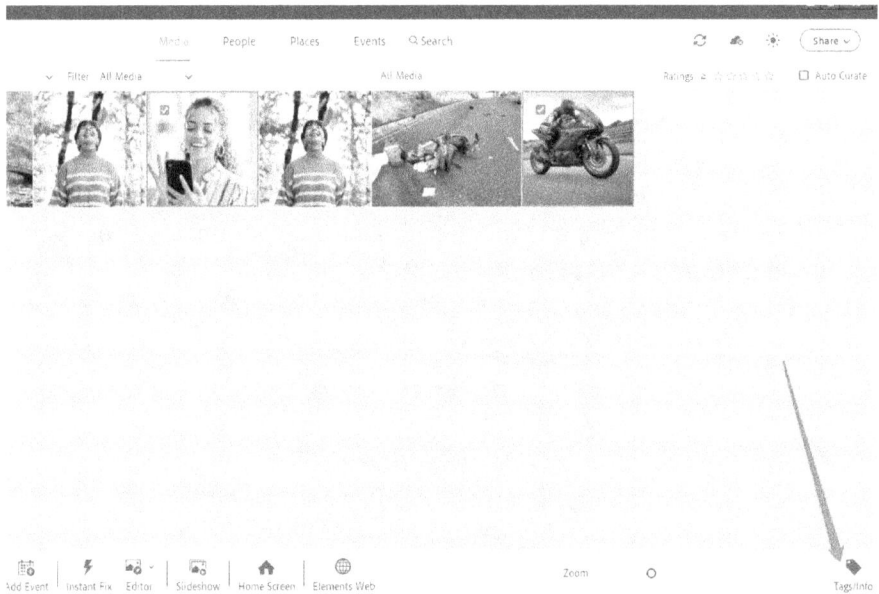

2. Select the **Plus Icon** beside the category type you want to access the tag dialog box of the category you pick.

81

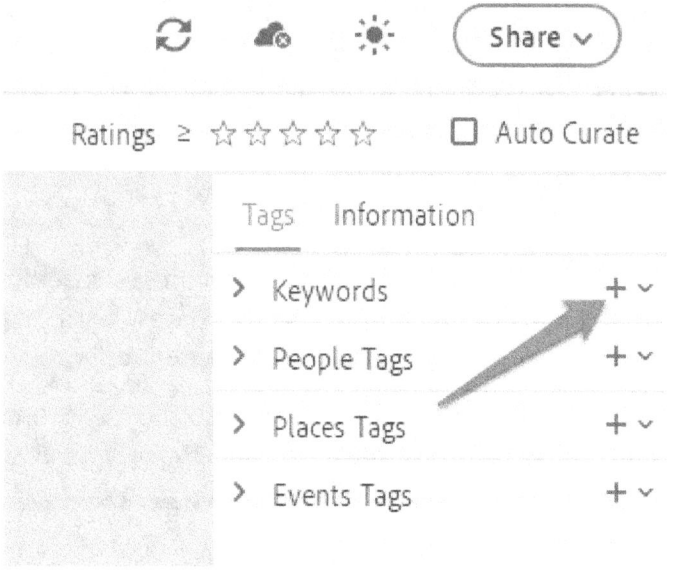

3. Provide the tag information according to the group type you select. For example, input text for keywords and describe the keyword, person name for People and choose the group the person belongs to, name for location, and event name such as marriage for events then type the dates for the event.

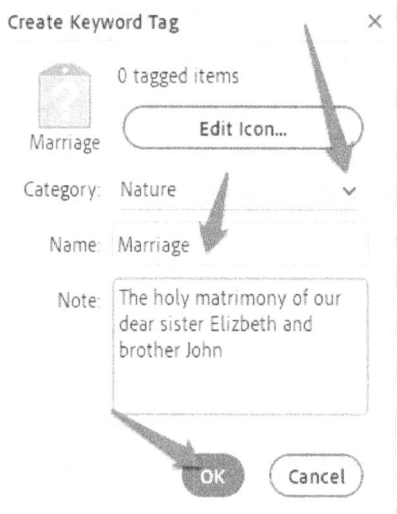

4. Click on the Ok button for confirmation.

ADDING AN ICON FOR YOUR TAG PHOTOS

Though Elements provides an icon for all your tags, but you can choose a different icon for your tag photos. To modify the preset icon of your tag photos to a different one, kindly follow the steps bellow:

➢ Right-click the concerned Tag in the Tags panel and select Edit to enter the Edit tags dialog box.

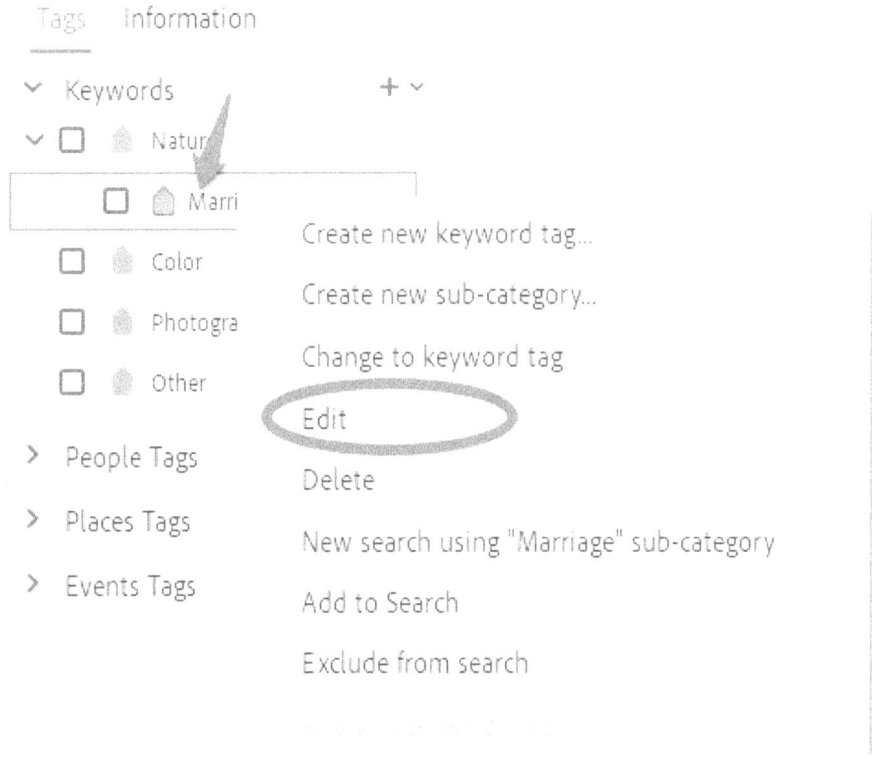

➢ Click the Edit Icon in the Keyword dialog box to access the Edit Keyword dialog box.
➢ Click the **Import** button to navigate to and from within the Picture folder and select a photo to be imported for the icon photos tag.

83

GENERATING A PHOTO ALBUM

Photo album assists you in perfectly storing and arranging your photo in the Organizer. Follow the steps below to create and add photos to the album:

> ➤ Choose the Photos you want to add to the album
> ➤ Click the Album button and select the Plus Icon My Album to access the New Album dialog box.

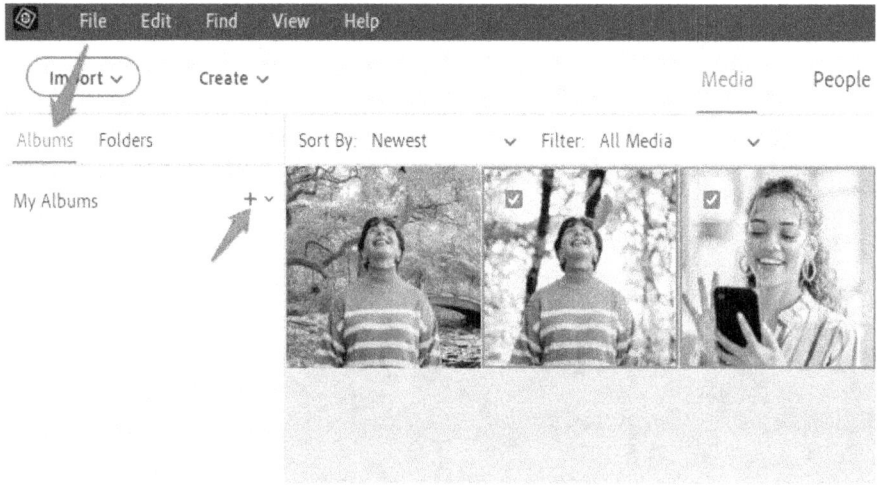

> ➤ A new album box will appear, insert the Album Name into the new album name box.
> ➤ Drag those Photos you have selected into the new album box and Click Ok for confirmation.

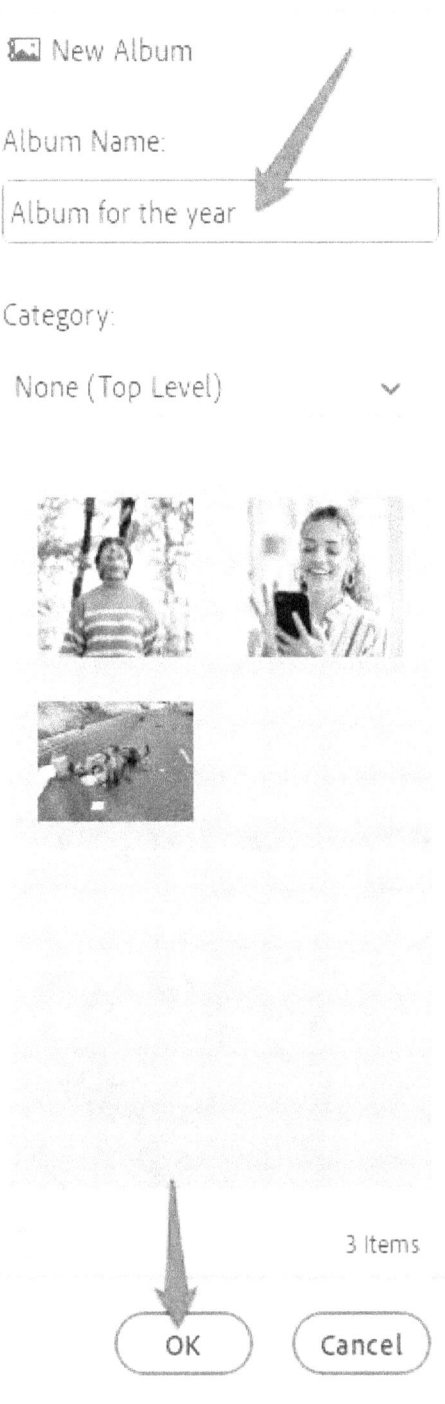

SEEING, RENAMING, AND DELETING A PHOTO ALBUM

You can carry out some tasks on the photo album you have created. An incidence may require you to see, rename, and delete an album. Follow the steps below to perform those tasks above:

➢ To see the photos of your album, click the concerned album.

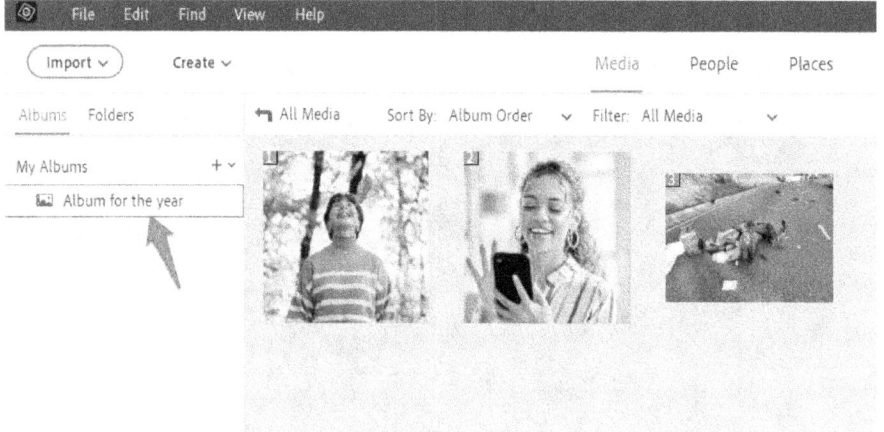

➢ To rename a photo album, right-click the concerned album and pick rename from the drop-down menu.

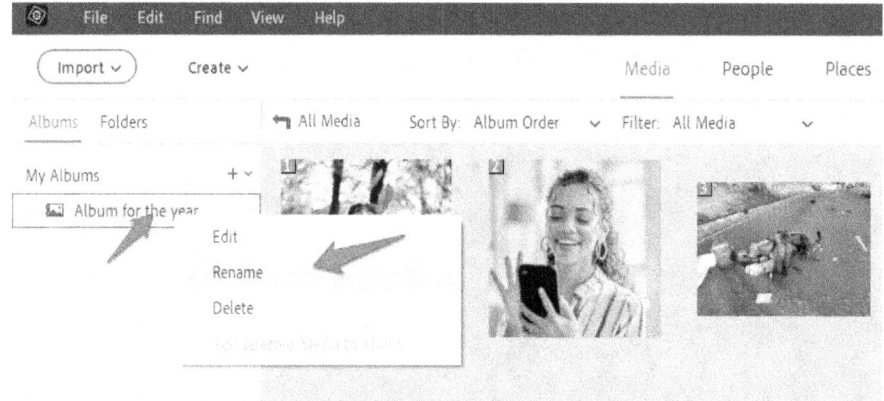

➢ To delete a photo album, right-click the photo then select delete from the drop-down menu.

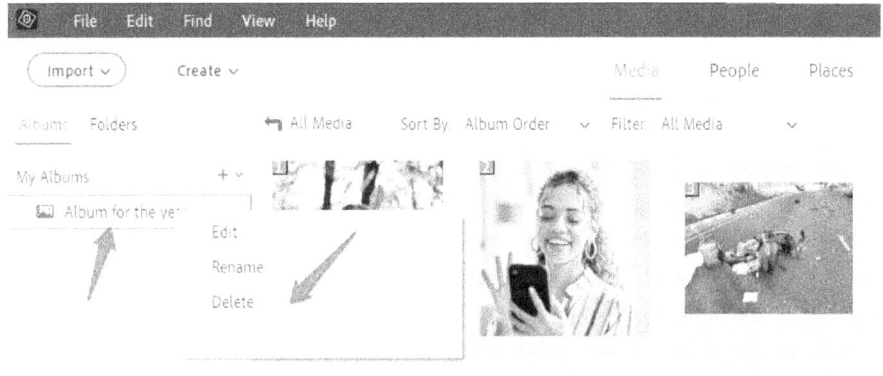

EDITING A PHOTO ALBUM

To edit a photo album, kindly follow the steps below:

> ➢ Right-click the album name, then choose Edit from the drop-down menu.

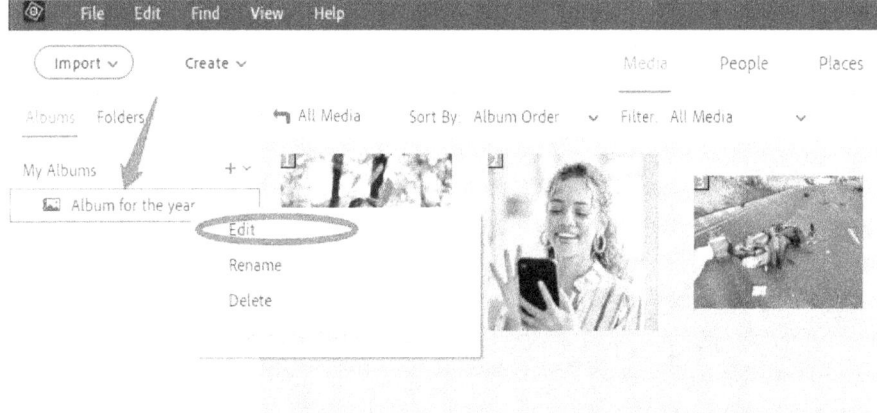

> ➢ After you have chosen the Edit button, the chosen album will be relocated to the panel bin of the Organizer.
> ➢ Pick and drag the images you want to include to the Album from the Media to add them to the chosen album automatically.

➢ If you want to remove images from the album, choose the unwanted images in the album panel and select the trash icon to forward the chosen images or pictures into the trash can.

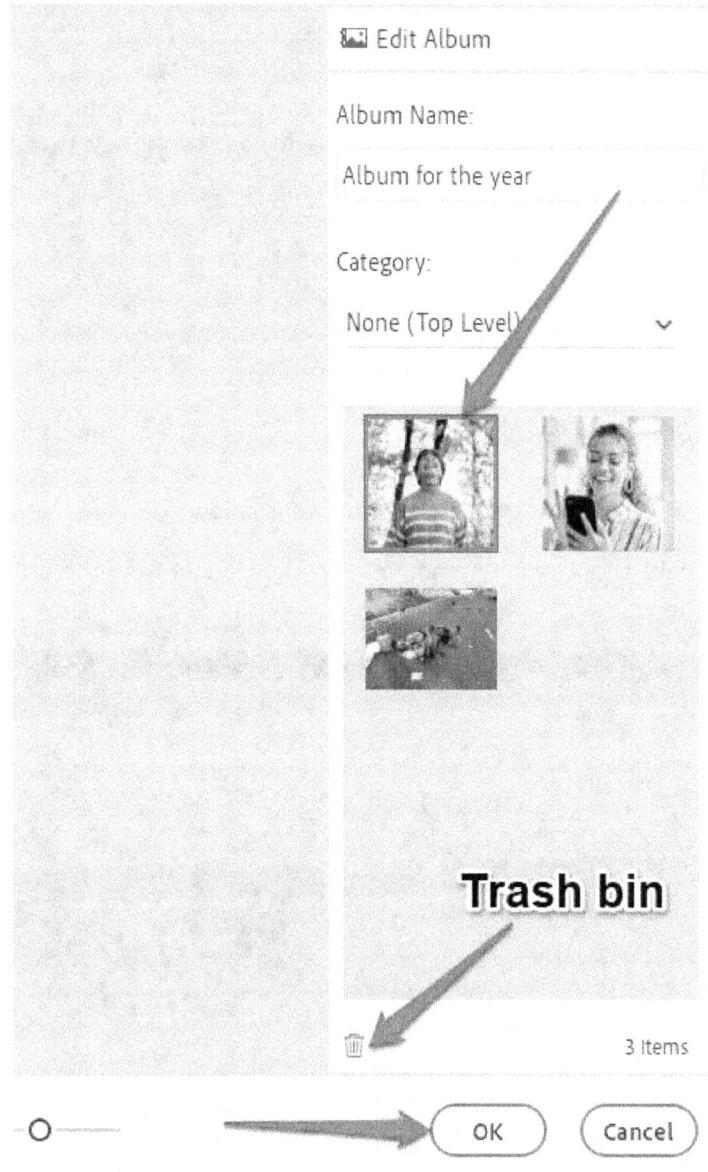

CHAPTER SEVEN

THE ORGANIZER CATALOG

The tank of all the pictures you send to the organizer is known as a **Catalog.** the more you send pictures or media to the Organizer the larger the Organizer's contents will be. There is only one catalog in Organizer and it is known as **Default Catalog.** it is essential to add more Catalogs to the default catalog to prevent it from getting filled.

BUILDING A NEW CATALOG

To build or create a new catalog, navigate to the Organizer and follow the steps below:

> ➤ Click the **File** menu and choose the **Manage Catalog** to enter the manage catalog dialog box.

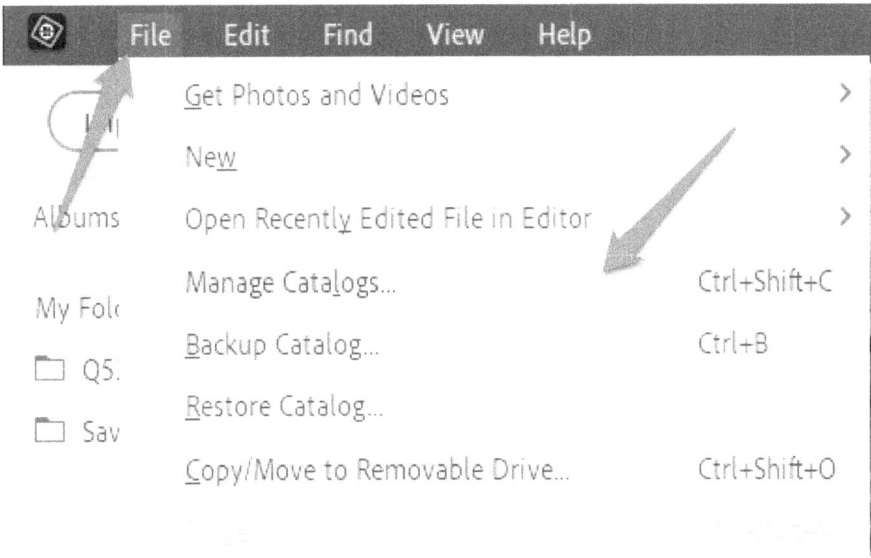

> ➤ Click the New button from the manage catalog box that appears to see the New Catalog dialog box.

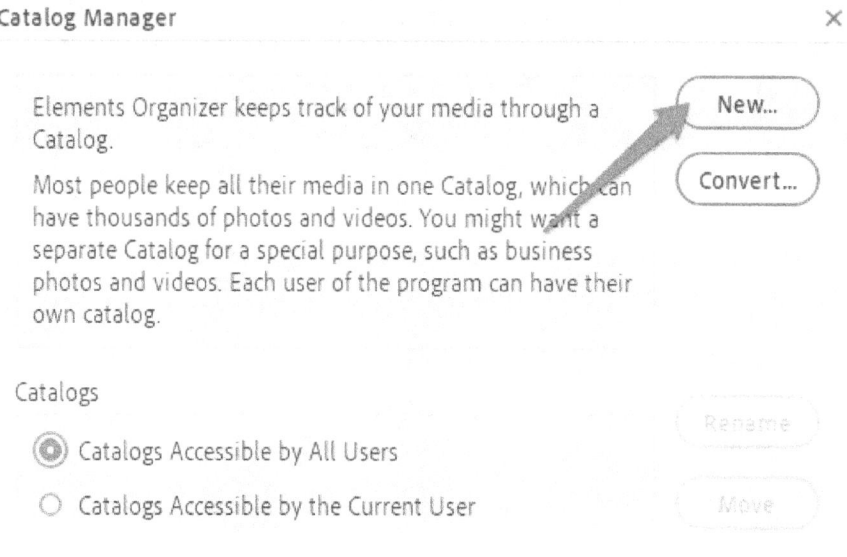

> Input the **Name** of the catalog into the file box, then click Ok.

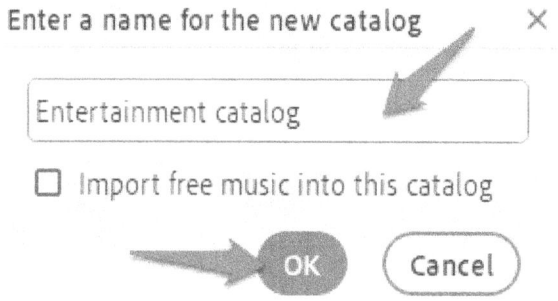

ADDING FILES TO THE CATALOG

The next thing to do after building a new catalog is to add a file or media inside it, follow these steps below to add the file to the new catalog:

> Click the **File tab** and select the **Get Photos and Videos** menu from the File fly-out list, then choose **From Files And Folders** to add new files to the Catalog to gain entrance to the Get Photos and Videos from Files and Folders dialog box.

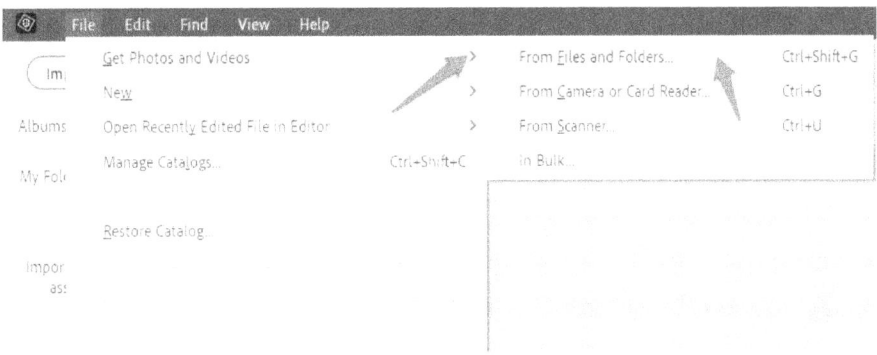

> Search through your hard drive and choose the photos you want to add to the new catalog, then click the **Get Media or Open** button to forward them into the new catalog.

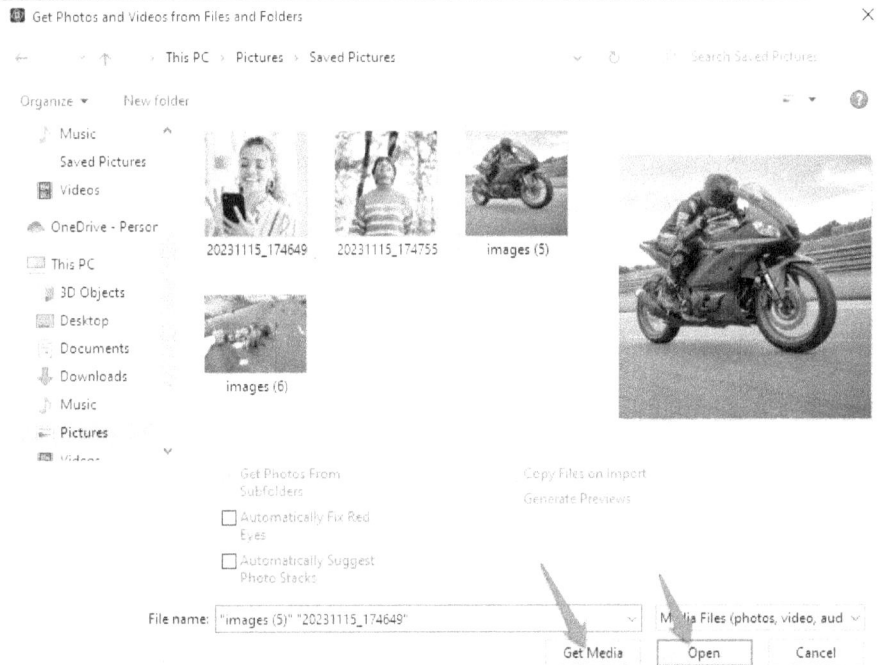

HANDLING ORGANIZER CATALOG

The easiest thing in Elements is to know how to manage the catalog, you can add photos to it, you can also delete photos from the catalog, and also send the catalog out of the Organizer, and so on. This aspect of this mini-book will reveal to you some things you can do with the Organizer Catalog:

1. **Opening Catalog:** you can choose the catalog you want to unlock in Media by selecting the File tab, then click the Manage catalog menu and pick the name of the catalog you want to unlock. Click on Open to unlock the photos in the concerned catalog in the Organizer window.

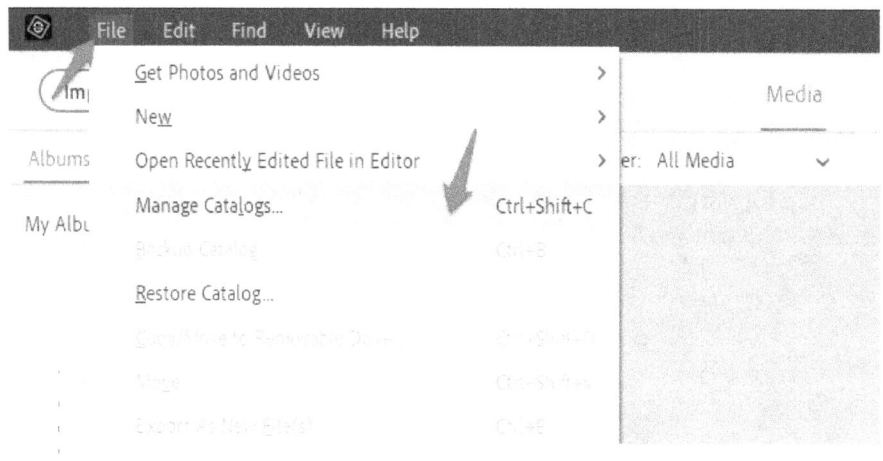

2. **Repairing And Improving A Catalog:** A catalog that cannot longer load the thumbnail of the Photos needs repairing while a catalog that is too slow while loading requires improvement. To repair and improve a Catalog, click on the Optimize and Repair buttons individually in the Catalog Manager dialog box and follow the onscreen steps to finish the process.

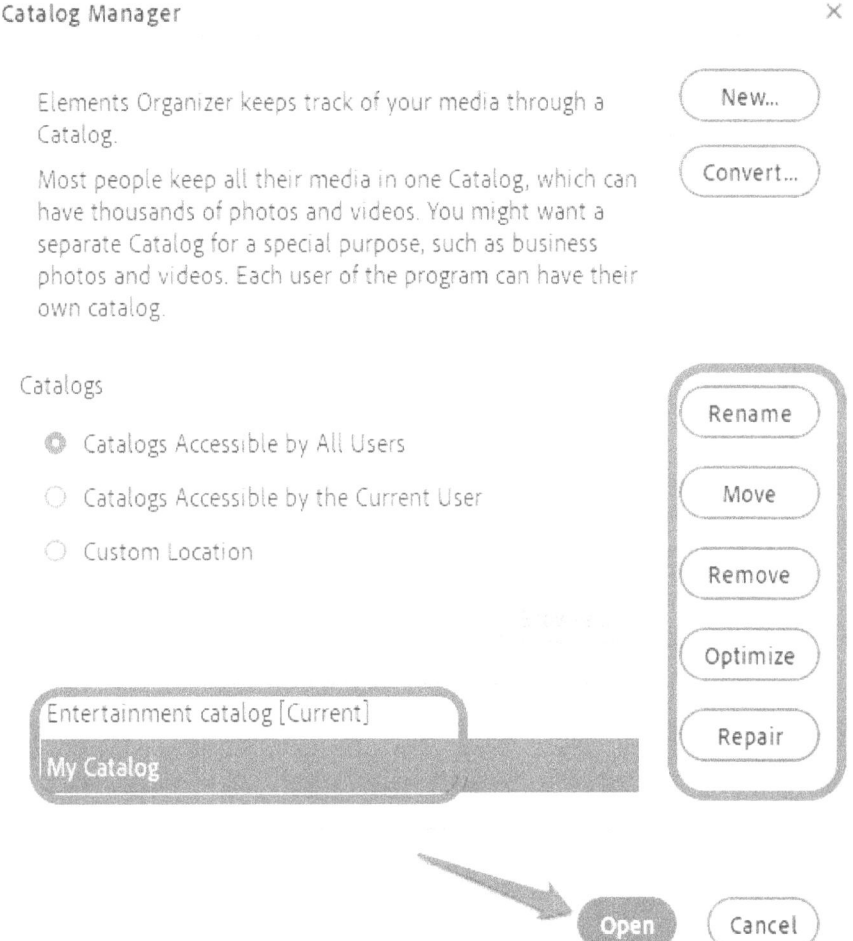

Catalog Manager   ✕

New...

Convert...

Elements Organizer keeps track of your media through a Catalog.

Most people keep all their media in one Catalog, which can have thousands of photos and videos. You might want a separate Catalog for a special purpose, such as business photos and videos. Each user of the program can have their own catalog.

Catalogs

◉ Catalogs Accessible by All Users

◯ Catalogs Accessible by the Current User

◯ Custom Location

Rename

Move

Remove

Optimize

Repair

Entertainment catalog [Current]

My Catalog

Open   Cancel

3. **Renaming And Removing A Catalog:** click on the individual buttons to rename and remove the chosen catalog.

WORKING WITH ORGANIZER VIEW

You can view the Organizer media in many ways through the View menu. The View menu gives you numerous views with attached options. I will just discuss a few of them below:

- **Details:** this reveals to you the date the File was generated and other details that are attached to each file. Click on the view and select details, to navigate to the details view.

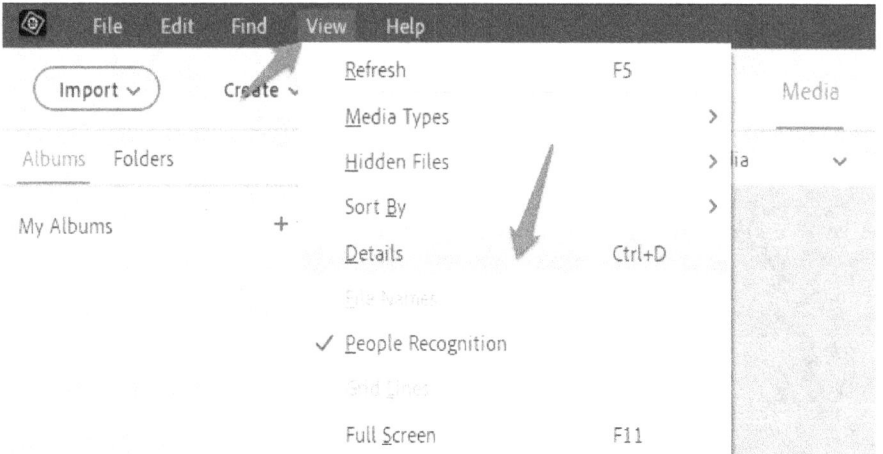

- **File names:** this option ascribes the name of each file to every file in the Organizer. To see the file name of each photo, click on the view tab and choose file names.
- **Timeline:** this is used to set the time when the photos are taken, click on the view, and pick the timeline. Then pull the horizontal bar to ascribe the time when your photos were taken.

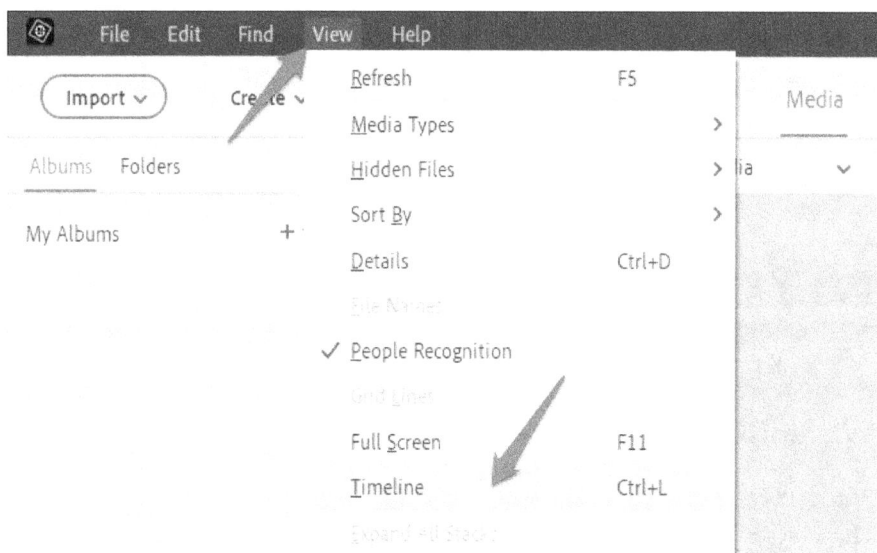

- **Media type:** it provides you the thumbnail pf each file, to move to media types, click on the View tab and choose Media types, then choose one or more sub-menu you need such as Videos, Photos, and so on.

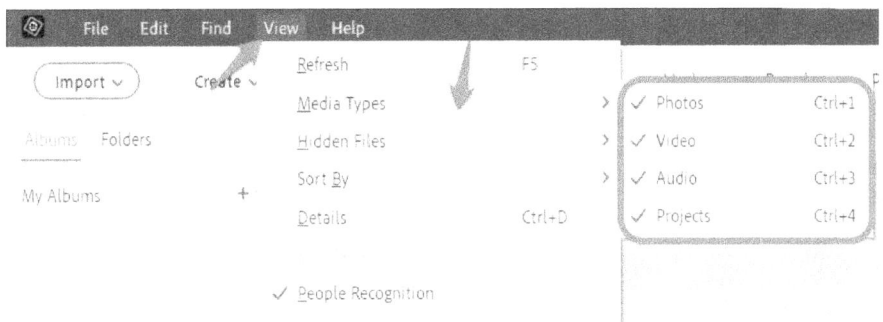

DISCOVERING PHOTOS WITH THE SEARCH BOX

Organizer gives numerous ways of finding photos but the common way of looking for photos is through the Search box. Kindly click on the Search box at the top of the Organizer screen, to search for any of the Organizer photos.

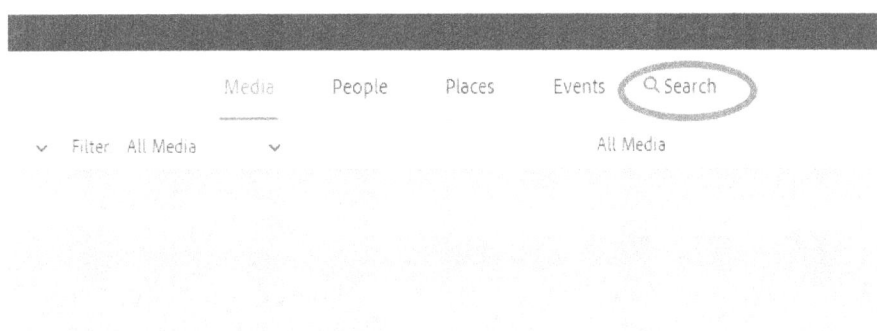

Immediately after you have clicked on the Search tab, the window will move to searching options mode showing you options for searching photos from the Organizer.

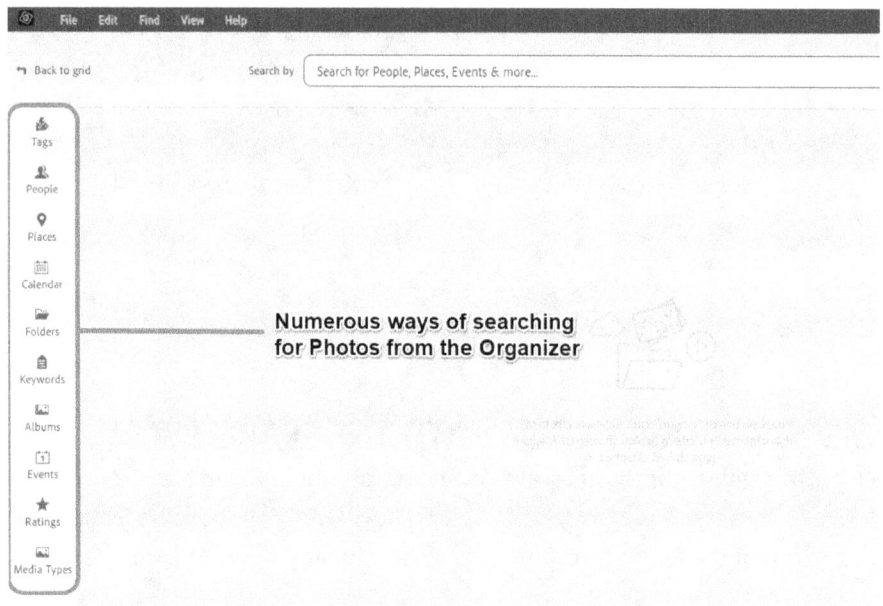

For instance, if you want to search for those photos you tag with a smart tag, and click on **Tags Icon** which is the first on the list, then if you want to search for photos you tag with the specified name of a person **People Icon,** and so on.

THE CAMERA RAW EDITOR

The Camera Raw Editor is an attached plug-in program that comes with Photoshop Elements to assist you with fast and brilliant image editing. It permits you to import raw image files to the Elements for editing and converting the files to the supported formats. The cameras and phones used to take those images were from numerous producers and many of these files are not supported by Photoshop Elements.

DEALING WITH NUMEROUS RAW FILE FORMATS

Raw files are mostly bigger compared to non-raw files such as PNG and JPEG because raw files have more data in them raw files are those images you save using digital camera format. Here are the raw files you will interact with while working on the Raw Editor:

- Sony (ARF)

- Nikon (NEF)
- Canon (CRW) or (CR2)
- Olympic (ORF)
- Panasonic (RW2)
- Hasselblad (3FR)
- Pentax (PEF)

UNLOCKING RAW IMAGES IN THE CAMERA RAW EDITOR

To unlock raw files such as RW2, CR2, DNG, and other formats on the Raw Editor, follow the techniques below:

➤ Select the **File tab** on the Photo Editor and pick **Open** then select the **raw file** you want to unlock inside the Open dialog box and click the **Open** button.

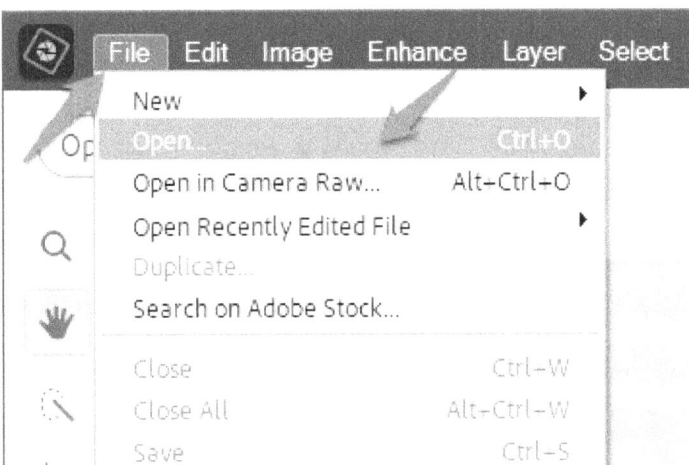

➤ Choose the **raw image** on the Organizer and click the **Edit** tab, then select **Edit with Photoshop Elements Editor** on the drop-down menu.

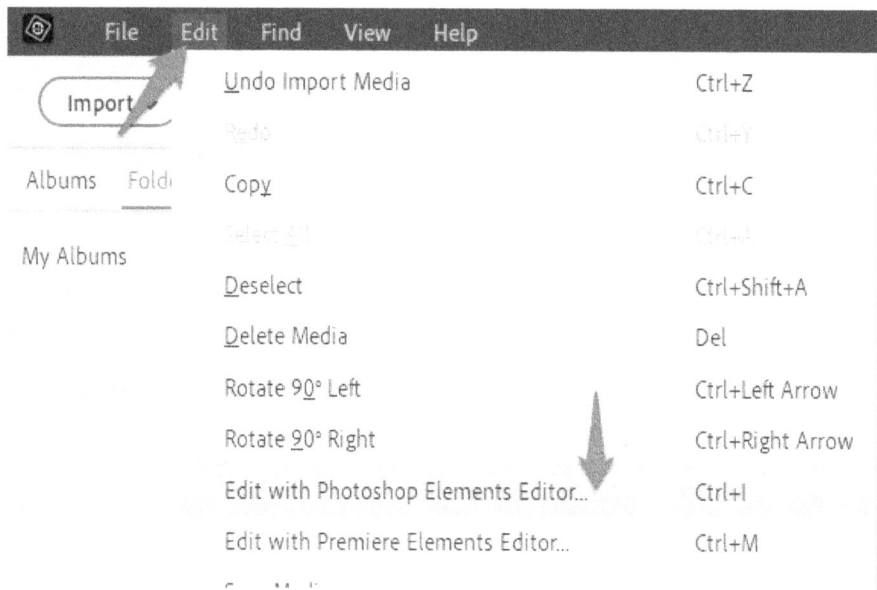

Note: If Adobe failed to load the raw files, that means Adobe does not support such Camera formats, so you need to convert the image to dng formats which is the supported format that Adobe identifies. And if you want to edit with Camera Raw Editor you will need to install the Camera Raw Editor from the **Help** tab at the top of the screen.

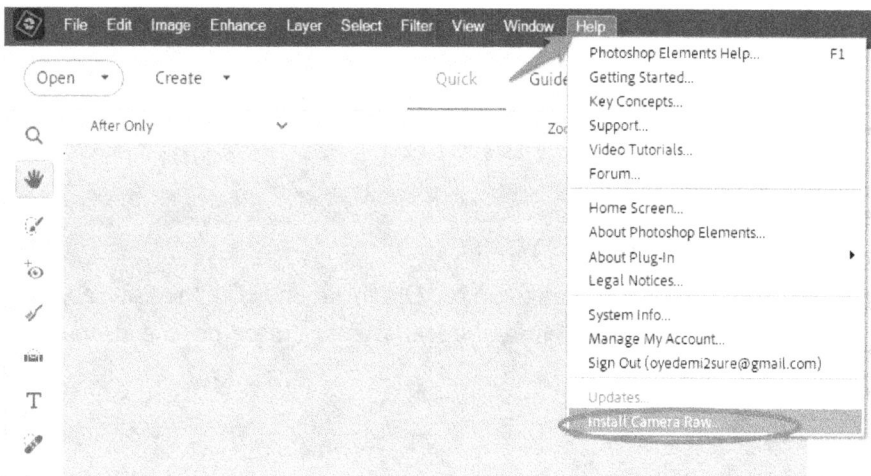

CHAPTER EIGHT

CONSTRUCTING AND MODIFYING THE SELECTION

This chapter discusses everything you need to know about selection which is the aspect of photo editing you cannot take with levity hand, making a selection with the different selection tools, and the reason why you need to use each selection tool and when to apply them. A selection is the part of the image you selected that you want to work on, in a state whereby you select the whole parts of the photo, the complete photo is selected but when an aspect of the photo is chosen, the part you choose is called the selected part while the area you did not select is known as the unselected part, and any editing you make will only reflect on the selected area. A selection will be obvious with the signal of a dotted borderline on the selection area of a photo.

CREATING A SELECTION WITH ELLIPTICAL AND RECTANGULAR MARQUEE TOOL

The **Elliptical Marquee** tool is used to choose an aspect of the image spherically such as a ball, clock, and so on, by drawing a circle, or globe over the necessary part while the **Rectangular Marquee** tool is used to choose an aspect of a photo by drawing rectangular border over the part you want to select. Follow the steps below to guide you in creating a selection with the Elliptical and Rectangular Marquee tool:

> ➤ Move to the tools box and choose either the Elliptical or Rectangular Marquee tool.

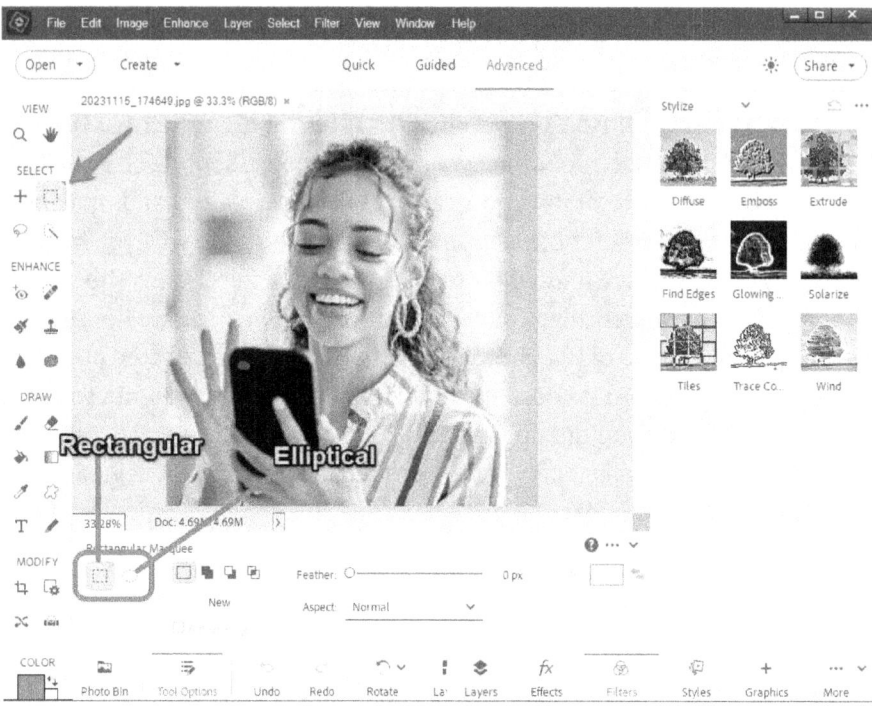

For the **Rectangular Marquee tool,** drag across the aspect of the photo you want to select then release the mouse immediately when you discover you have captured the aspect you need. See the image below:

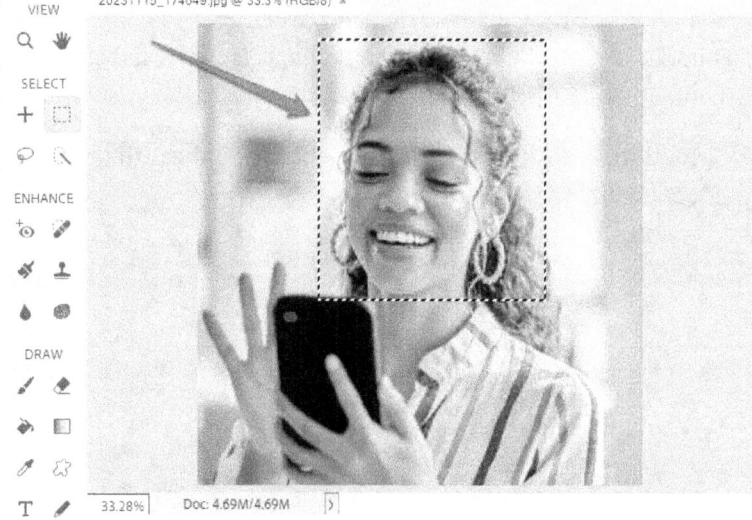

For the **Elliptical Marquee tool,** kindly drag across the aspect of the photo you want to pick, then release the mouse when you discover you have captured the aspect you need. See the image below:

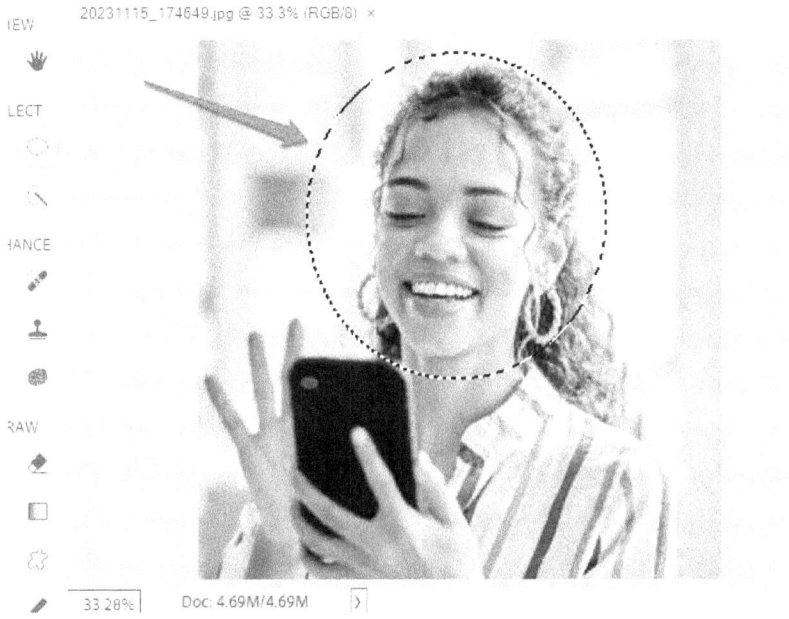

FUNCTIONING WITH MARQUEE OPTIONS

Marquee options are numerous options you can make use of to change the effect of both Marquee tools such as softness and sharpness measures through feathers and other options. The following are the Marquee options you need to understand when using Rectangular and Elliptical Marquee tools:

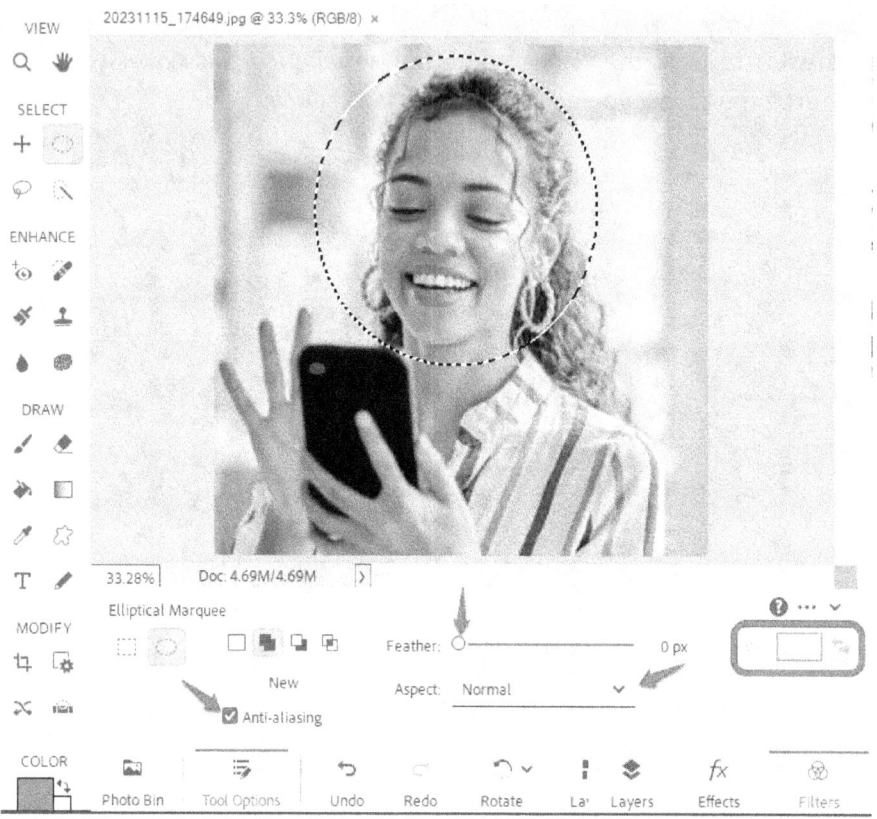

- **Feathers:** this is the option that is used for measuring the softness of the selection edges, all you need is to drag the slider, the higher the range the higher the softness.
- **Anti-Aliasing:** this is used to make softer the edges of the selection you made with an Elliptical tool or any other unbalanced shape.
- **Aspect:** This Option has three splitting-up functions and they are explained below:

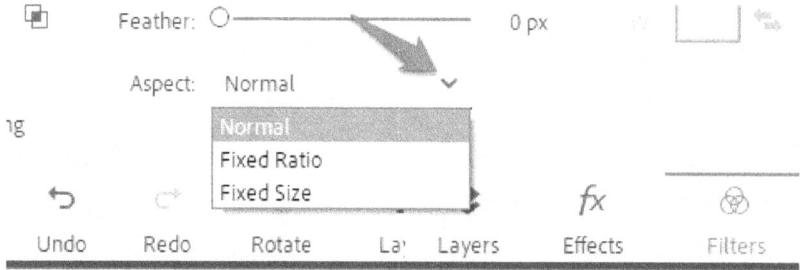

1. **Normal:** it is used to perfectly drag a selection to any size, and also the Marquee default option.
2. **Fixed ratio:** this permits you to input a certain ratio for the width and height of the selection.
3. **Fixed-size:** you can input any value into the height and width of your selection.
• **Width and height:** this is used in place of fixed ratio and fixed-size, that is to say, you need to enter a particular value into a fixed ratio or fixed size to accurately make use of fixed ratio and fixed size.

CONSTRUCTING ANY SHAPE SELECTION WITH LASSO TOOLS

Elements give opportunity for its users for selecting an aspect of a photo by drawing freely on any aspect of the photo for a perfect selection such as the line of any side, curve of any form, and so on rather than rectangle and sphere selection. Lasso gives three ways for freehand drawing which are, Lasso, Polygonal Lasso, and Magnetic Lasso. These three tools are discussed below:

FREELY SELECTING ANY SHAPE WITH A LASSO

The Lasso tool is created to freely draw any shape on the image. Follow the steps below to freely draw and pick aspects of an image with the Lasso tool:

➢ Click to choose the Lasso tool from the tools box.
➢ Position your cursor on the aspect where you want the drawing selection to begin.
➢ Pin down by pressing the mouse button and trace around the aspect of the photo you want to choose, don't release the mouse button.
➢ When you are done selecting the area you want to choose, return the cursor to the starting area and let down the mouse button, and finish the selection process.

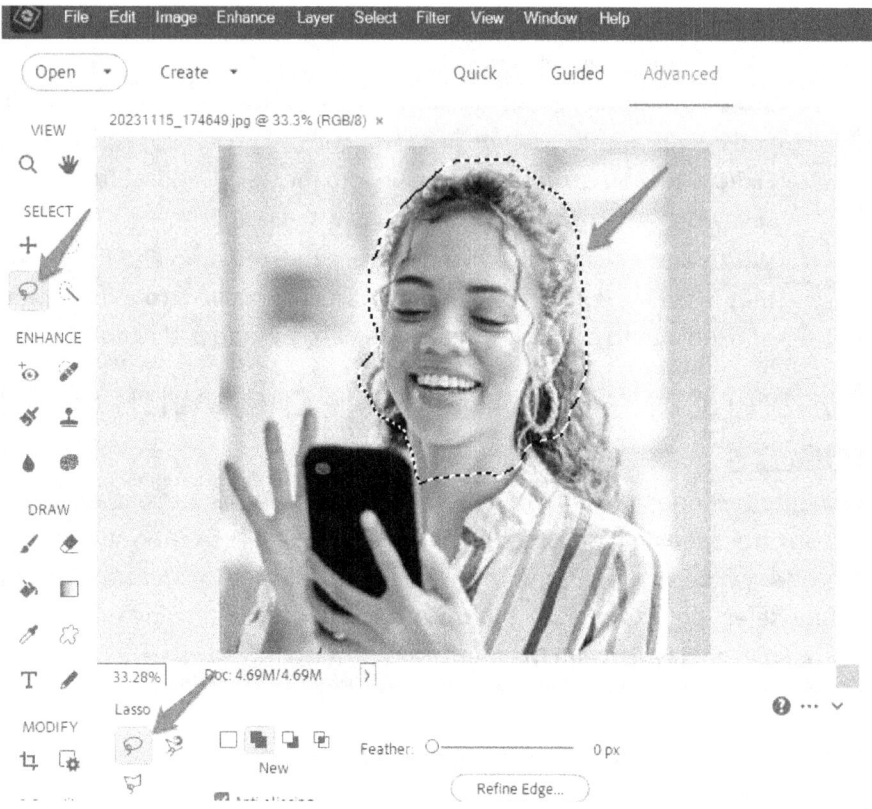

USING THE POLYGONAL LASSO

A polygonal lasso is created to choose any straight aspect or line of an image. Follow the steps below to apply the Polygonal Lasso tool:

➢ Click to pick the Polygonal Lasso tool from the tools box or in the tool option after you have chosen the lasso tool.

➢ Position the cursor at the point where you want to start the selection, then click and release the mouse at the very point.

➢ Navigate to the end point and click the point, shift to the next point you want to select, and click the mouse, you navigate from one point to another and left-click them to select it, you do not drag when you are selecting an aspect of a photo with Polygonal Lasso tool but you have to move.

➢ Return to the last point and click the starting point to close the selection or double click the last point to close the selection process.

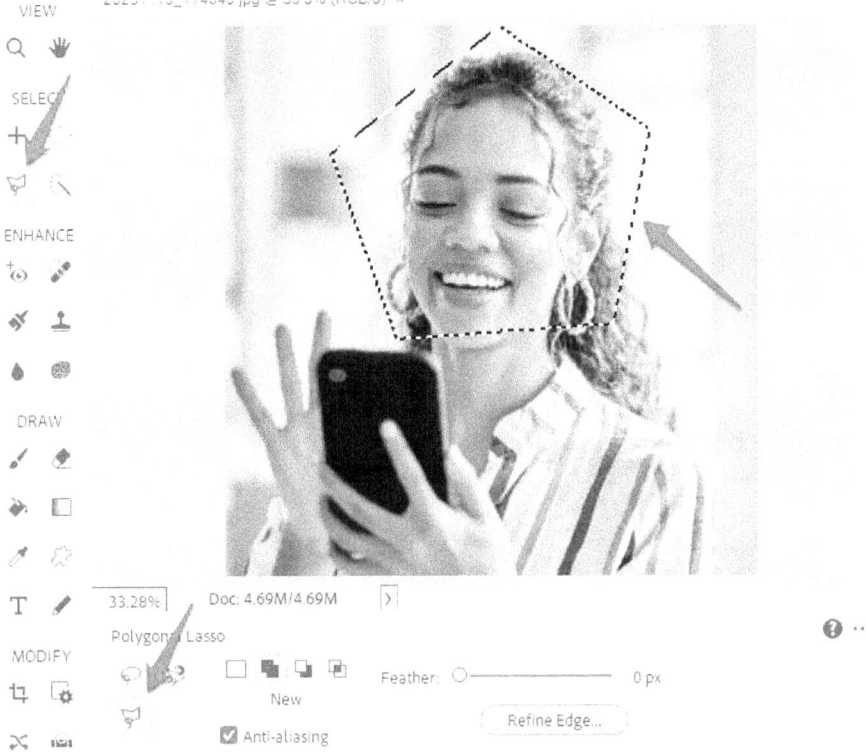

MAKING USE OF THE MAGNETIC LASSO

The Magnetic lasso is used for drawing a selection on an aspect of the photo to balance the difference between the background of the two points. Follow the steps below to make use of Magnetic Lasso for selection:

➢ Click to choose the Magnetic Lasso tool from the tools box.
➢ Position the cursor on the edge where you want to start your selection, then navigate your cursor around the background object you want to choose. Be selecting and dropping anchor so that what you have selected will not be damaged.
➢ Go back to the starting point and click it to close the selection.

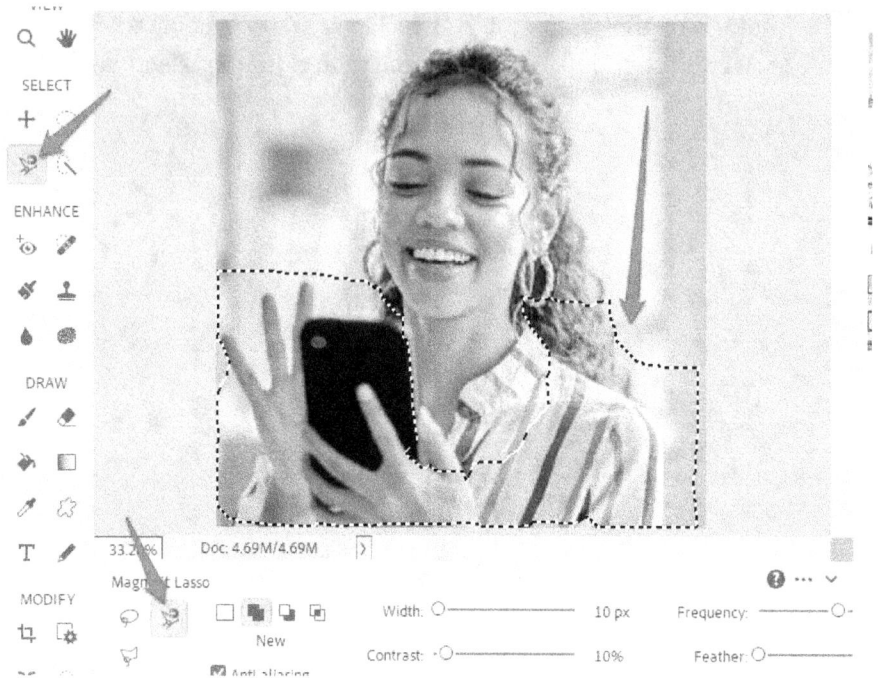

THE MAGIC WAND

The Magic wand selects the color of a pixel area you selected automatically and applies such color pixels to the entire photo. Magic Wand always works with the Tolerance; the Tolerance is the range of color that is present in a photo. Follow the steps below to make a selection with the Magic Wand and modify Tolerance:

> Click to pick the Magic Wand tool from the tools box.
> Choose the area of the photo that has the pixel colors you want to copy, and the background color changes instantly. Nevertheless, if you discover the pixel color selected is lower than your specification you can increase the tolerance setting and if the pixel color is higher than what you expect decrease the tolerance setting.
> Choose the aspect again to sub-change the background pixel color, all the previous magic settings will be erased immediately after you reselect.

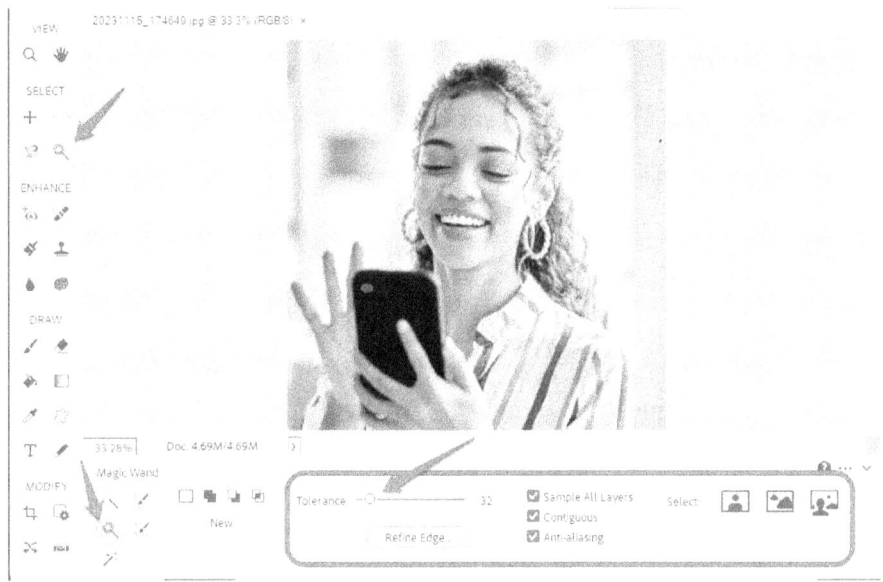

The following are other settings you can modify while dealing with Magic Wand aside from tolerance settings:

- **Sample all Layers:** click this option to several possible layers of the selected aspect, otherwise, Magic Wand will choose pixels of the current layer.
- **Contiguous:** if you choose this option it will make Magic Wander choose pixels of the close selection otherwise it will pick all the pixels that are visible to the tolerance.
- **Anti-Aliasing:** this is used occasionally to soften the edges of the selection you made with the elliptical tool or any other unbalanced shape.
- **Refine edge:** this is a refining Option used for fine-tuning and refining the edges of your selection by dragging the smooth slider to change the edges of the selection.

CHANGING A SELECTION

Photoshop Elements permits you to change any of your selections to allow you to the exact area of the image that you want to select. For example, if you select beyond what you aim to select, you will have to subtract from the selection, and if you select below what you aim to select, you will need to add to the selection

ADD TO AND SUBTRACT FROM A SELECTION

You can decide to Add to and Subtract from a selection regarding the issue you are facing. I will be using Marquee, Lasso, and Magic Wand as an example regarding this:

➢ **ADD TO:** for Marquee, hold down the **Shift** key and drag across the aspect of the image to add more selection. For Lasso, hold down the **Shift** key and **click** around the aspect of the image to add more selections, and for Magic Wand, hold down the **Shift** key and click the aspect of the image to add more selections.

➢ **SUBTRACT FROM:** For Marquee, hold down the **Alt or Option** key and drag around the selected part of the image to subtract from the selection. For Polygonal Lasso, hold down the **Alt or Option** key and click around the selected part of the image to subtract from the selection. For Magic Wand, hold down the **Alt or Option** key and click the selected aspect to subtract from the selection.

➢ **INTERSECT SELECTION:** To intersect two selections, hold down the **Shift and Alt** keys on Windows and the **Shift and Option** keys on macOS and drag over the two selections. For Marquee and Lasso tools. You will need to click the two selections for Magic Wand.

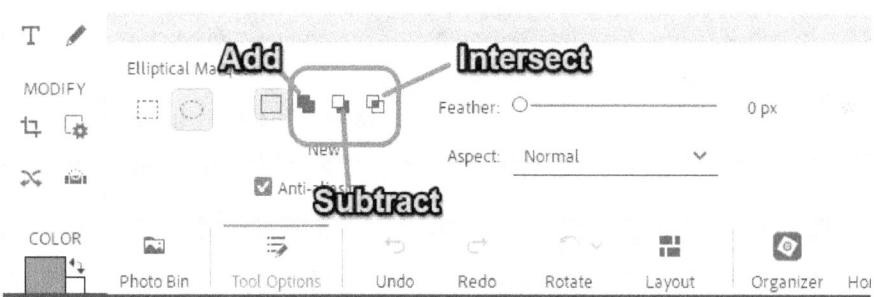

APPLYING A SELECTION BRUSH FOR PAINTING THE AREA OF AN IMAGE

A Selection Brush is a perfect tool for painting across the area of an image. Follow the steps below to learn how to use a Selection:

1. Click to pick the **Selection Brush tool** from the **tools box.**
2. Apply the tool options to set the Selection Brush options. The tool options are as follows:
   - **Size:** input the size value into the size box or set the brush size by using the slider.
   - **Brush preset picker:** this permits you to choose a picker from the drop-down menu for your Selection Brush.
   - **Mode:** choose a selection to paint across the area you want to select or select a Mask for the painting over the area you don't want to select.
   - **Hardness:** choose the brush adjustment from 1-100% for the Selection Brush.
3. You can now paint the area you want to select or the area you don't want to select.

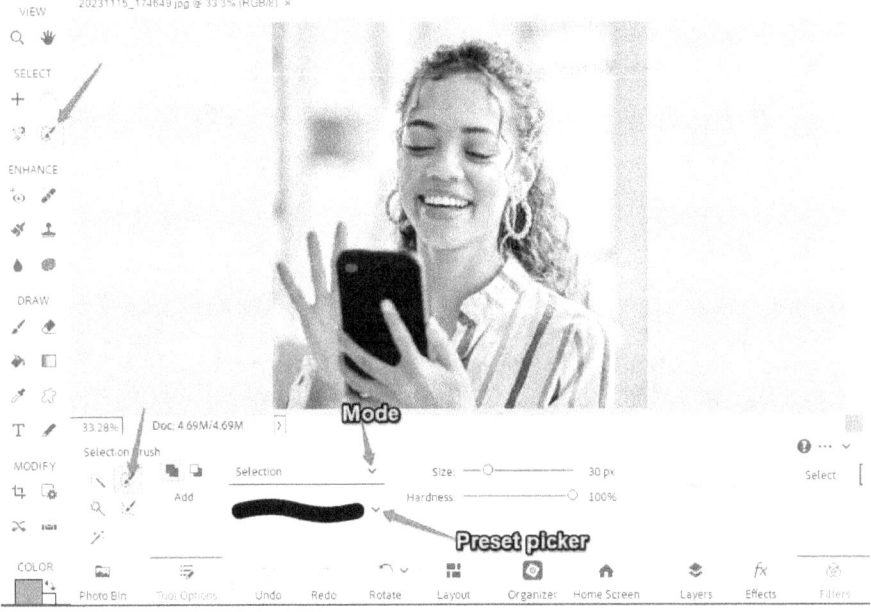

INSTANTANEOUS PAINTING WITH QUICK SELECTION TOOL

A quick selection tool is created to select an aspect of the image by comparing the textile and color of the selected aspect. Follow the procedure below for painting a selection with a Quick Selection tool:

1. Select the Quick Selection tool from the tools box.
2. Set the option for the Quick Selection tool from the Tool options box as orated below:
   - **Sample all Layers:** click on this option to add all possible layers of the selected aspect, or else the Quick Selection tool will choose pixels of the current layer.
   - **New Selection:** this is the default option when dealing with the Quick Selection tool, it permits you to build a new selection.
   - **Brush Setting:** this comprises numerous settings for the Quick Selection tool such as hardness, border, angel, and so on.
   - **Size:** input the size value into the size box or apply the slider to set the Quick Selection size.
   - **Auto Enhance:** this will assist you to fine-tune or perfect the area of selection.
3. Drag across the selected area to paint it.
4. You can apply tool options to add to or subtract from your selections by clicking on the individual button in the toll options.

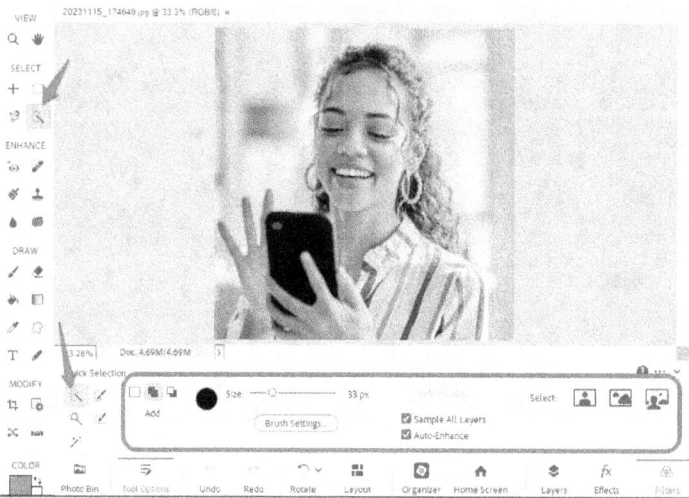

USING THE AUTO-SELECTION TOOL

The Auto-selection tool will automatically select the part of the image. Below are the steps to guide you on how to apply the Auto Selection tool:

➢ Select the Auto Selection tool from the tools box.
➢ Click on any other tool you want to use for making a sample selection, it can be any of the following **Polygonal Lasso, Lasso, Rectangular, or Elliptical Marquee Tool.**
➢ Enter other essential settings to properly implement the operation of the Auto Selection tool such as:
  - **Sample all layers:** select this option to several possible layers of the selected area, or else the Auto Selection tool will hand-pick pixels of the current layer.
  - **Constraints Selection:** this option deals with Marquee tools only by providing you with a perfect Elliptical or rectangular shape selection.
➢ Make a sample selection with any of the tools in the second step above.

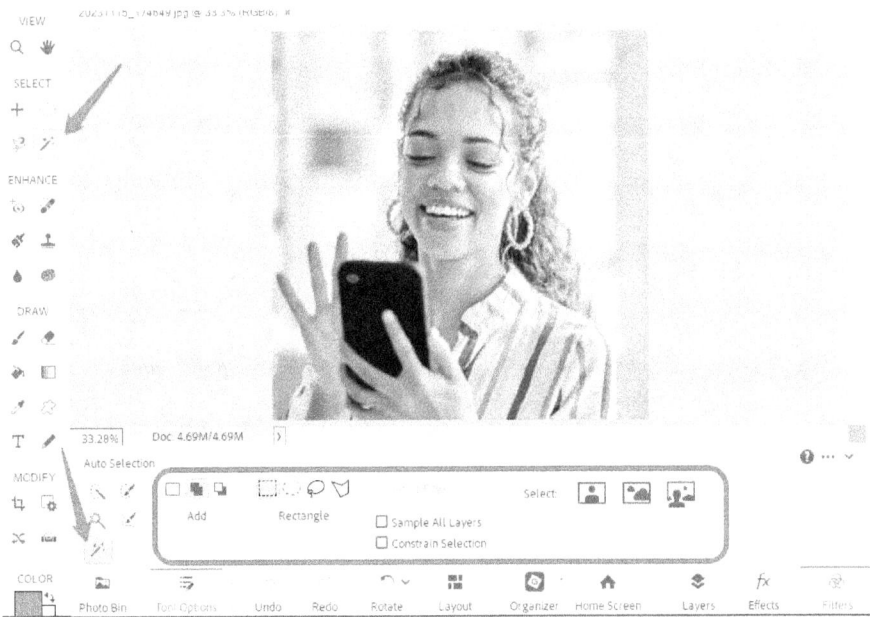

➤ You can make use of refined edges to enhance the selection of the edge in the tool option, and you can also add to or subtract from your selection in the tool option.

THE REFINE SELECTION BRUSH TOOL

The Refine Selection Brush tool is created for pruning the edges of the selection you made by merging or removing your selection to boost and advance your selection. The below steps reveal to you how to refine the edges of selection with the Refine Selection Brush tool work:

1. Select the aspect of the part you want to select with any of the selection tools I have discussed above.
2. Click to pick the Refine Selection Brush tool in the tools box.
3. Input and modify the essential options in the tool options to make edge refining work better, such as **Size, Snap strength, Selection edge, Add or subtract, Smooth, and View.**

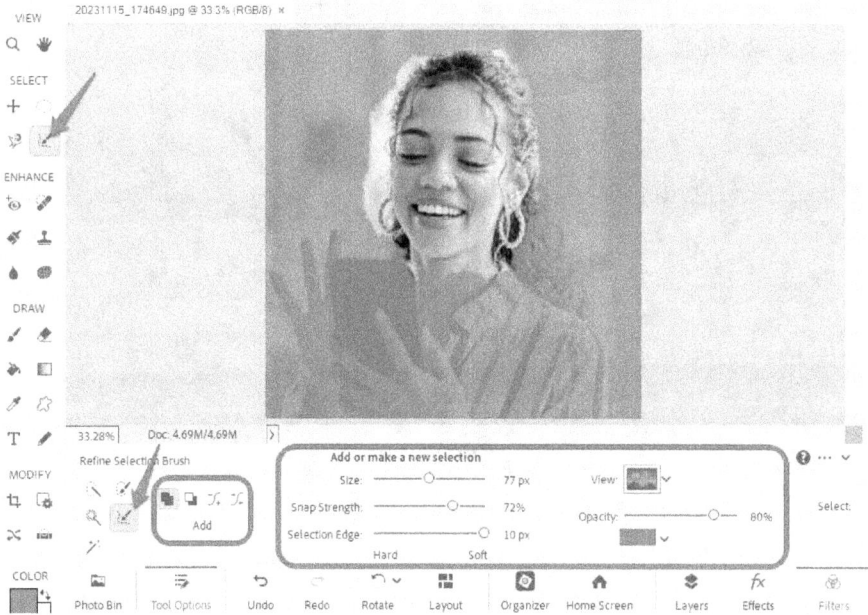

4. You can also use Refine Selection continuously till you have the perfect look you want.

THE COOKIES CUTTER TOOL

The cookie cutter tool assists you in remodeling your photo into the shape you want by cutting out some aspects of your image. Follow the steps below to make use of the Cookies Cutter tools:

➢ Pick the **Cookies Cutter** from the tool options by selecting the **Crop tool** in the tools box.

➢ Set up essential options for Cookies Cutter, those options are:
- **Geometry option:** for setting up a variable for drawing shapes.
- **Shape:** this is for choosing numerous shapes from the Custom shape collection.
- **Unconstrained:** this is used to eradicate all constraints when drawing
- **Crop:** this is used to crop an image
- **Fixed Size:** to state precise size
- **Feather:** this is used for measuring the selection edges, apply it by dragging the slider
- **From the center:** start drawing the shape from the center.

➢ You can now construct that particular shape you want by dragging the mouse over the image.

➢ Apply any of the side handles to regulate the size of the shape, when you notice you already have the shape you want, click on the enter button on the keyboard for confirmation.

113

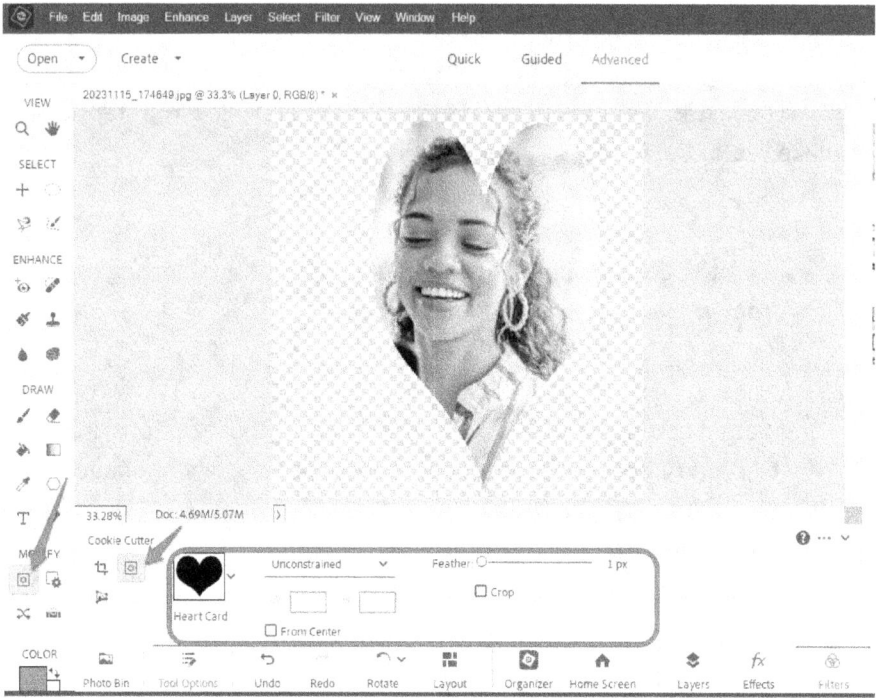

THE ERASER TOOLS

This is another amazing Elements tool created to erase a particular aspect of an image, the tool is divided into three, namely: **Eraser tool, Magic Eraser tool, and Background Eraser tool.**

APPLYING ERASER TOOL

This permits you to erase a particular aspect of your image, for instance, the color, background, or photo. Follow the steps below for using the Eraser tool:

> ➢ Select the Eraser tool from the tools panel
> ➢ Then regulate the tool with the following options:
>> • **Brush Preset Picker:** this permits you to choose the brush you will be using for the erasing.
>> • **Size:** this permits you to set the brush size by dragging the slider.

- **Opacity:** this is used to adjust the transparency level of the Eraser color.
- **Type:** this allows you to choose the category of the type you want.
➢ When you have applied all the options above, drag the tool across the area you want to erase.

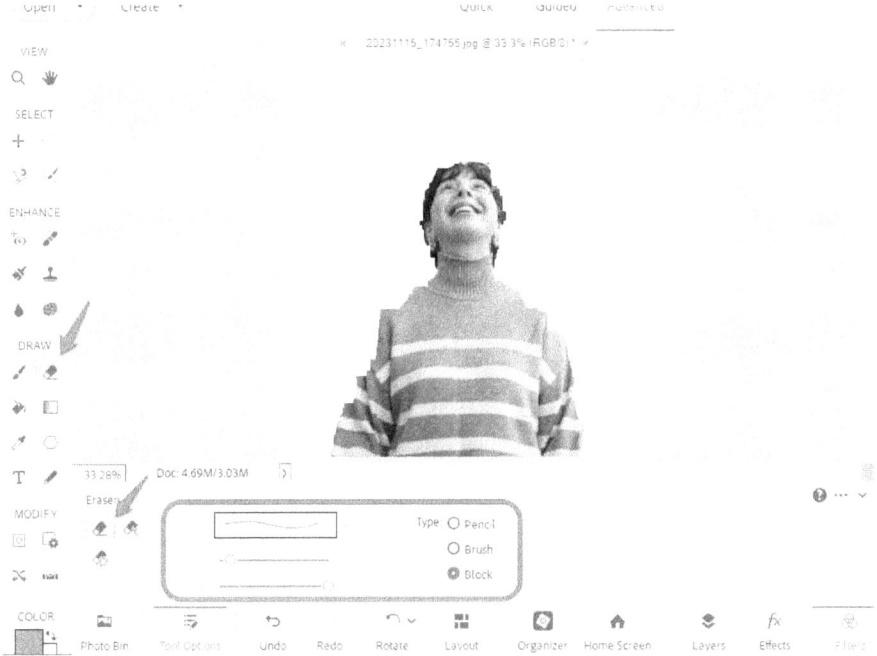

THE BACKGROUND ERASER TOOL

To make use of the Background Eraser Tool, follow the steps below:

➢ Select the Background Eraser Tool in the tool box.
➢ Apply the Layer panel to choose the layer you want to erase.
➢ Then regulate the Background Eraser tool from the tool options, which are:
- **Brush setting:** this contains numerous settings for the background Eraser such as size, border, and so on
- **Limits:** this option offers you two options, which are contiguous and discontiguous. Contiguous erases any equal colored pixel that is next to the hotspot while discontiguous

erases all equal colored pixels irrespective of their position in a photo

- **Tolerance:** this is used to measure he degree through which the color will be undistinguishable compared to the hotspot color before the concern color will be eradicated.

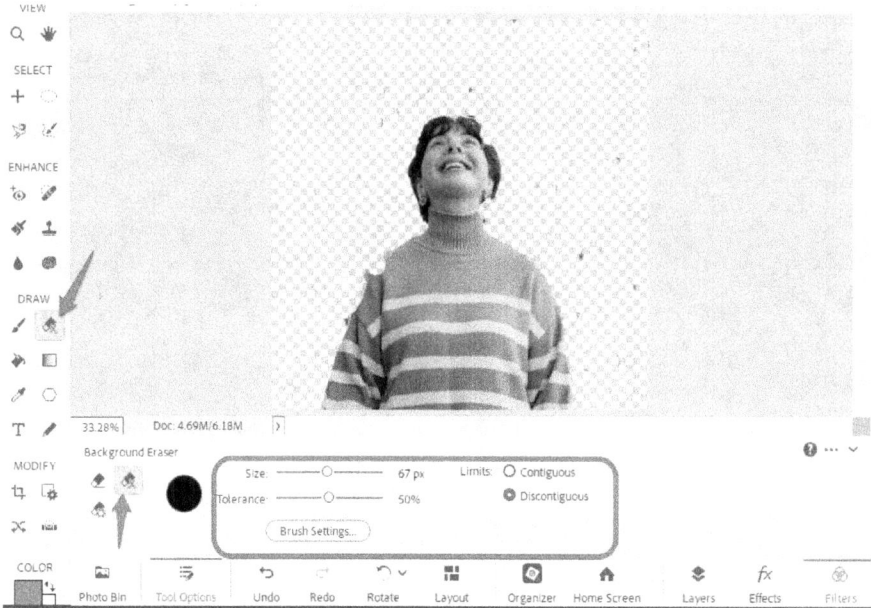

> then drag the tool to erase the color pixel you do not need any more.

APPLYING A MAGIC ERASER TOOL

To apply the Magic Eraser tool, follow the steps below:

> select the Magic Eraser tool in the tools box.
> Regulate the Magic Eraser tool as important such as: **Sample all Layers and Anti-Aliasing.**

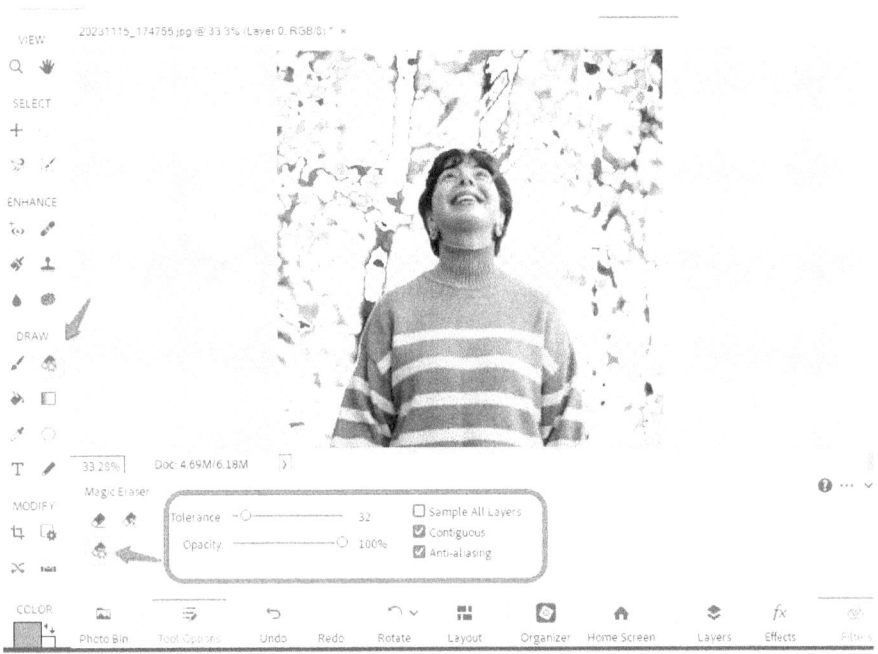

REFINE THE EDGES OF YOUR SELECTION

The refine edge button can be located in the tool options of **Lasso**, **Magic Wand**, and **Quick Selection tools**. It is used to smooth and refine the edges of a selection. To view the Refine Edge dialog box, click the Refine edge button in any of the above-mentioned selection tools. Then navigate around the options to see their effectiveness.

SAVING YOUR SELECTION FOR FORTHCOMING PURPOSES

Element permits you to choose any aspect of the image in the process of your editing, it may happen to be the selection you will need in the future, therefore, you have to save such a selection. Follow the steps below to save a Selection:

> ➢ Select the aspect of the image with any Selection tool.
> ➢ Click on the **Select tab** then click on **Saving Selection** to access the save selection dialog box.

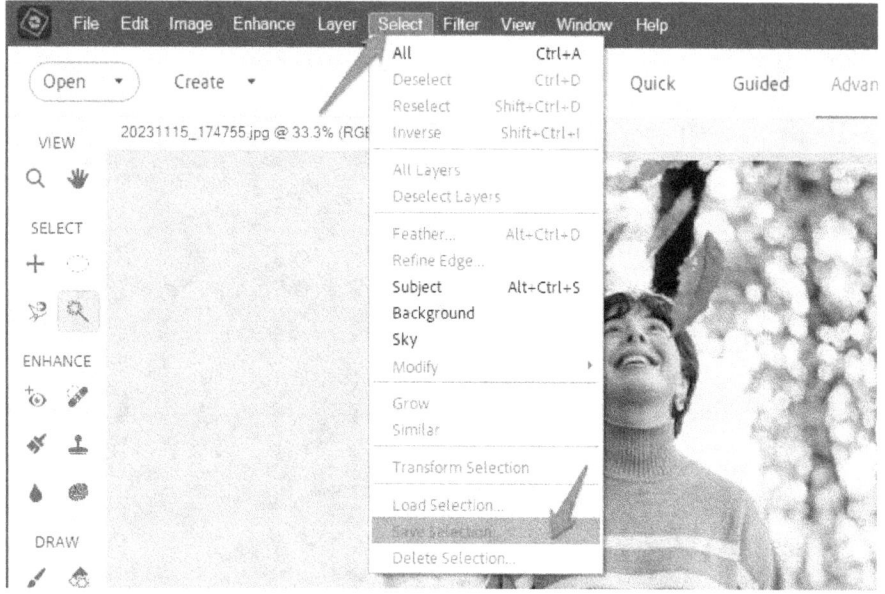

> ➢ Move to the **Operation Section** and Click on New **Selection.**
> ➢ Input the name you want into the name field and click the Ok button.

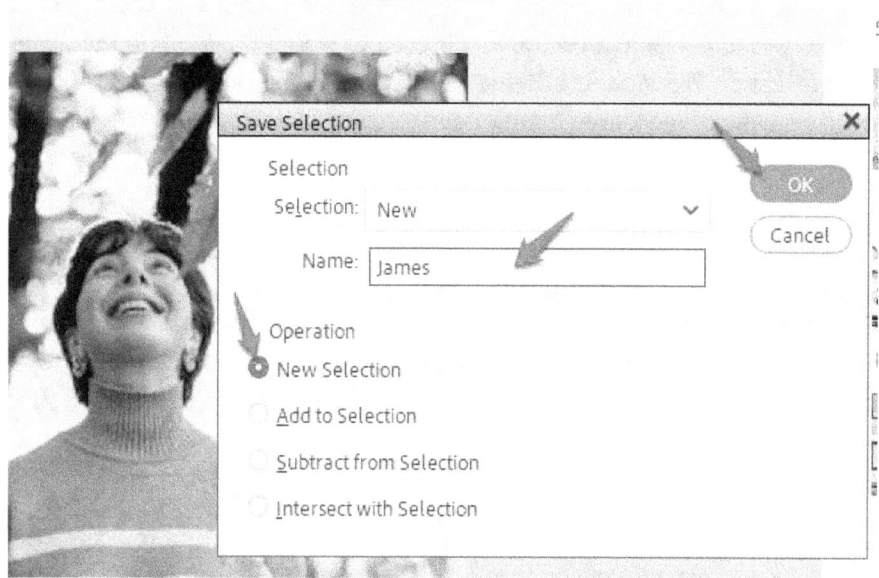

LOADING A SAVE SELECTION

To gain access to your Save Selection anytime you want, kindly follow these steps below:

1. Pick the **Select tab** then click on **Load Selection.**

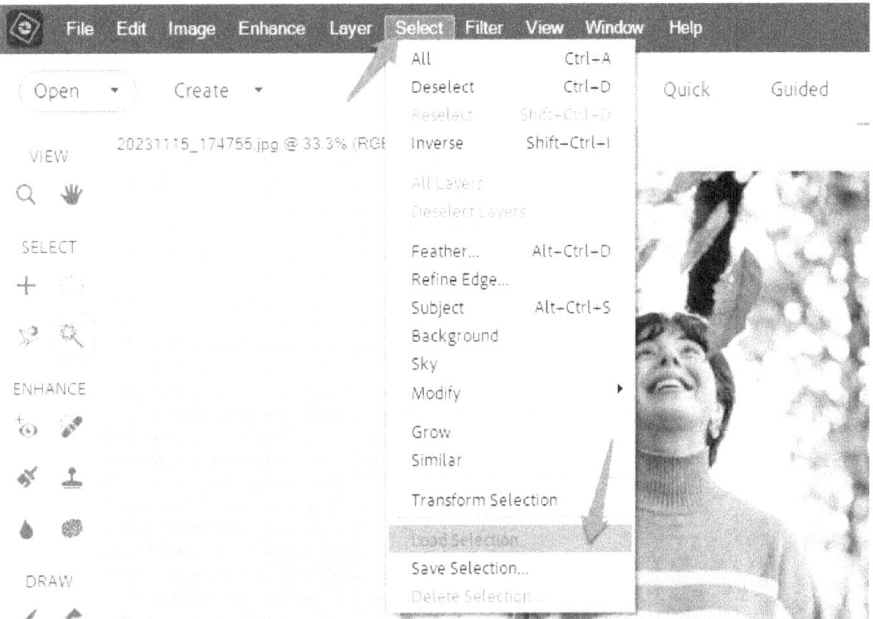

2. Click on the Selection you want from the selection collection you have saved on your PC.

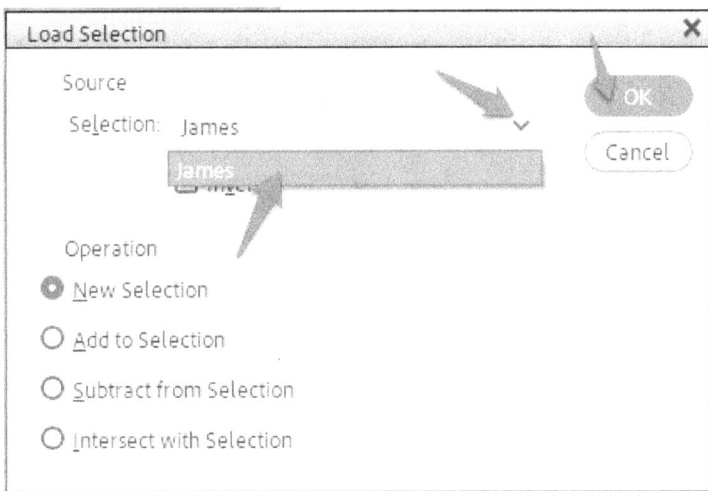

CHAPTER NINE

THE LAYERS

Layers simply mean dividing an image into diverse sections which are described as Layers by stacking them over one another, it means a photo has been divided into diverse elements for numerous editing, so when you combine all the layers of the photo, they will turn to a photo.

THE LAYER PANEL

A layer panel is a housing of numerous Layers where layer operations are being carried out, and also it is where layers of the image are shown and organized in a specific order. To view the layer panel, follow the steps below:

➢ Navigate to the Windows tab.
➢ Then click Layers from the drop-down list.

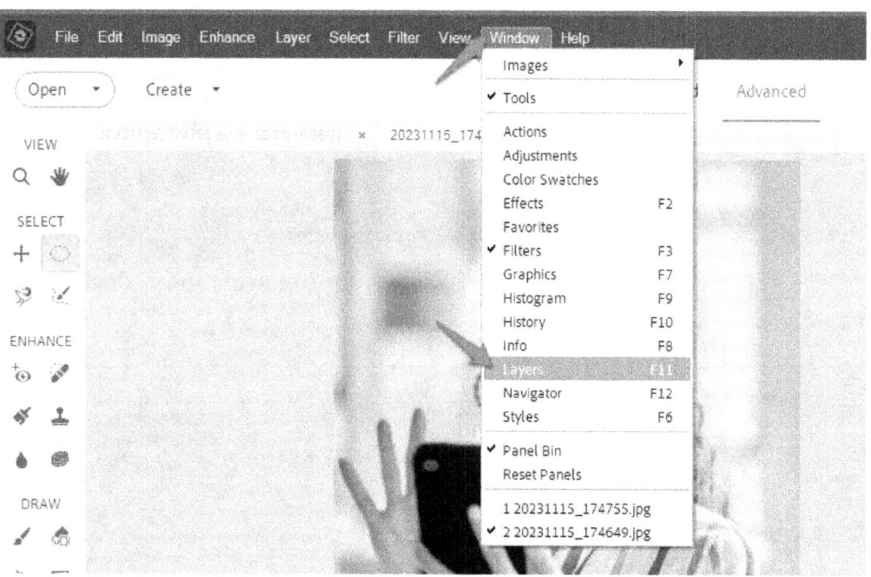

Immediately you click the layer, the Layer panel will appear. See The Layer panel as displayed below:

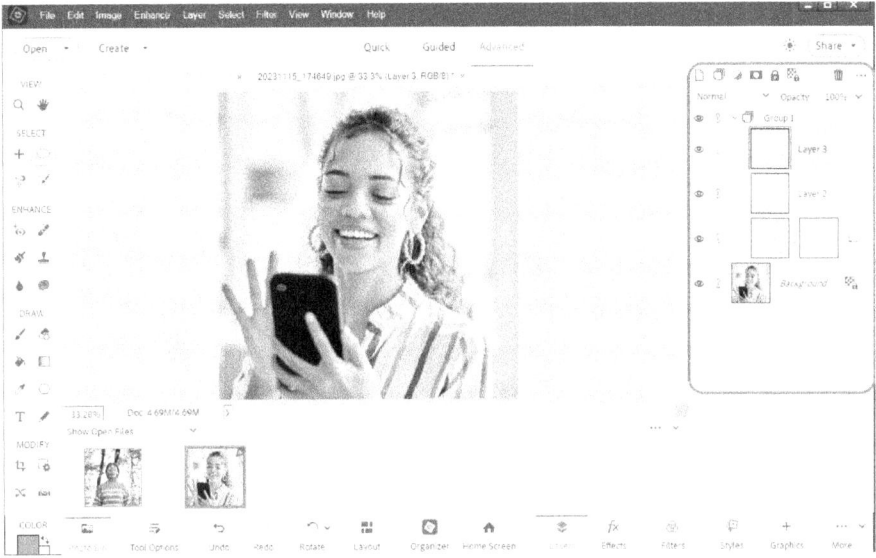

THE LAYER TYPE

Layer Panel offers you five Layers you can work with, which are

- Image Layer
- Adjustment Layer
- Fill Layer
- Shape Layer
- Type Layer

Let's look at the layers one after the other:

IMAGE LAYER

This is the layer that has image information and it is very essential. Observe the below steps to create an Image Layer:

➢ Select the **Windows tab** and pick **Layer** to access the Layer tab.

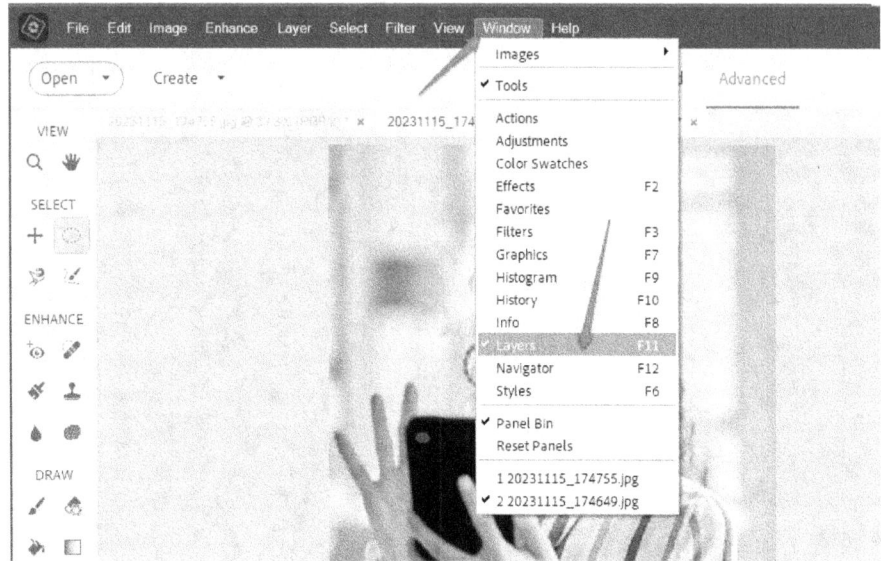

> ➤ Click on the specific Image in the photo bin that you want to use as an image layer.

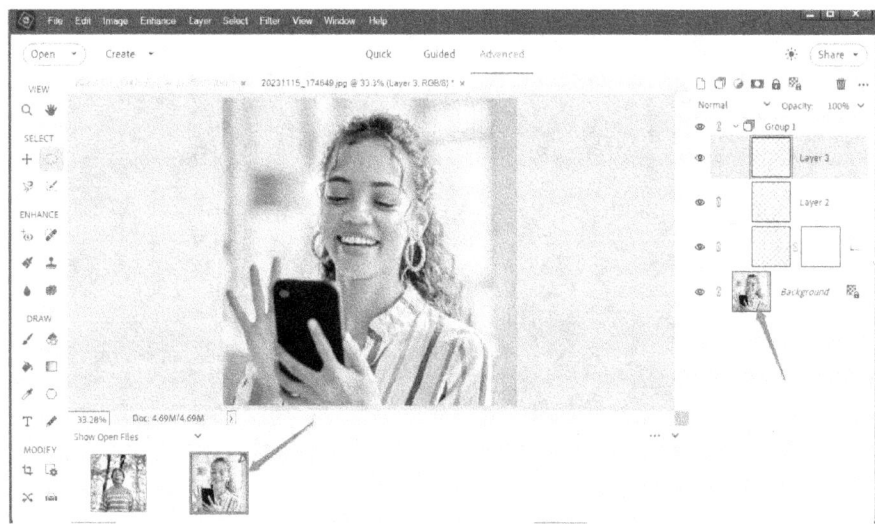

> ➤ It will appear as background in the layer panel, double click the background and give it any name of your choice, or leave it as its default name.

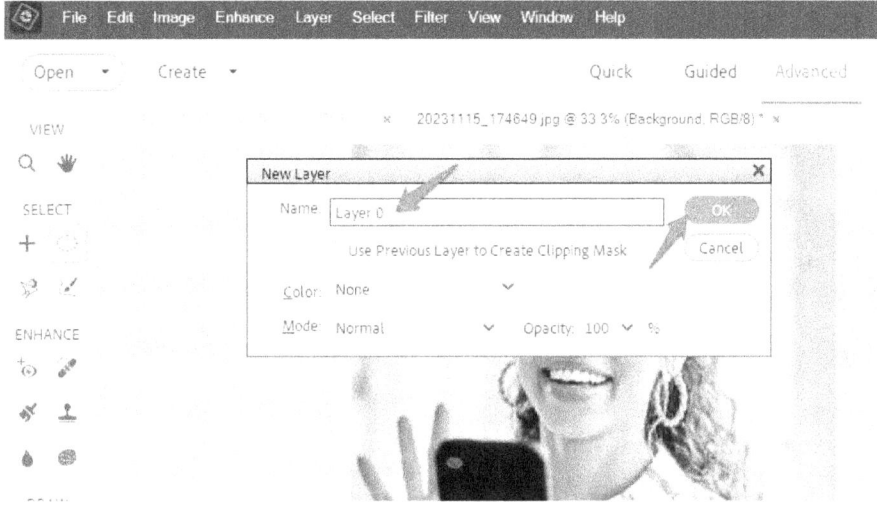

ADJUSTMENT LAYER

The adjustment Layer is mainly used for correcting the contrast, brightness, hue, and saturation of all layers beneath it. It is one of the essential layers in the layer panel. To view the adjustment layer, follow the steps below:

- ➢ Click on the image you want to modify or adjust
- ➢ Navigate to the layer panel and click the **fill or adjustment layer** at the top of the panel
- ➢ Then choose the adjustment type you want to work on from the drop-down list. See the image below

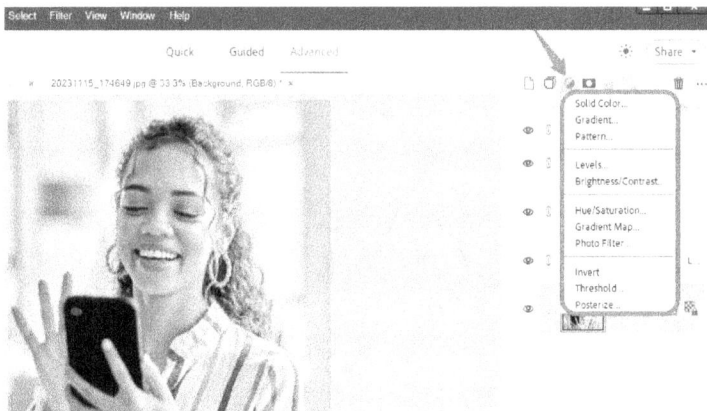

For instance, I select the **levels** from the drop-down list to adjust the total value of the image.

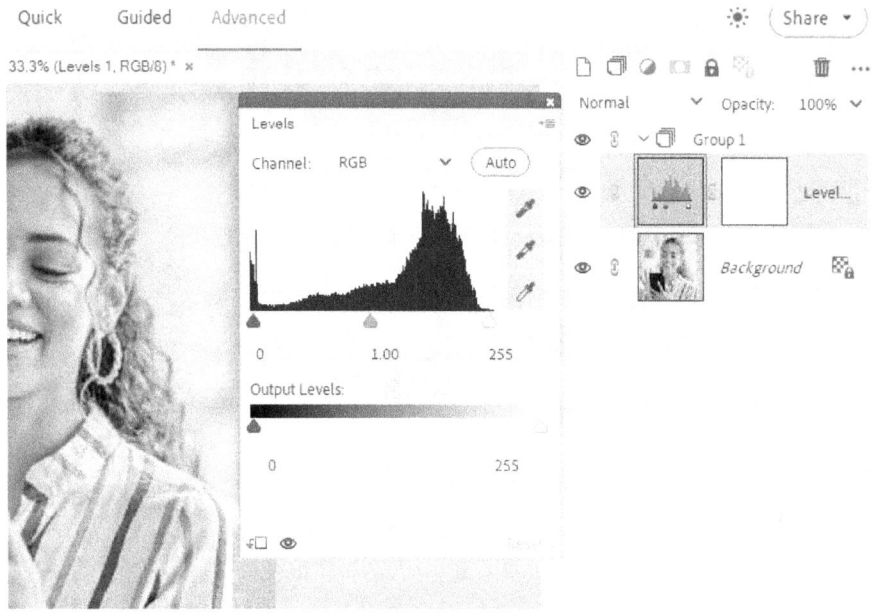

> ➢ To edit the adjustment panel again, double-click the panel in the adjustment panel.

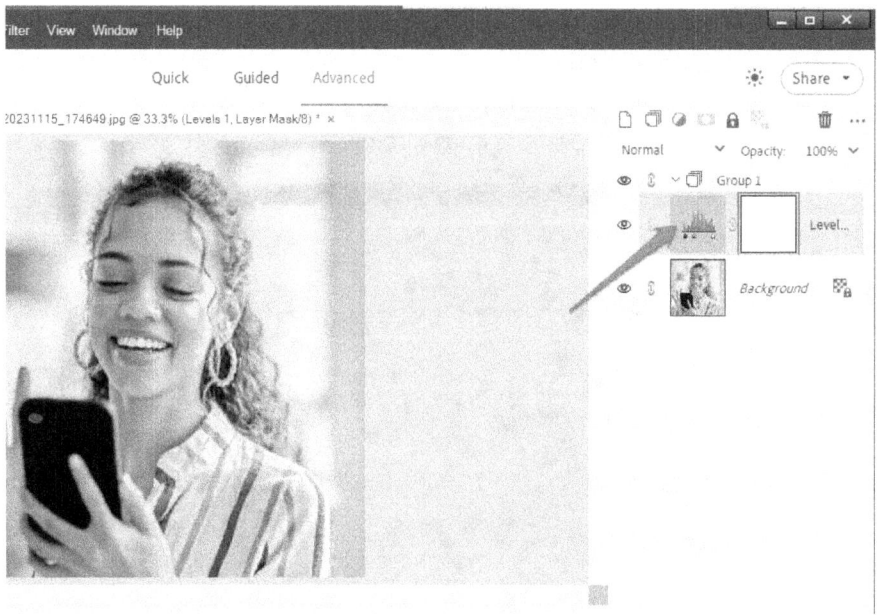

FILL LAYER

The fill layer is created for adding a gradient, colors, and patterns to the image, it works very similarly to the Adjustment layer. You can also carry out numerous operations such as duplicating, editing, deleting, and so on. To apply the Fill Layer, follow the steps below:

- ➢ Click the image you need to modify
- ➢ Go to the Layer panel and click on the **Fill or Adjustment layer.**
- ➢ Then choose the fill type you want from the drop-down menu such as **Solid Color, Gradient, and Pattern.** See the image below:

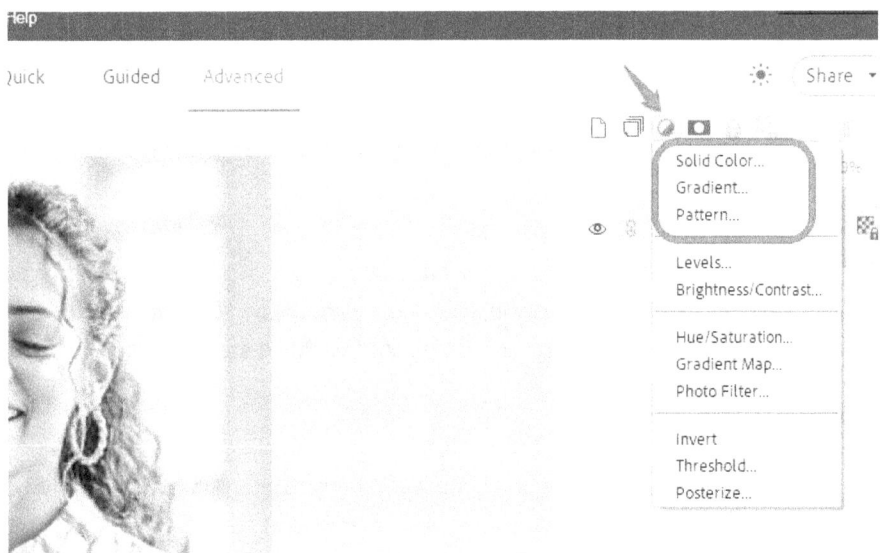

SHAPE LAYER

This layer permits you to attach numerous shape layers with paths rather than pixels in another layer. You can also resize the shape to any length without any depreciation. Follow the steps below to learn how to use the shape layer.

- ➢ Click to choose any **custom shape or shape** in the tools box.
- ➢ Drag the shape tool on the image to draw the shape.

Immediately the shape will occupy its layer, you can now move or edit it, and adjust it with opacity and blend mode.

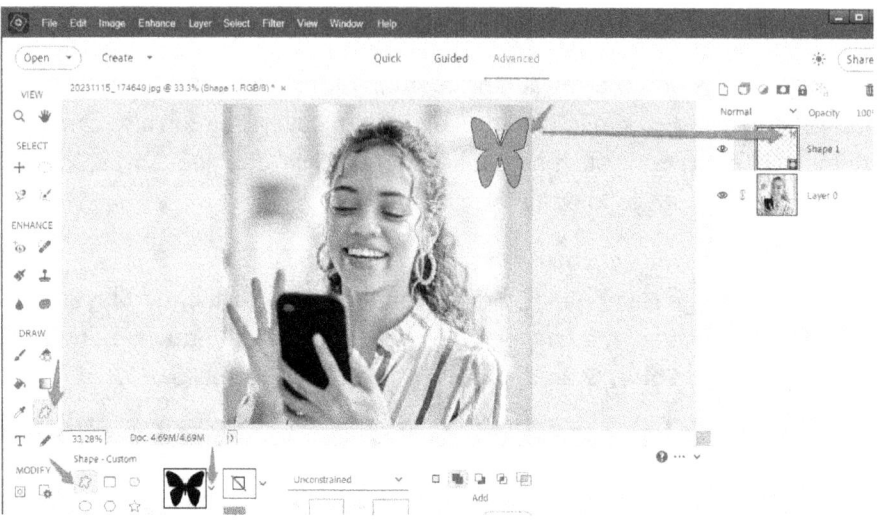

TYPE LAYER

This layer can be used anytime you want to insert the word into your image. It is designated with the T icon in the Layer Panel. The font and size of the text in the Tool Options can be adjusted, follow these steps to use the Type layer:

- ➢ Pick the Type Tool in the tools box.
- ➢ Click the actual place on the image where the words will be shown.
- ➢ Input the Texts and click on the Confirm icon to create a type layer which will appear as a T icon in the Layer Panel.

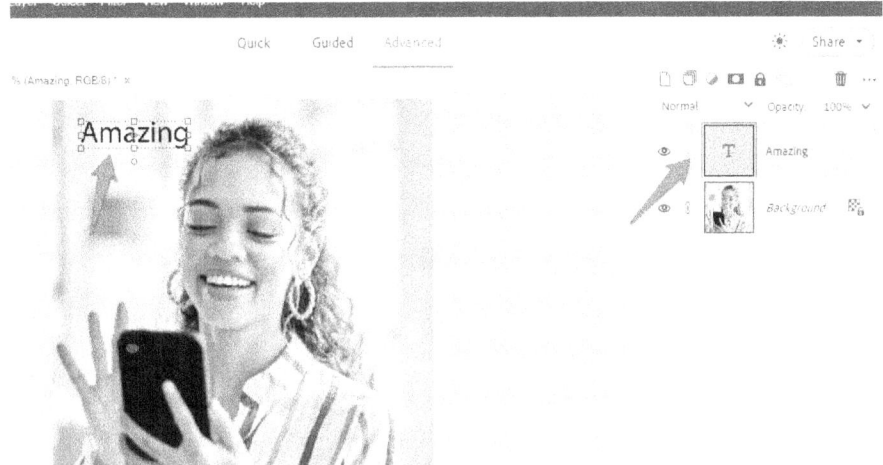

DEALING WITH LAYER MENU AND LAYER PANEL MENU

The layer panel menu and layer menu can assist you in carrying out some editing activities that you cannot do with the layer panel. This section is created to show you some editing activities that are entrenched in the layer menu and layer panel menu.

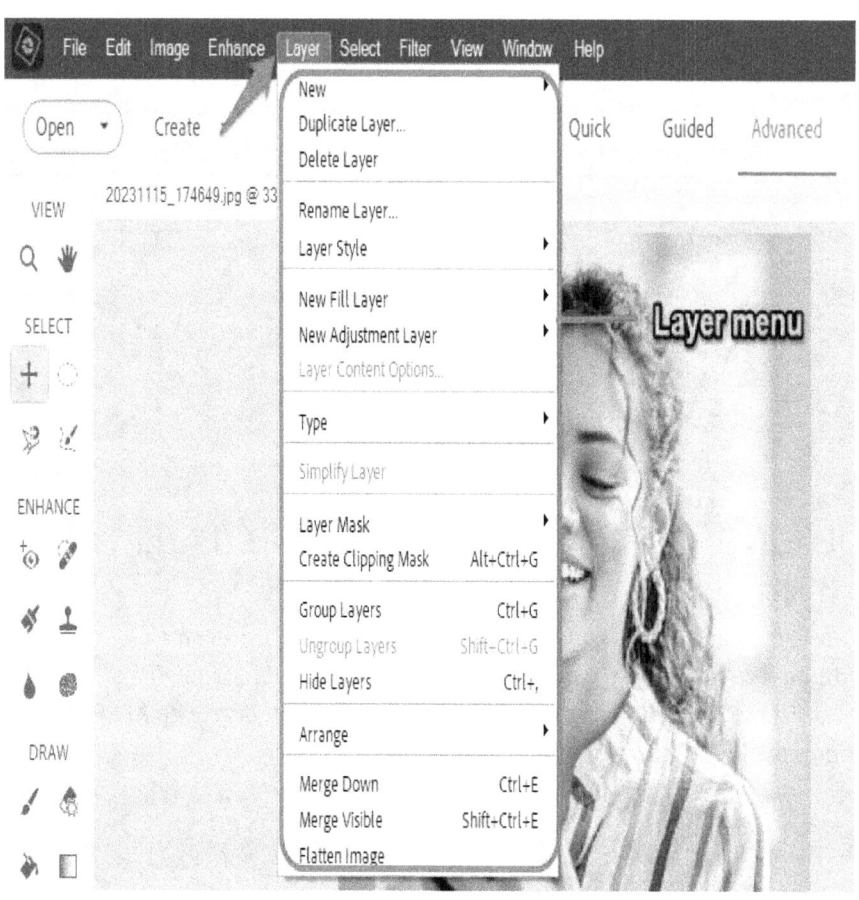

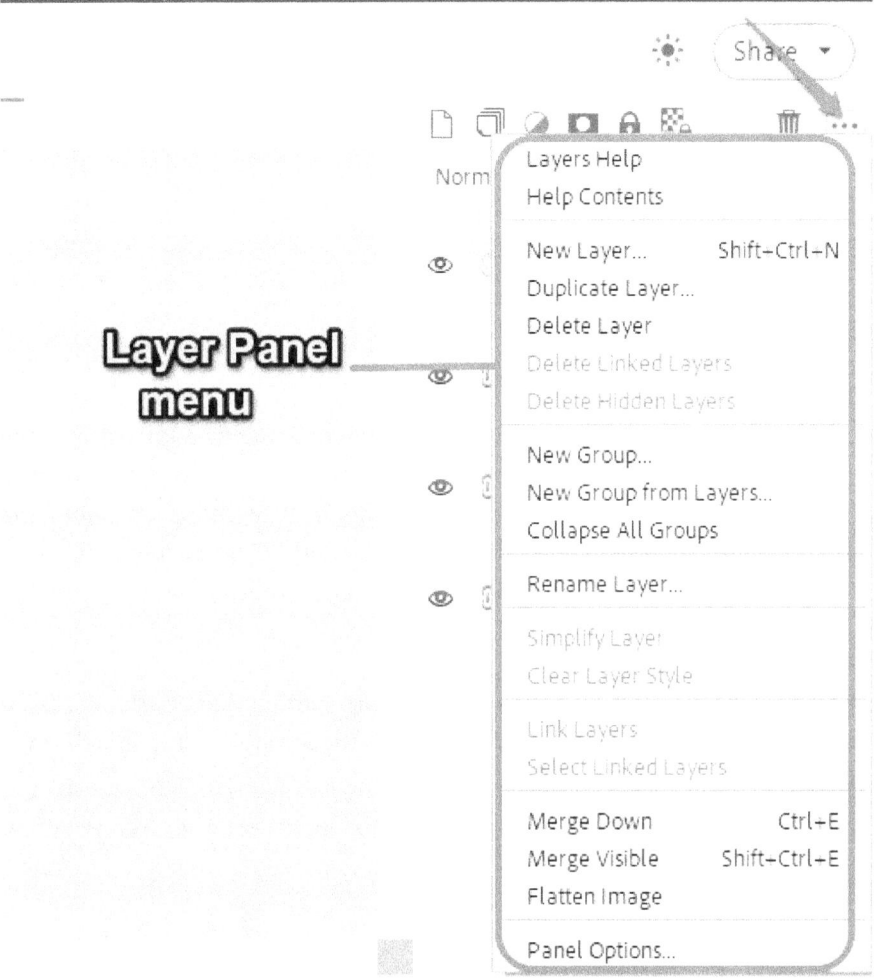

Below is a little explanation about the Layer menu and Layer Panel menu:

> **Delete Linked Layers/Delete Hidden Layers:** delete linked layers is used to delete the layer connected while deleting the hidden layer allows you to delete all the layers that have been hidden from the layer panel.
> **Arrange:** this is the command for layer assembling order by using options like Bring, to Front, Send to Back, and so on.
> **Layer Style:** this is the button for managing the styles and effects that you have applied to the layers.
> **Type:** This signifies the submenus of the Type layer you have on the layer panel.

➢ **Rename:** This is needed when you want to rename the layer you choose on the panel.

➢ **Panel options:** this assists you in carrying out particular panel options such as the display and selection of layer mask on the adjustment layer.

➢ **Flatten image:** this is used to bring together the visible layers into a single background.

➢ **Merge visible:** this button is used to chain visible layers into a single layer.

➢ **Simplify layer:** apply this command to convert the fill, shape, or type layer to the actual image layer.

➢ **Create Clipping Mask:** The clipping mask uses the lowest layer to create a mask for the above layers. The layer at the top will clip to the opaque aspect of the layer beneath without revealing the transparent aspect of the layer beneath. This is done by using numerous image layers to fill the shape or type layer.

THE SELECT MENU

The select menu deals with selections but in another way, particular layer commands are fixed in the select menu. Those commands are enlightened below:

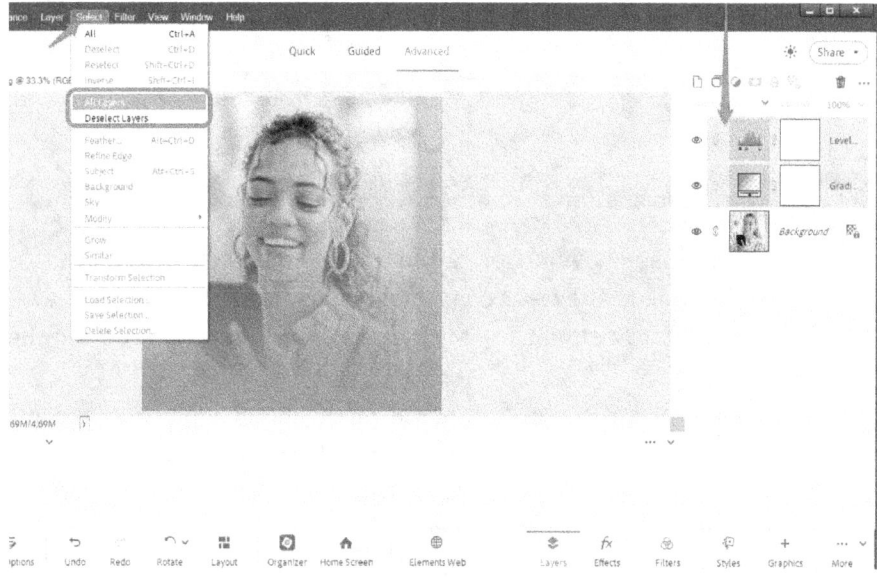

➢ **All Layers:** click this option to choose all the layers or contents of a certain file, to do this click on the select tab and choose All layers on the drop-down list.

➢ **Deselect Layers:** select this option to choose no layer contents of a certain file.

TRANSFORMING LAYERS

Transforming layers has to do with the adjustments you did on your layers such as Rotating, Resizing, Distortion, or scaling. Follow the steps below to learn how to transform layers:

➢ Choose the **Layer** you want to transform. To apply transformation over **numerous layers**, link the layers in question with the link layers.

➢ Select the **Image** tab and pick over the **Transform** menu, then choose Free **Transform** on the submenu.

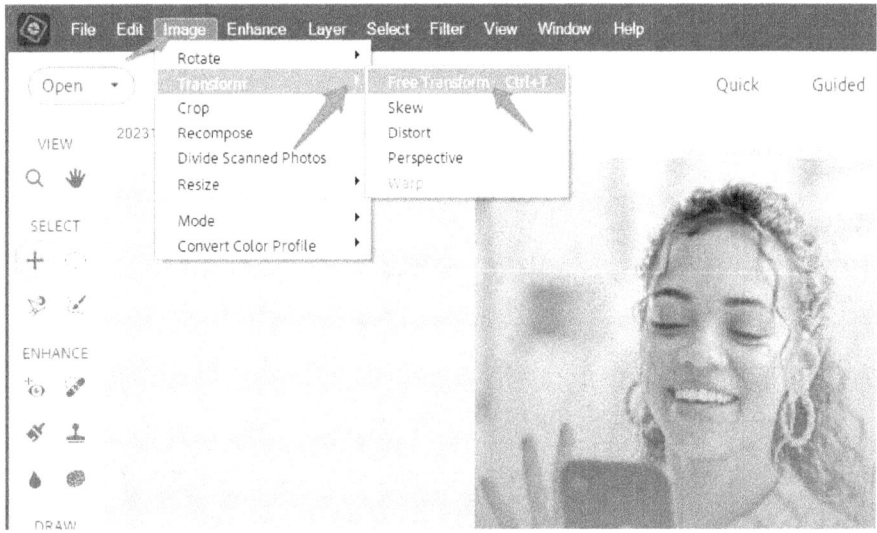

You can now perform the following transformations on the chosen layers:

• **Rotate the contents:** position the mouse on the edges of any of the corners till the mouse turns to the curve arrow, and drag to rotate the way you want.

• **Distort, Skew, or apply perspective:** right-click the bounding box and choose the equivalent option from the context menu.

• **Resize the contents:** drag the corner handles for resizing.

131

- **Constraint the proportion:** press the Shift key while dragging any of the corners.

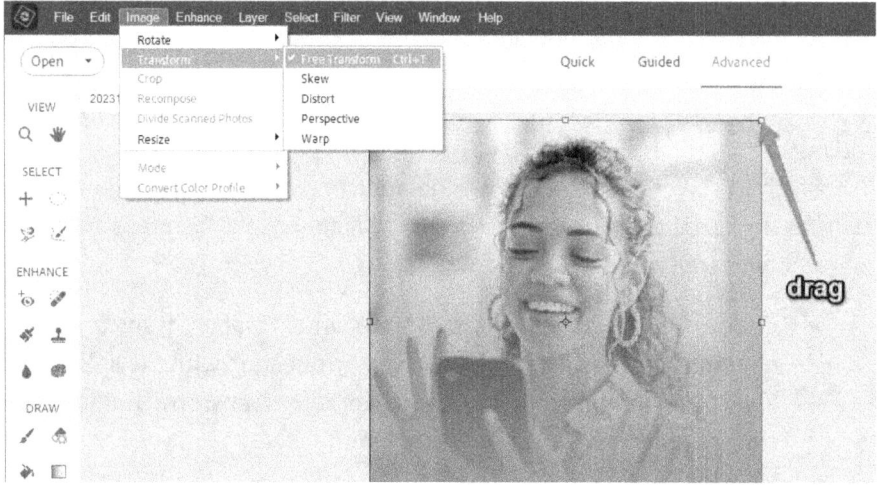

> Double-click anywhere within the bounding box to validate the changes.

CONSTRUCTING A NEW LAYER

You can create or construct a layer in two ways, which are:

> Creating a layer from a blank file
> Creating a layer from an existing file

To create a layer from the above two options, kindly follow the steps below:

1. Select the **Layer tab** and Click on a **New** menu, then choose a **Layer** from the drop-down menu.

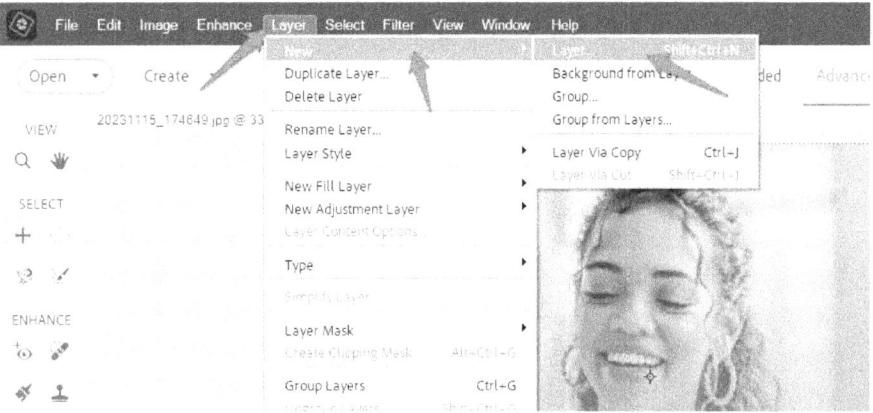

2. Then fill in the details in the Create New Layer dialog box to construct a new layer as described below:

- Input the name for the new layer in the name box, or leave it as default.
- **Color:** Pick the color from the color selection for your new layer.
- **Opacity:** drag the Opacity slider for the opacity setting
- **Mode:** this is an option for mode adjustment.

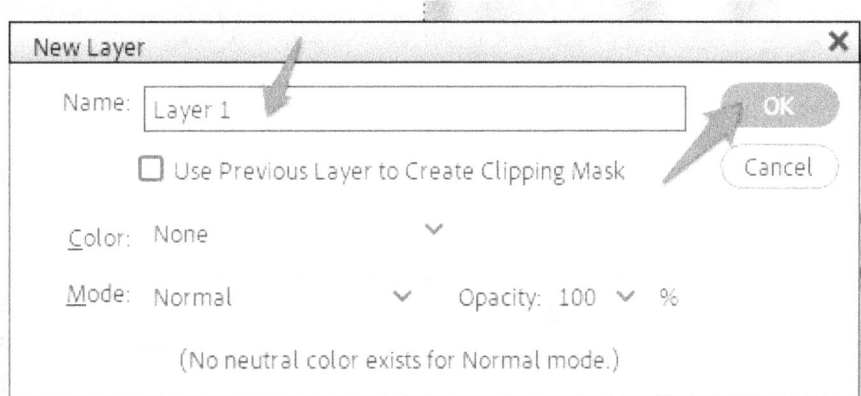

Substitute:

1. Select the **Create New Layer** from the Layer panel to call upon Layer 1 in the Layer Panel. Then double-click to rename Layer 1.

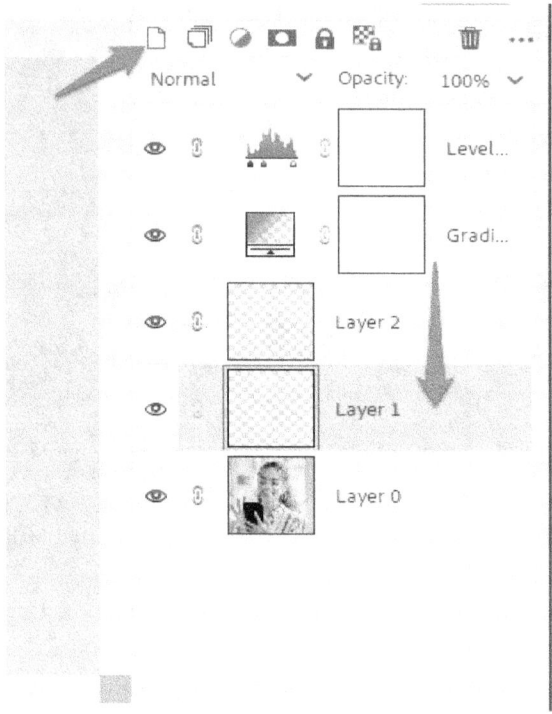

After you have acquired the layer, the next thing to do is to put some selections or elements into the layer. To put selections or elements into the layer that you have created, follow the options below:

> **Copy and paste a selection:** build a selection on a background layer or different layer within the same file or diverse file, then follow the steps below:

- Click the **Edit tab** and select **Copy** on the source file and source layer.

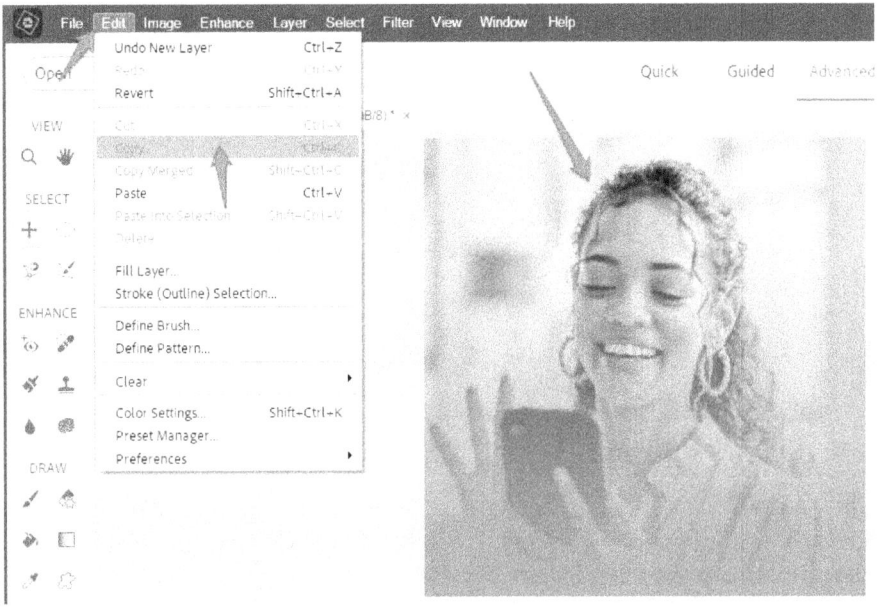

- Choose the **destination layer** which is the blank layer and click the **Edit** tab then select **Paste** on the drop-down menu.
- The elements or selections you copied will be pasted to the blank layer.

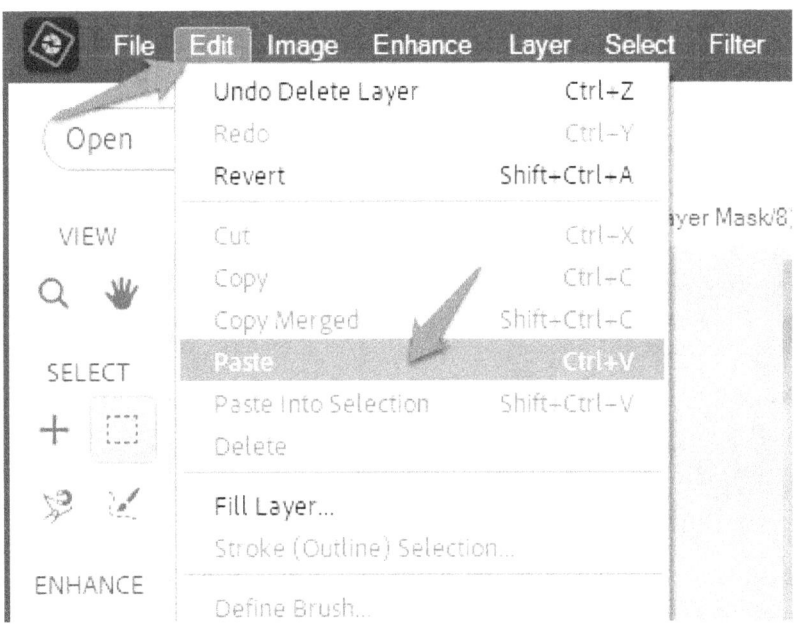

➢ **Cut and paste a selection:** build a selection on a different layer or background layer within a different file or the same file, then follow the steps below:
  • Click the **Edit** tab and select **Cut** on the source file and source layer.
  • Choose the **Destination layer** which is the blank layer and click the **Edit** tab then select **Paste** on the drop-down menu.
  • The elements or selections you cut will be pasted to the blank layer.

MERGING LAYERS

This is the process of combining the visible layers into a single image to manage system memory. Follow the steps below to merge layers:

➢ Fixed all the layers you want to combine to be visible by removing the slanting line and hide the layers you do not want to combine by positioning the slanting line on those layers.
➢ Click the **Layer** tab and select Merge Visible.

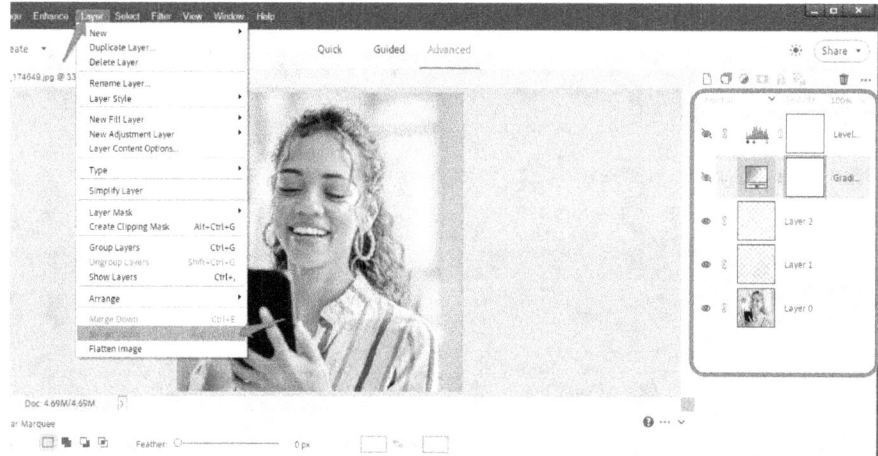

FLATTENING LAYERS

This is the process of combining all the visible layers of your image with the background. The instruction below reveals to you how to flatten images:

➢ Fixed all the layers you want to flatten to visible mode.
➢ Click the Layers tab and choose Flatten image.

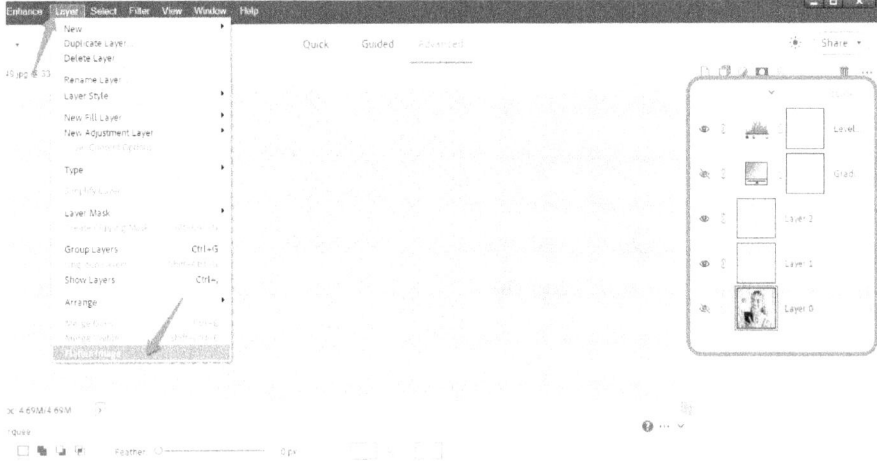

CHAPTER TEN

IMPECCABLE IMAGE TRANSFIGURATION

This chapter is created to show you the easiest way to speedily transform an image in the most appropriate way such as removal of the unwanted pulse from the image, rectifying color issues, cutting the unwanted aspects from an image with a cropping tool, straightening bend photograph, and so on.

THE CROP TOOL

The crop tool allows you to cut out any of the image aspects that you did not want in your image. Follow the steps below to learn how to apply a crop tool for cutting aspects of an image.

> ➢ Click the **Crop Tool** in the tools box.
> ➢ Make use of the necessary settings for the tool resolution and aspect ratio under the tools Options which are discussed below:
>> • **Pixel:** this option allows you to set your image pixel either in inches or cm.
>> • **Resolution:** Apply this option to set your image resolution.
>> • **Grid Overlay:** this is used to encompass your image with the Overlay before cropping.
>> • **Preset size:** this is the size of the manufactured photo; you only need to make a setting for selecting any of the preset sizes in the process of cropping to get a certain image size after cropping.
>> • **Width and height:** this option allows you to specify the width and height measurement of the image you want to crop.
>> • **Rule of thirds:** it allows you to locate an important aspect of the image where one out of the four-point of both the vertical and horizontal view.
>> • **Use photo Ratio:** this is an option selected to maintain the actual ratio of the image in the course of cropping.
>> • **No Restrictions:** this permits you to cut an image into any size without restriction.

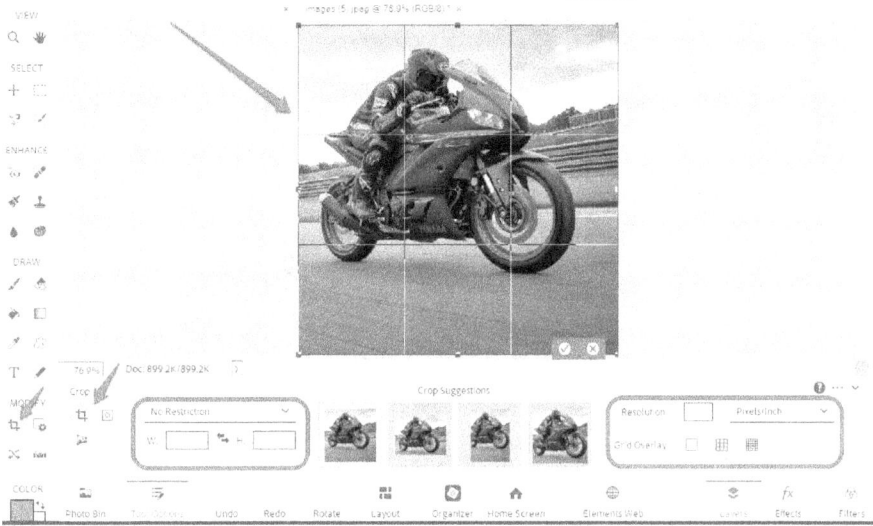

> ➤ Drag the mouse to encamp the part of the image you want and release the mouse, the crop selection will provide you with two parts which are the outer and inner parts. The outer aspect is a wall to the inner aspect while the inner aspect is the area of the image that you need.

> ➤ You may have to adjust the selection by dragging any of the Marquee handles, immediately after you have the appropriate selection you will have to click the confirm button to endorse the process or press cancel to reject the process.

STRAIGHTENING A PHOTO

Straighten a photo is important when you discover your phone is not balanced well, you will need the service of the straighten tool for both vertical and horizontal arrangements, below are the steps on how to use it:

> ➤ Choose the **Straighten Tool** from the tools box, then change or adjust the following settings:

- **Remove background:** this is used to remove unwanted background from the image.

- **Original size:** this assists in rotating an image at its actual size without removing the background canvas.

- **Grow or Shrink:** Grow is for increasing the image size while shrink is to decrease it.

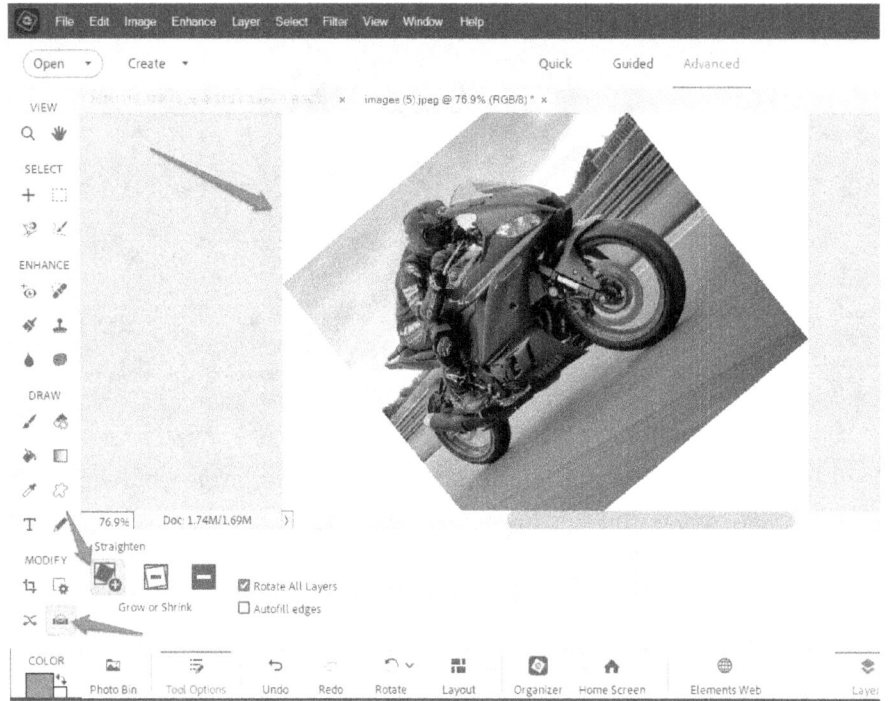

➢ Draw straight lines over horizontal or vertical lines over the face of the image to straighten the bent image.

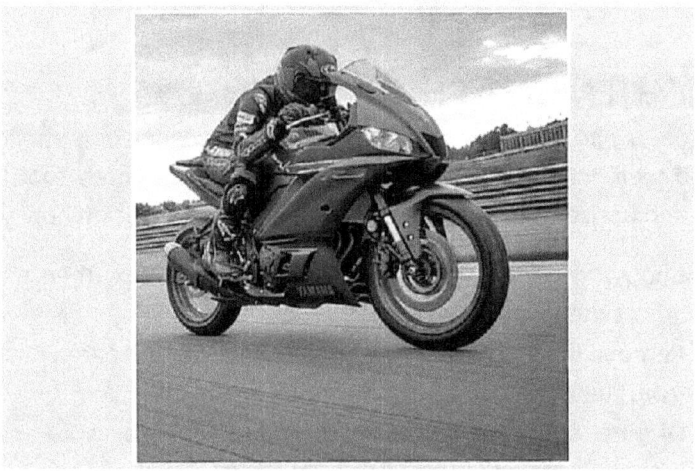

RECOMPOSING AND RESTRUCTURING AN IMAGE

Elements permit you to recompose your image in such a manner that a particular aspect that is not needed will be removed without losing a pinch from the essential element. This is how image restructuring works:

➢ Click the **Recompose tool** from the tools box.
➢ Select the **mark for protection** from the tool Options and apply it to brush across the region you want to protect.
➢ Then choose the mark for removal brush and apply it to brush over the region of the image you did not need in the image.
➢ Then specify the recompose setting Options such as **Threshold, Size, Width and Height, and No Restriction.**

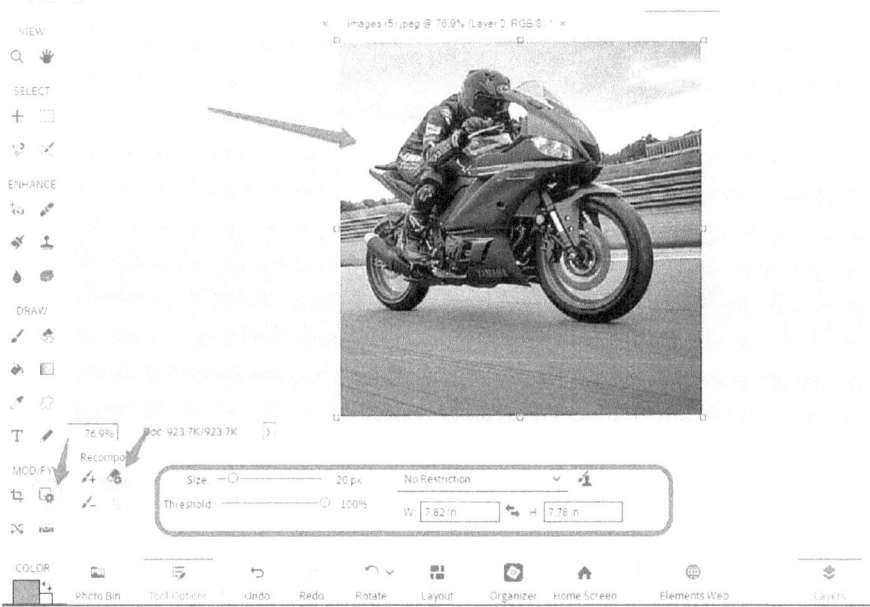

➢ Drag the corner side of the image inside to recompose the image.
➢ Then click on the confirm button for endorsement.

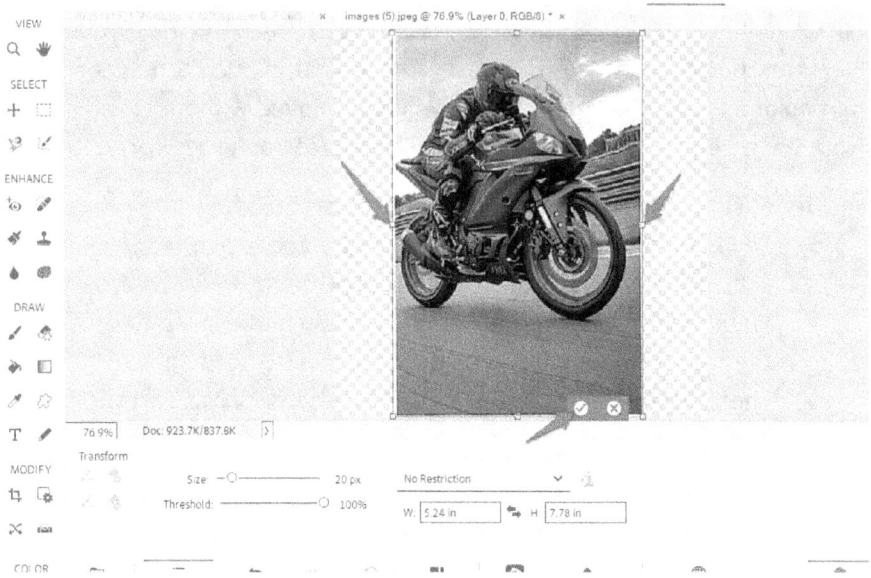

THE AUTO COMMANDS

The auto command is an essential feature that Elements uses for correcting particular image indiscretions such as lightning, contrast, color adjustment, and so on. Let's quickly look at them one after the other.

THE AUTO SMART TONE

The auto-smart tone is spontaneously used to change the tonal values of your image. To change the tonal values of your image, follow the below steps:

> Click on the **Enhance** tab and pick the **Auto smart tone.**

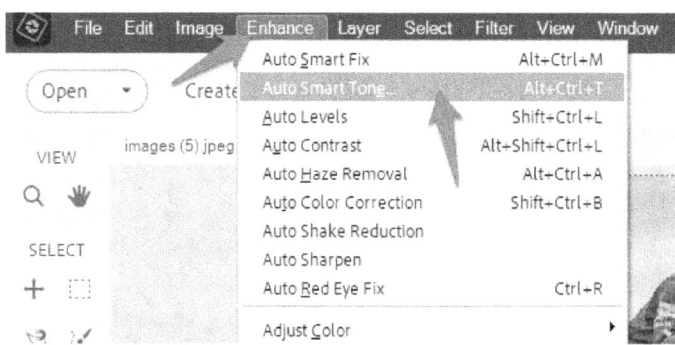

➤ Regulate the **controller slider** by moving it around to sharpen the development.

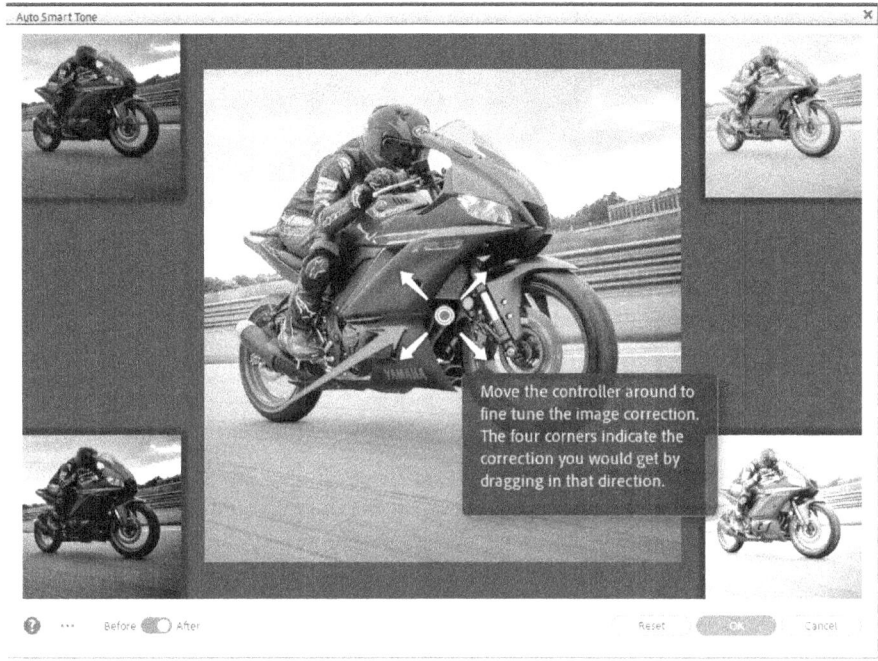

➤ Click the OK button for endorsement.

THE AUTO SMART FIX

This is generated to pass affect various adjustments on an image, for example, contrast, shadow, color balance, and so on. To do this, click on the **Enhance tab** and select Auto Smart Fix.

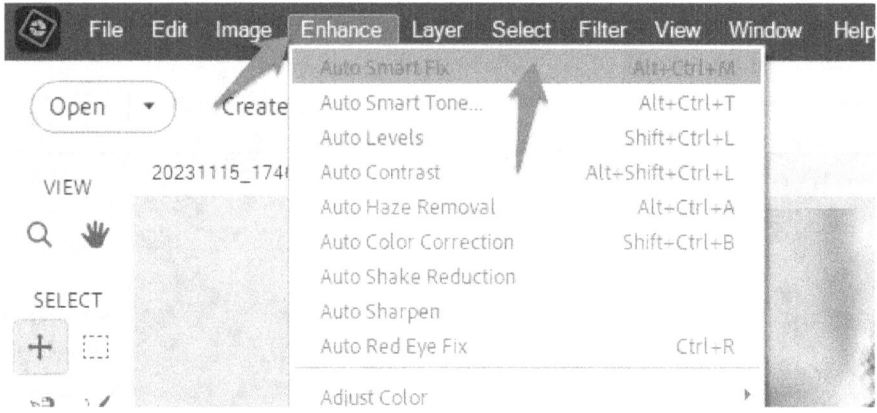

AUTO LEVEL

The Auto level works by adjusting the entire contrast that you can locate in an image by renovating the darker and lightest pixels in an image.

AUTO CONTRASTS

The Auto Contrast corrects the entire contrast of an image but without taking knowledge of the image color.

AUTO HAZE REMOVAL

The Auto Haze removes fog and Haze in your image.

AUTO RED-EYE FIX

This feature spontaneously looks for red-eye and fixes it instantly, red-eyes happens when the person you want to snap glance directly into the camera flash. You can also make use of the Red-Eye tool in the tools box. See the image below:

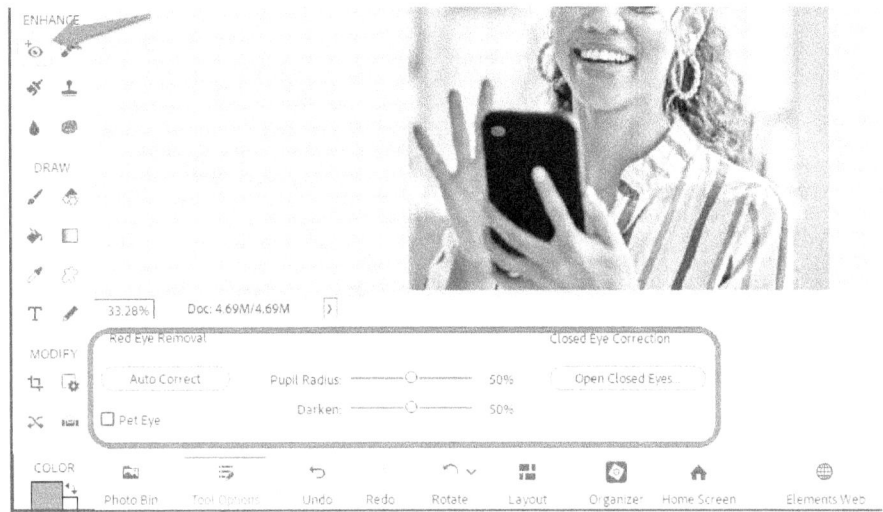

IMAGE MOVING WITH THE AWARE CONTENT TOOL

The Aware Content Tool allows you to move an aspect of an image, follow the below steps to make use of the Content-Aware Move tool:

➢ Choose the image you want to move or pick the part of its object and click on the **Content-Aware Move Tool** in the tools box.

➢ Select between **Extend** or **Move mode** (the Extend mode allows you to extend the aspect of the image you chose and compare it with the nearest aspect, then mix them into an existing object while Move mode permits you to move the chosen aspect of an image to a new place and used the content-aware pixels to replace the empty hole).

➢ Regulate the healing setting to determine the level of elasticity of how the pixels will move around and how the holes will be conserved with the Content-aware tool.

145

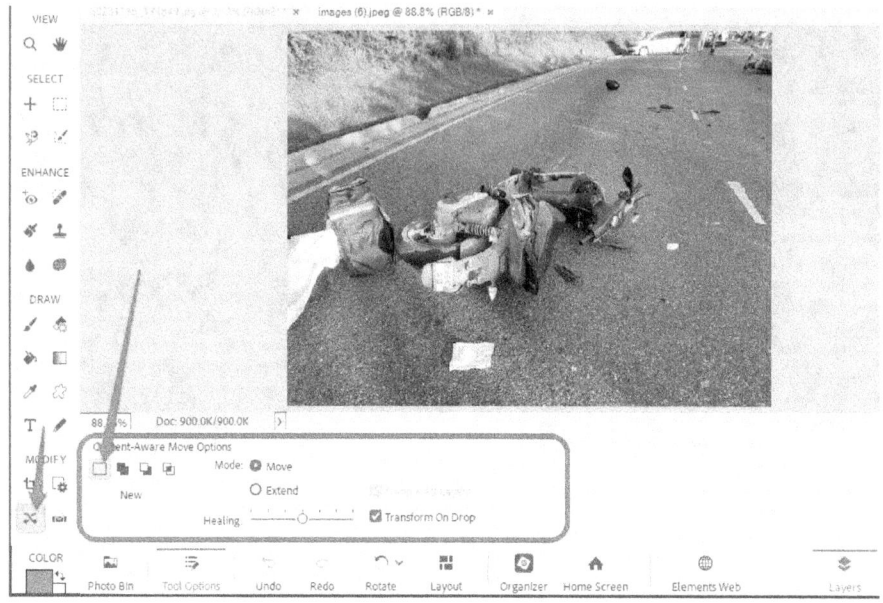

- ➢ Drag around the aspect of your image that you want to move or extend. You can change your selection by applying Transform on Drop in the tool option to change the selected aspect by dragging the transform box. To refine your selection, click on the path operations in the tool options and click on the confirm button.
- ➢ Nevertheless, if you do not want to use Transform on drop option, the thing you need to do is to move your selection portion to the preferable aspect and deselect the selection.

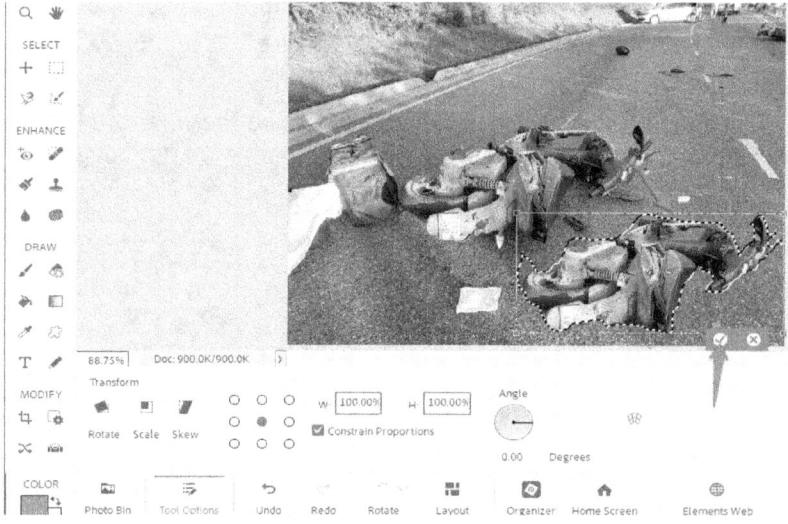

146

➢ If it is needed to fix some mistakes, you can use the **Healing Tool** to do that.

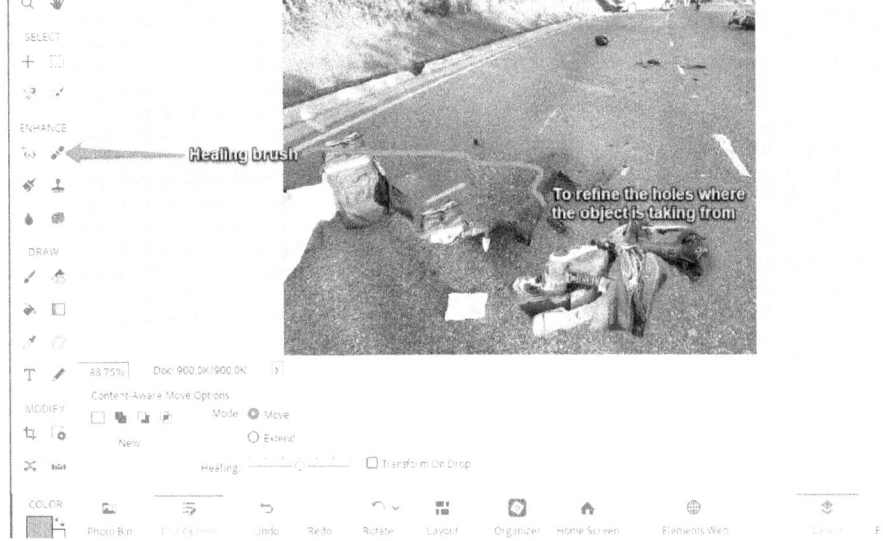

FIXING COLOR, CONTRAST, AND SHARPNESS PHYSICALLY

This aspect of the book takes you through the steps to physically fixing the color, contrast, and sharpness of an image. The benefit of using manual or physical fixing is that it offers you more options and elasticity compared to automatic to arrive at the desired outcome.

REGULATE LIGHT THROUGH SHADOWS/HIGHLIGHTS

There are numerous ways to regulate the imbalance of light in your image. Manual fixing offers you numerous options to handle the light of your image. Below are the steps on how to regulate light through shadows/highlights in both Quick and Advance modes:

➢ Click on the **Enhance tab** and pick the **Adjust lighting** menu.
➢ Then choose the **shadows/highlights** from the drop-down list to enter the shadows/highlights dialog box.

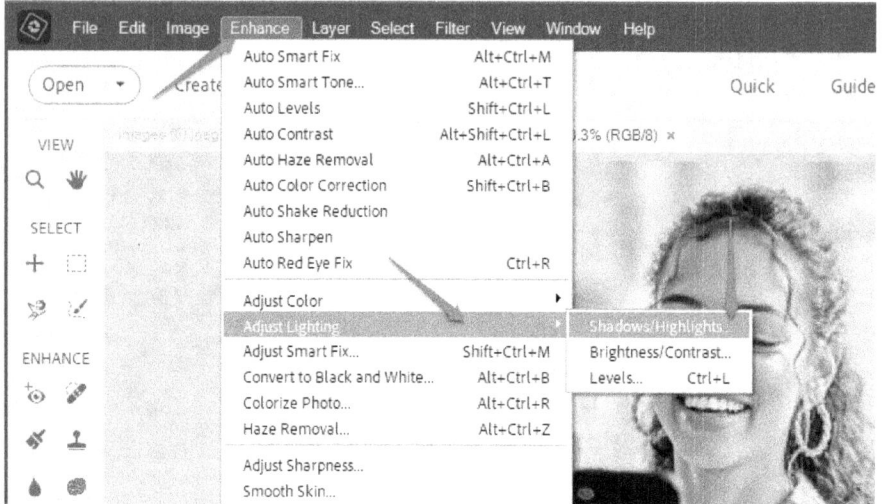

> ➢ Put a mark on the preview check box, then drag the **Shadows Slider** to regulate the dark area, the **Highlights slide** to adjust the light area, and the mid-tones for the middle tone area Adjustment.
> ➢ Click OK for endorsement.

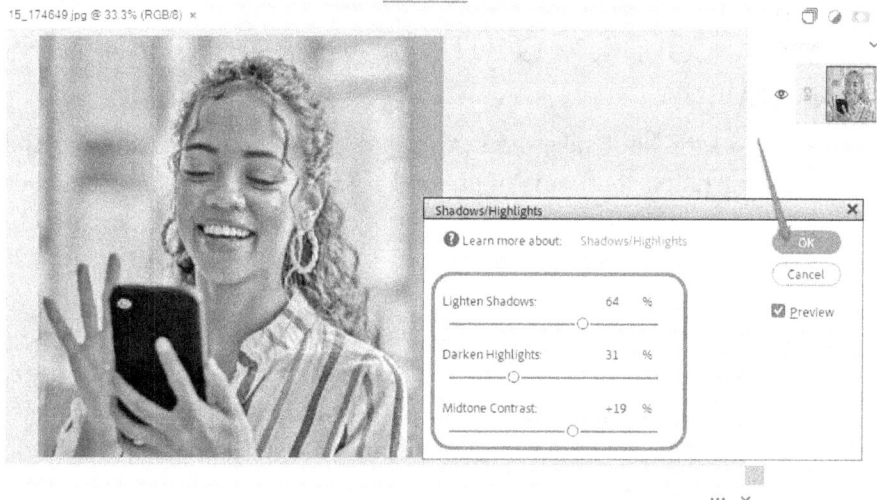

ADJUSTING LIGHTING THROUGH CONTRAST/BRIGHTNESS

To make use of contrast/brightness in adjusting light, kindly follow the below steps:

1. Select the **Enhance** tab and click on the **Adjust Lighting** menu.
2. Then choose **Brightness/Contrast** from the drop-down menu to enter the brightness/contrast dialog box.

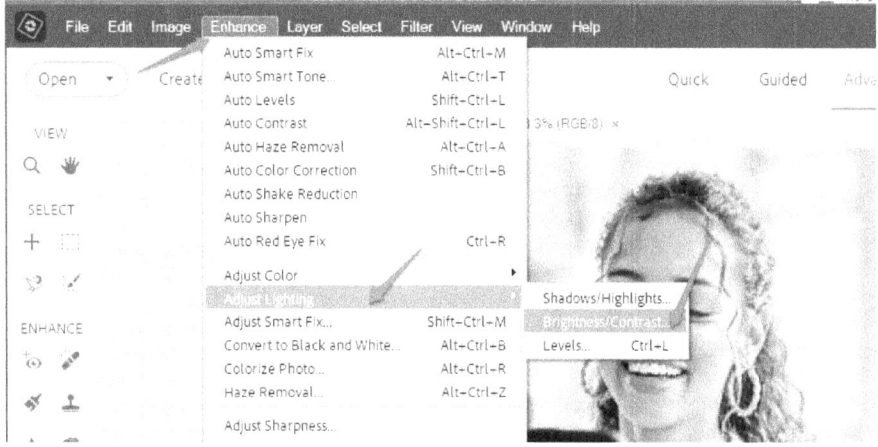

3. Position a mark on the **preview box** and regulate the **Slider.**

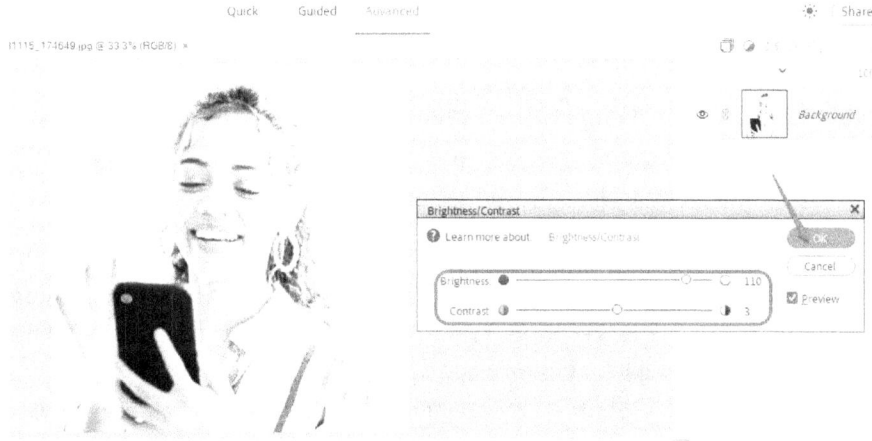

4. Click on OK for endorsement, and have the outcome instantly.

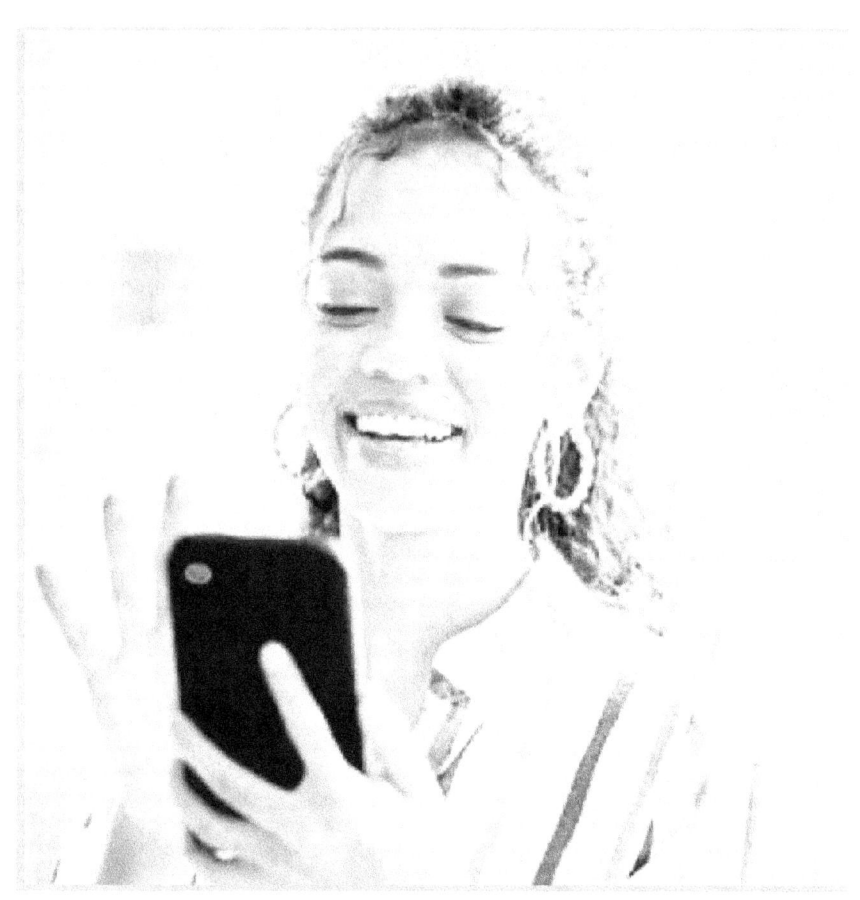

REGULATING LIGHTING THROUGH LEVEL

Level works better than brightness and contrast in adjusting image lighting. Follow the below steps for adjusting lighting with levels.

- ➢ Click the **Enhance** tab and click on the **Adjust Lighting** menu.
- ➢ Choose **RGB** from the channel list, nevertheless, you can choose individual colors such as, green, red, and blue from the channel list but choosing **RGB** works perfectly.
- ➢ Regulate the Contrast by dragging the triangle sliders in the output levels.
- ➢ Regulate the **mid-tones** by dragging the **middle triangle** in the input slider.

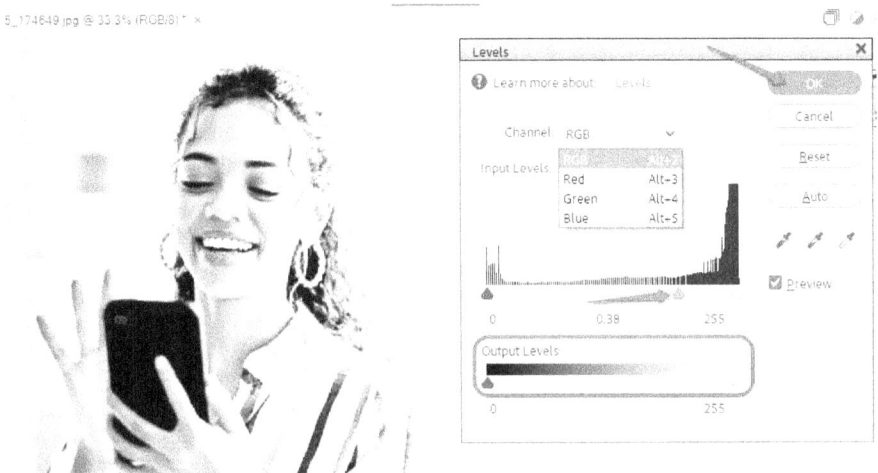

> ➢ Then click OK for endorsement.

DEALING WITH THE COLOR ADJUSTMENT

This aspect of the book deals with the techniques of working with colors, removal, and changing of colors. Remove color cast assists to send the polluted light out of your image by following the steps below:

> ➢ Select the **Enhance** tab and click on the **Adjust Color** menu.
> ➢ Choose **Remove Color** Cast from the drop-down menu to enter the Remove Color Cast dialog box.

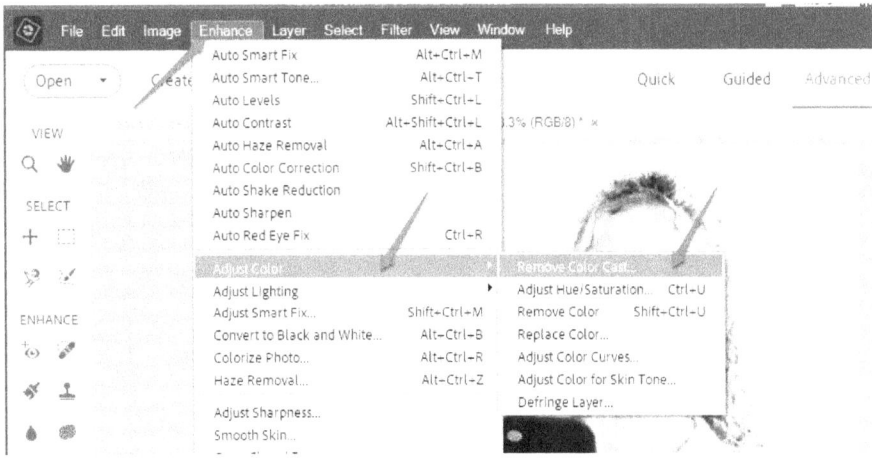

- ➢ Click on the **Eyedropper icon** and apply it to click the aspect of the image you want to adjust and the color cast will be removed spontaneously.

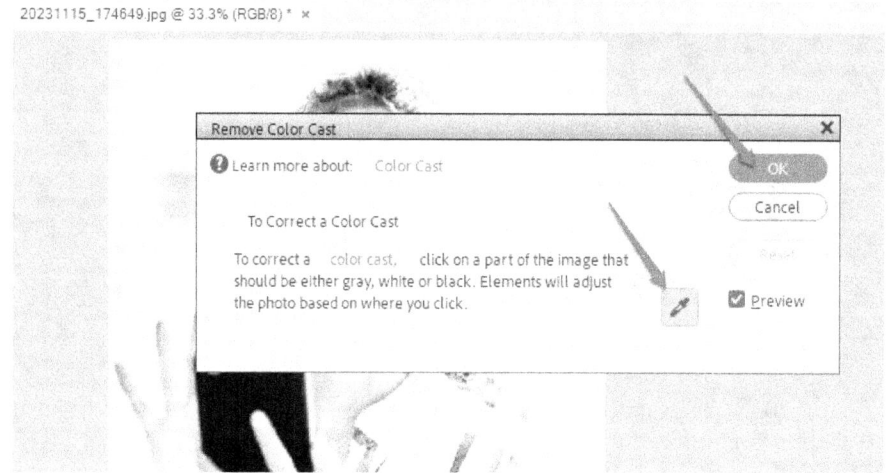

- ➢ Click OK for endorsement.

ADJUST HUE/SATURATION OPTION

Hue/Saturation is used to change the color of your image by examining the saturation (the productivity of your image) and Hue (the color of your image). Follow the steps below to apply Hue/saturation to change the color of your image:

- ➢ Select the **Enhance** tab and click on the **Adjust Color** menu.
- ➢ Then click **Hue/Saturation** from the drop-down menu to gain access to the Hue/Saturation dialog box.

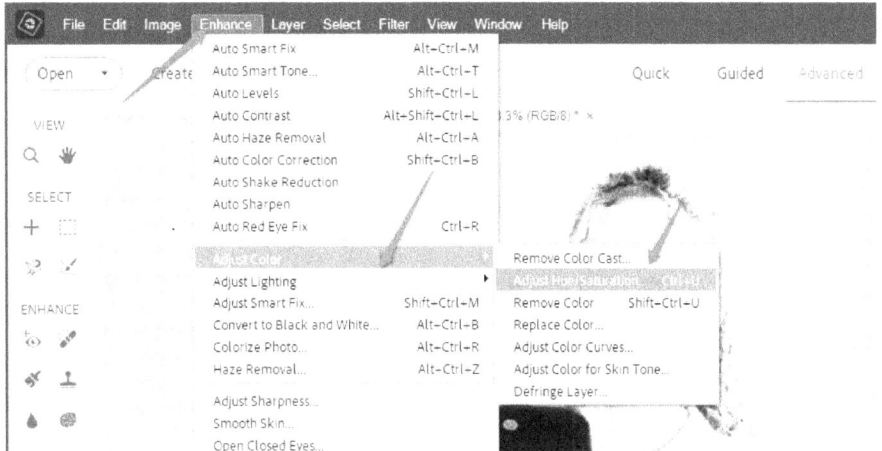

➢ Click on the **Master** menu to change all image colors or choose an **individual** color you desire to adjust.

➢ Drag the following sliders depending on the color features you want to adjust:

- Hue
- Lightness
- Saturation

➢ Put a mark on the colorize box in case you want to change the color to a new color.

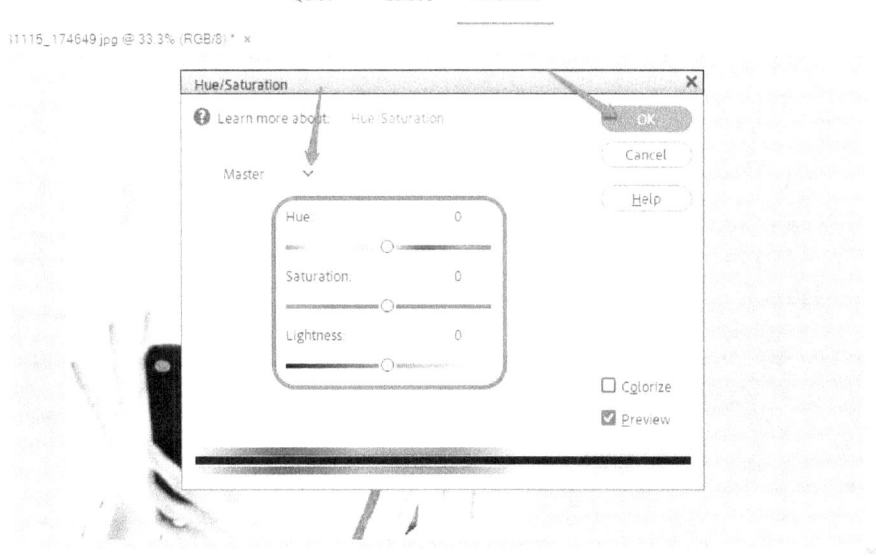

153

THE REMOVE COLOR

If you want your image to turn out to be pure black and white color. It can be done with **Remove Color**. Follow the steps below to apply Remove color in removing image color:

➢ Choose the **whole, portion, or the whole layer** of the image you wish to remove its color.

➢ Select the **Enhance** tab and click on the **Adjust Color** menu, then choose **Remove color** from the drop-down menu to change your selection to black and white color instantly.

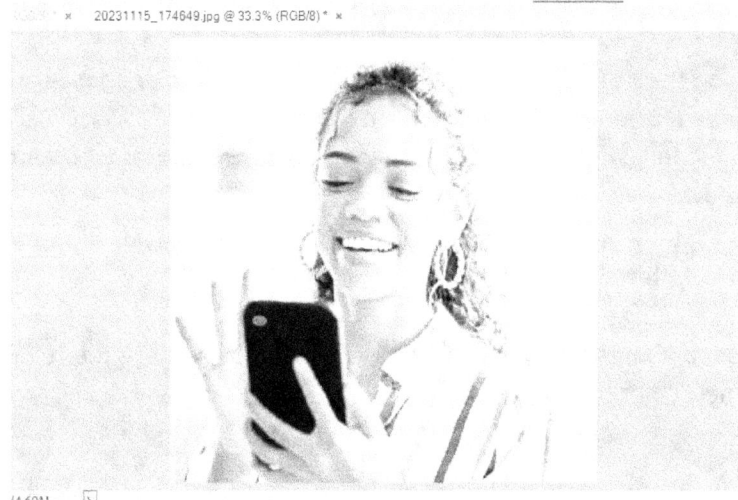

THE REPLACE COLOR

This Elements feature permits you to replace the original color of your image with another color. Follow the steps below to know how to apply the Replace color:

➢ Use the **Mask To Create A Selection** (this has been explained under the layer mask).

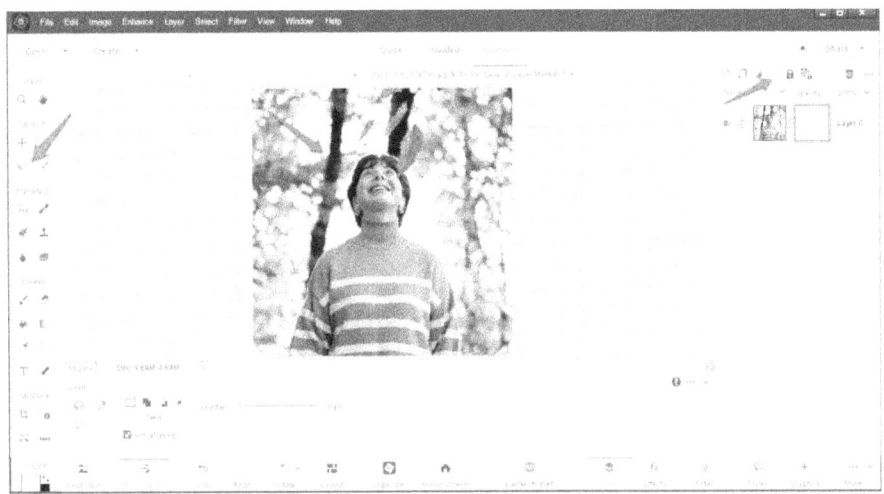

- ➢ Select the **Enhance** tab and click on the **Adjust Color** menu, then choose **Replace Color** from the drop-down menu to enter the Replace dialog box.
- ➢ Position a mark on the **Preview** check box and choose replace color options which are:
- • **Image:** this will allow you to view the entire image clearly in the preview area.
- • **Selection:** picking this option will make you see the area selected as white, and unselected as black, and the aspect incompletely selected will be gray in the image preview section
- ➢ Select the **Eyedropper tool** and use it to click on the color you want to select for your selection or the entire image.
- ➢ Use the **Plus + Eyedropper** tool to include numerous colors and the minus – Eyedropper tool to delete colors and click OK.
- ➢ Drag the Hue slider to adjust the color and the saturation to change the color productivity.
- ➢ Drag the **lightness slider** to lighten or darken your image.
- ➢ Check the outcome heading to view what you have done, and if you love the outcome, click OK for endorsement.

THE COLOR CURVE

This Elements feature is created to correct the whole tonal range of an image by changing the color of the color elements which are Mid-tones, Highlights, and Shadows. Follow the steps below to use the color curve in changing or adjusting a layer, the entire image, or the selected part of an image:

> Click the **Enhance** tab and Click on the **Adjust Color** menu, then choose **Adjust Color Curve** from the drop-down menu to gain entrance to the Adjust Color dialog box.
> Select the curve adjustment you want, then change your image color style from the Select a style section.
> Drag any of the sliders you want to use for refining your image color and continue observing the preview window.
> Click OK for endorsement.

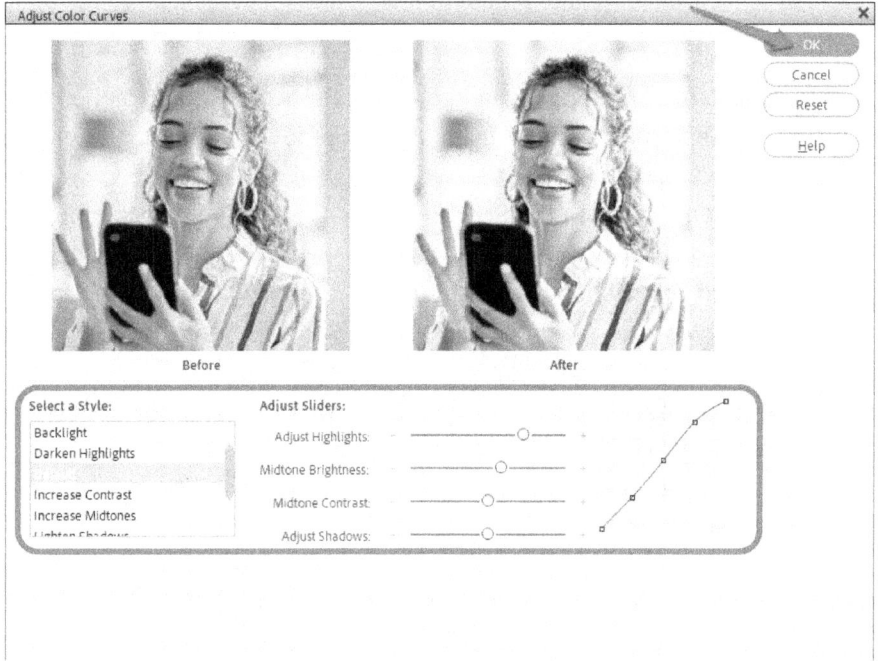

ADJUST COLOR FOR SKIN TONE

To use this option, follow the steps below:

> Choose the aspect of the image that needs to be adjusted, in case your image is without layer, the entire image will be selected.

- ➢ Click the **Enhance** tab and click on **Adjust Color Menu,** then choose Adjust Color Skin Tone from the drop-down menu to enter the Adjust Skin Tone dialog box.
- ➢ Click the aspect of the image you want to adjust and it will be adjusted instantly.

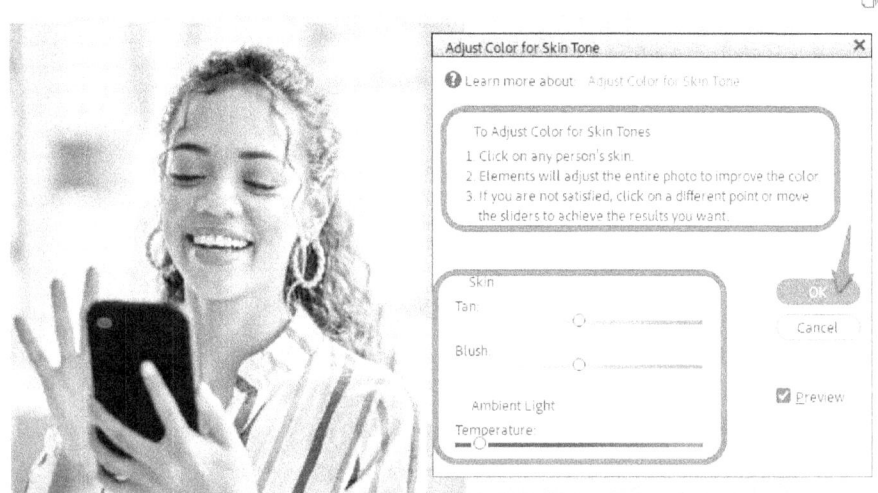

- ➢ You can adjust the following options by dragging the slider which are: **Tan, Blush, and Temperature.**
- ➢ Click OK for endorsement.

DEFRINGE LAYERS

Fringe is the group of weak edges that frame the selection that you copy or move into another document or layer, it always comes with any selection you copy so it is expedient to defringe any selection you copy or move into another document or layer, follow the steps below to do that:

- ➢ Move or copy and then paste such a selection into a fresh or existing layer.
- ➢ Select the **Enhance** tab and Click on the **Adjust Color** menu.
- ➢ Then select the **Defringe Layer** from the drop-down menu to enter the Defringe layer dialog box.

157

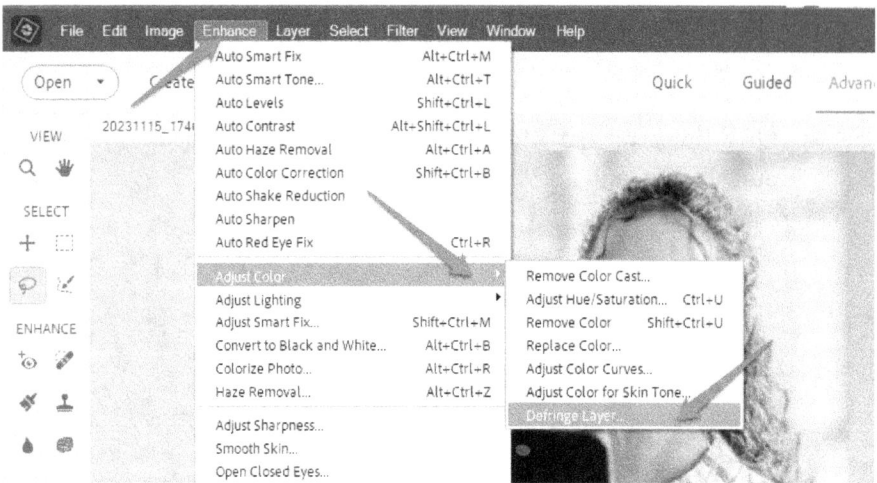

➤ Input the correct Defringe pixel values into the width box.

ADJUST SHARPNESS FOR AN IMPROVED VIEW

Adjust Sharpness assists in improving the sharpness of the image caused by the use of shadows/highlights, it permits you to improve the sharpness of the image with a precise adjustment. Below are the instructions for using Adjust sharpness:

➤ Click the **Enhance** tab and click the **Adjust Sharpness** to enter the Adjust Sharpness dialog box.

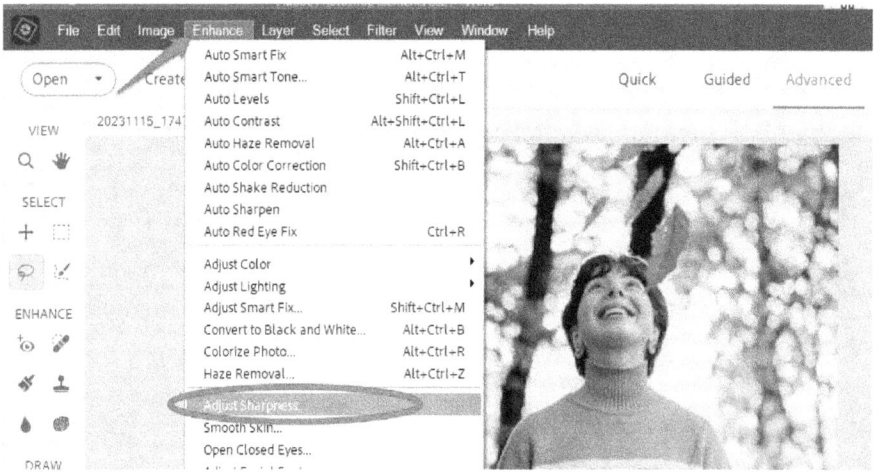

➢ Adjust the following sharpness options in the dialog box such as **Amount, Radius, Preset, Remove, Angle, and shadows/highlights** by dragging their sliders left and right and selecting options from the box provided.

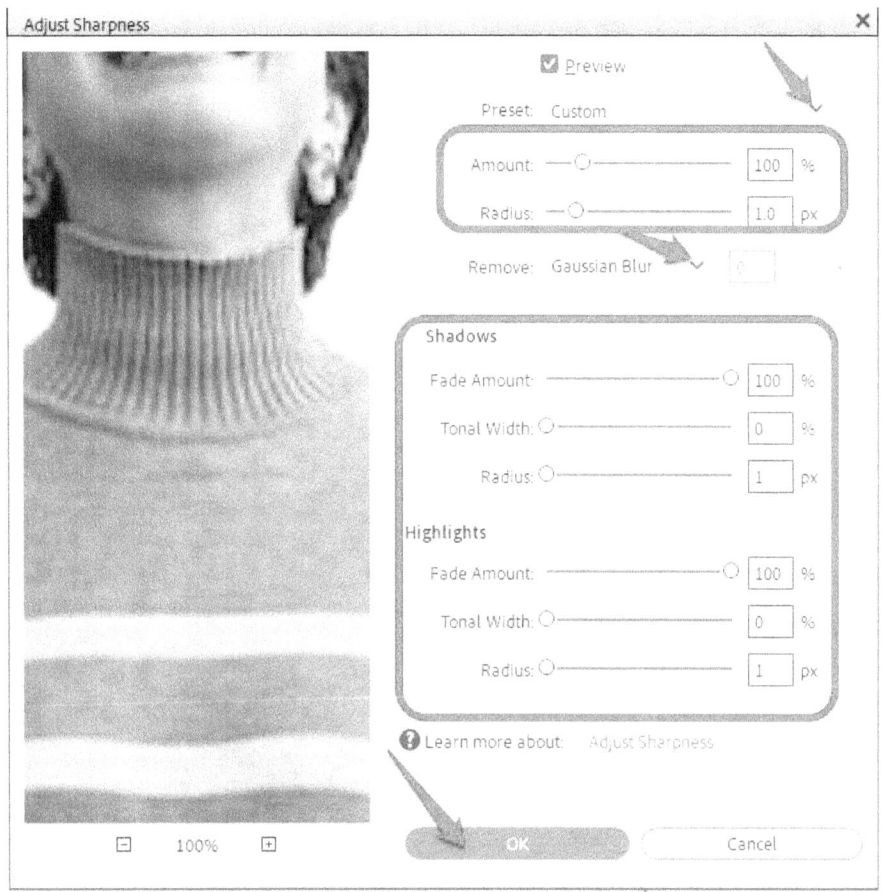

➢ Click OK for endorsement.

SMOOTH SKIN FEATURES

This is a wonderful feature that presents an image more smoothly and outstandingly than it should normally by fine-tuning and improving all the imperfections and wrinkles. Follow the steps below to transform rough skin into fresh and smooth skin:

- ➤ Unlock the **Image** that needs skin improvement
- ➤ Move to the **Enhance** tab and choose **Smooth Skin** to enter the Smooth Skin dialog box.

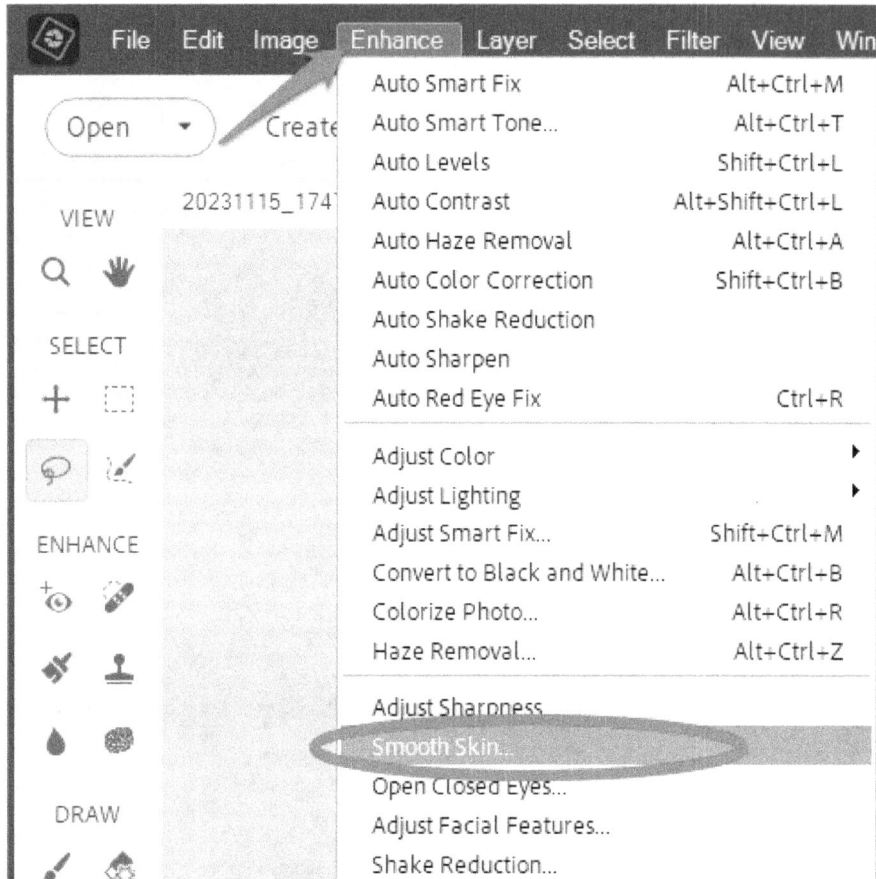

- ➤ Drag the **Smoothness Slider** to change the value of smoothness you need. The circled area is the aspect you are about to change.
- ➤ View the outcome of the Adjustment you made above by switching between the **Before and After** buttons.
- ➤ Click OK for endorsement or **Reset** for cancellation and start afresh.

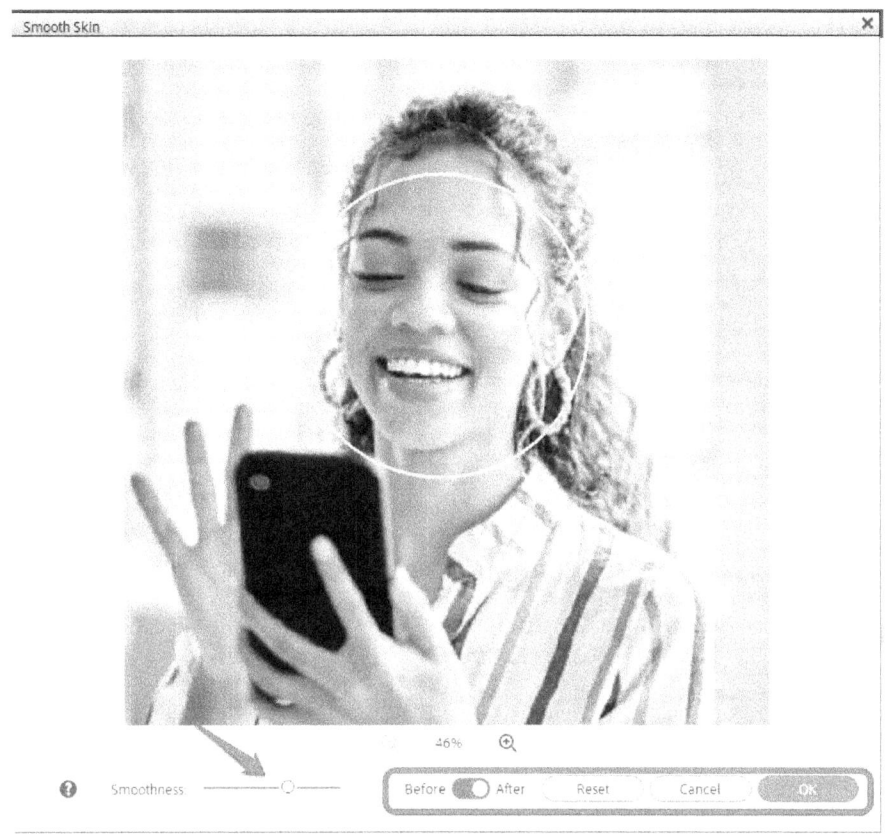

ADJUST IMAGE FACIAL FEATURE

Follow the instructions below for adjusting an image with a rough face:

> ➢ Move to the **Enhance** tab and choose **Adjust Facial Features** from
> the drop-down menu to gain access to the Adjust Facial Feature
> dialog box.

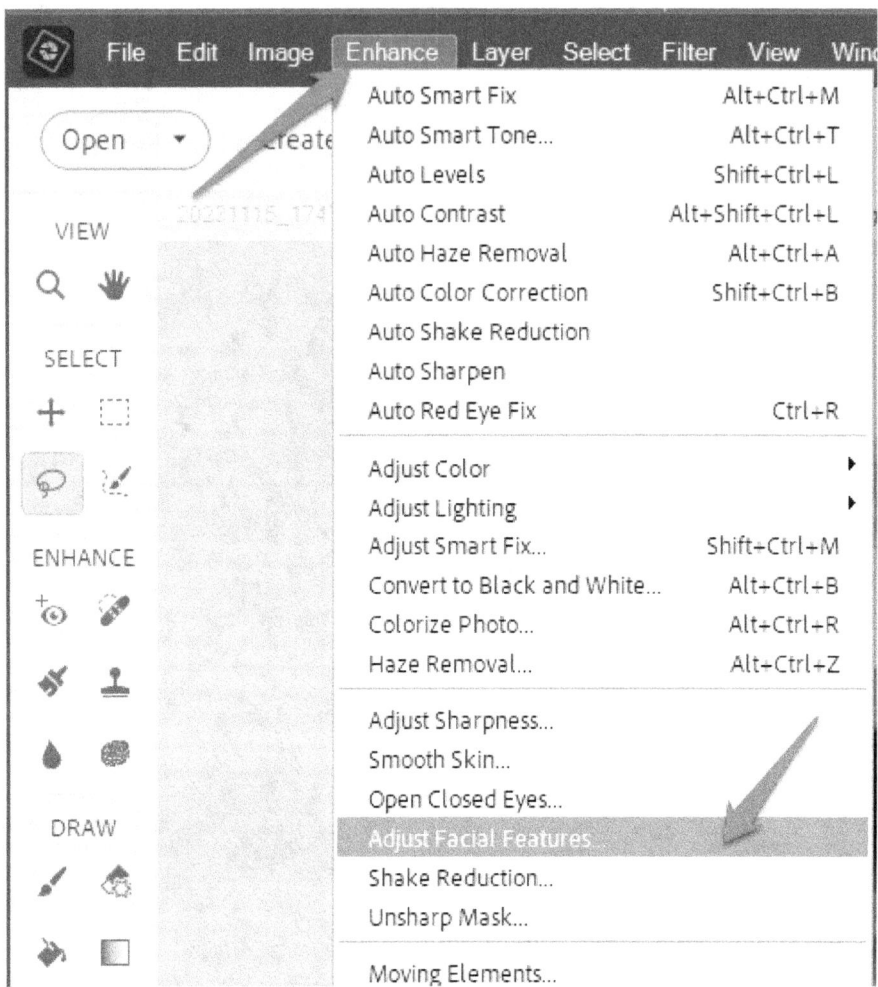

- ➢ Drag the **Slider** to change and improve the facial features you have on the image.
- ➢ View the outcome you are having by clicking on the before and after buttons.
- ➢ Click OK for endorsement.

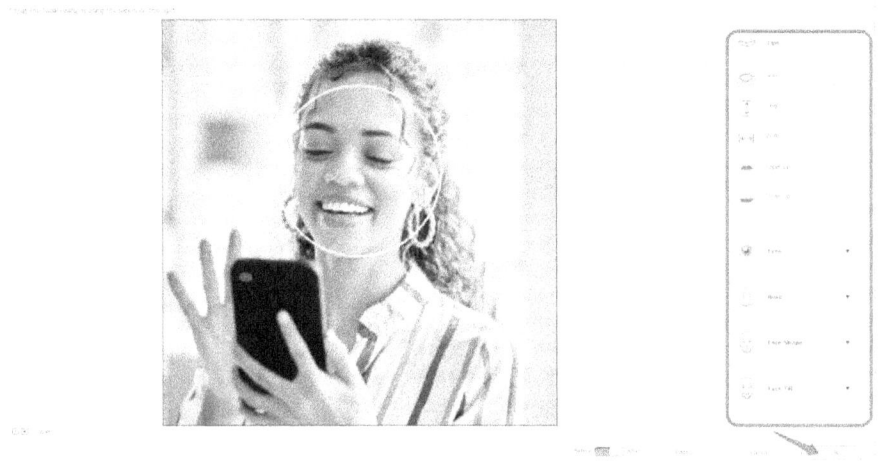

OPEN CLOSED EYE

This is an amazing Elements Feature that assists you in fixing eye issues. Below are the steps on how to use the open-closed eye feature:

➢ Unlock the **Closed Eyes Image** you want to replace with the opened eyes.
➢ Choose the **Eye Tool** in the tools box and Click on **Open Closed Eyes** in the tool options to enter the open-closed eye dialog box.

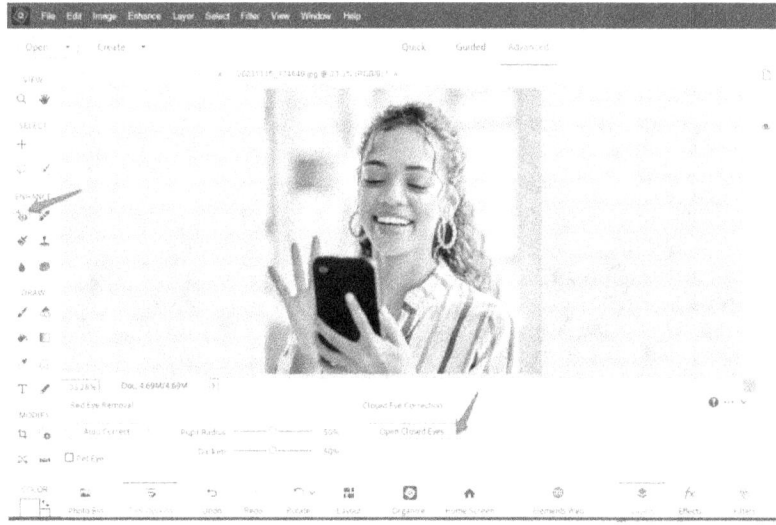

➢ Choose the **Image** that has the open eye you want to use in replacing the closed eye.

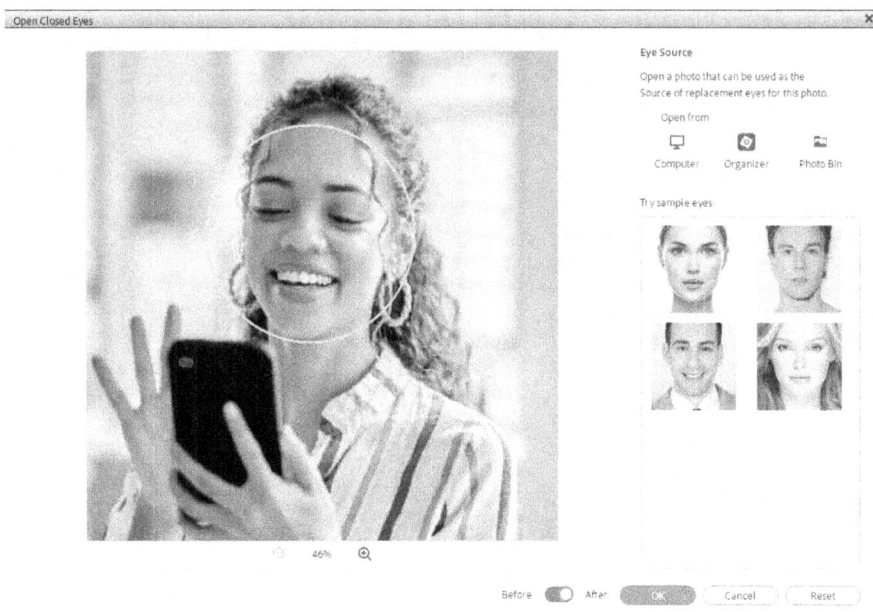

➢ Then click on the **image with open eyes** to copy the open eyes into the closed eye spontaneously.

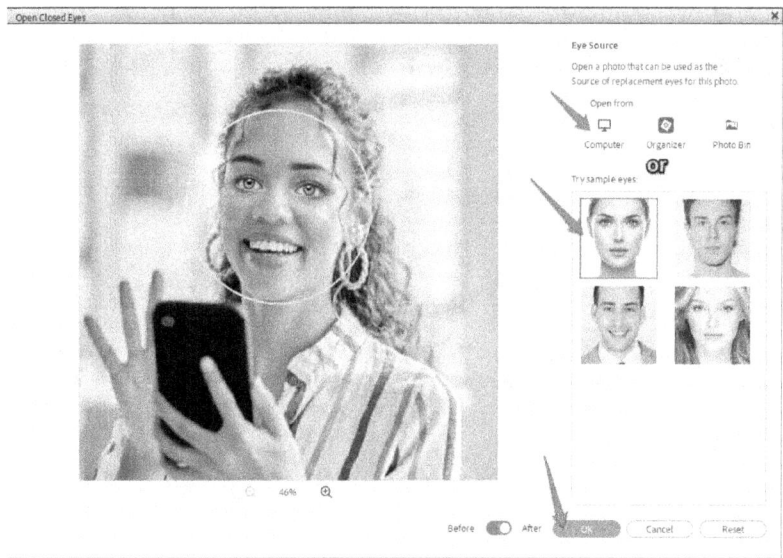

➢ Click OK for endorsement.

CONCLUSION

I am certain you will agree with me that Photoshop Elements 2024 is filled with widespread editing tools for creating eye-catching images. I hope this mini-book has solved numerous questions that might be bothering you about Photoshop Elements. I am sure you can now work with layers, build eye-catching images and improve your design, Boost contrast enhance color, and sharpen your images with all the essential tools embedded in Photoshop Elements 2024.

INDEX